Frances Trix is Professor Emerita of Linguistics and Anthropology at Indiana University and Distinguished Senior Scholar at the Center for the Study of the Middle East. She has been the recipient of a number of distinguished grants and was a Fulbright Research Fellow in Istanbul, a Woodrow Wilson Fellow at the Wilson International Center for Scholars in Washington, DC and received the Lifetime Achievement Award from the Albanian American National Association. In the winter of 2015–16, she spent time working in refugee transit camps on the Macedonian border and is the author of numerous books, including *Urban Muslim Migrants in Istanbul* (2016) with I.B.Tauris.

D1602201

"Do not neglect to show hospitality to strangers, for thereby some have entertained angels unawares."

Hebrews 13:2

"Whatever of good and abundant wealth you spend should be for parents and near relatives and orphans and the needy and the wayfarer."

Qur'an 2:26

EUROPE AND THE REFUGEE CRISIS

CRISIS

Local Responses to Migrants

FRANCES TRIX

I.B. TAURIS
LONDON • NEW YORK • OXFORD • NEW DELHI • SYDNEY

I.B. TAURIS
Bloomsbury Publishing Plc
50 Bedford Square, London, WC1B 3DP, UK
1385 Broadway, New York, NY 10018, USA

BLOOMSBURY, I.B. TAURIS and the I.B. Tauris logo
are trademarks of Bloomsbury Publishing Plc

First published in Great Britain 2018
Paperback edition published 2020

A catalogue record for this book is available from the British Library.

A catalog record for this book is available from the Library of Congress.

ISBN: HB: 978-1-7845-3993-1
PB:978-0-7556-1775-3
ePDF: 978-1-7867-3586-7
eBook: 978-1-7867-2586-8

Series: International Library of Migration Studies

Typeset by OKS Prepress Services, Chennai, India

To find out more about our authors and books visit
www.bloomsbury.com and sign up for our newsletters.

This book is dedicated to people everywhere who are working with refugees.

Frontispiece The Wahoud Family from Homs, Syria.
Photo by Leisa Thompson.

CONTENTS

LIST OF ILLUSTRATIONS

ACKNOWLEDGEMENTS

For the research for this book I made two journeys to Germany, a pilot study and a longer study. For the longer study my dear friend, Erika Stevenson, a German American from the Sudetenland who lives in Indiana, contacted friends in her later hometown of Bruchsal, Germany who were both kind and wise in helping me. Here I am especially grateful to Rosewitha Wallace who set up crucial interviews that framed my research experience, and Maria Frank-Seiferling who opened her home and accompanied me in Bruchsal. Earlier for the pilot study, my good friend Dr Siglind Bruhn, who lives in Germany, helped with train schedules and bus lines, and found articles on towns with good records on refugees for which I am most grateful. She also provided a welcome refuge at the end of my long journey when I was exhausted.

I thank the patience and love of family, especially my son and mother-in-law, and the kindness and the thoughtfulness of friends. Indiana University came through at the end of my long research journey, so that this work was partially funded by the Office of the Vice Provost of Research at Indiana University Bloomington through the Retired Faculty Grant-in-Aid Program.

I also thank Iradj Bagherzade, publisher of I.B.Tauris, for suggesting I write a book on the new refugees. I thank Thomas Stottor, my editor, for his work, his insights, and his continuing stalwart support throughout. I also thank a most erudite and thoughtful reader whose careful comments improved the manuscript.

For those at Legis.mk in Macedonia, your work was crucial in supporting the refugees in their travels through to Western Europe.

You should not be forgotten. Thank you for letting me work with you. I will be back.

To the many volunteers and others who work with refugees in Germany, I salute you for your continuing work. For those who took the time to talk with me, I am most grateful. To the refugees, my prayers are with you.

PROLOGUE

"What do you think of the new refugees?" I asked the husband of the German couple I had been talking with in the lower part of the Frankfurt long-distance train station. We were sitting on a wooden bench in the darkness of the lower station and, as the white trains sped past, there was a certain intimacy.

They were a handsome middle-aged couple. He was solid and broad-shouldered, and she wore a cross around her neck. I had asked for their help in finding the correct train as mine was delayed and the trains went by so fast. The husband told me that they lived in a town near Bamberg in northern Bavaria. "It is a lovely part of Germany I hear," I told them. They smiled.

We talked and then I asked the man what Germans thought of the new refugees. He said that in pubs what they actually thought was that "they" should be put on ships and sent to America since "we" had caused this by invading Iraq. I appreciated his frankness. I said certainly the US invasion of Iraq was a terrible decision and had destabilized the Middle East, but it was not the cause of the Syrian civil war now. And civil wars are the worst of all wars.

I talked some about the new refugees. He said the Turks had not done so well in Germany. I had views about the Turks in Germany but did not want to go there then. So instead I just said, "The refugees from Syria are different. Not all Muslims are the same, and certainly not all Arabs are the same either," I noted.

He allowed as how people tended to generalize.

I said I thought that the Syrian refugees would make good citizens. He said he thought that most of the educated ones wanted to go on to the west, to America or Canada. "No," I said. "I worked in refugee transit camps last winter and they wanted to go to Germany or Sweden. They preferred those countries above all others."

I added though that Canada was very fine. I had grown up in America on the Canadian border and always took an interest in Canada. He asked if Canada took just the educated ones. "No, Canada takes disabled refugees as well. It is a principled country." I explained how groups of six or seven couples banded together in Canada to sponsor a refugee family.

Then he told me how his family had come to Germany from Siberia. I would never have guessed. So, he said, when we talked about refugees, he guessed he too was one of sorts.

I told him that I was there to document the good things that Germans were doing with the new refugees since Germans now had the most experience. "Who is supporting you?" he asked. "A church?" I told him that I might get some support from my university for travel, but I was paying for this myself since it needed to be done.

He looked at me. "It is good there are people like you," he said. "You are needed." My train had just come in. He and his wife helped me confirm the number of the train. It was fifteen minutes late. The man came with me to the door of the train. I thanked him for his help. We shook hands.

The Power of Negative Example

My journey to Germany to research how people were dealing with the large influx of new refugees and to learn from the best programs drew initial inspiration from a negative example.

Indiana Governor Mike Pence announced after the attacks in Paris in mid-November 2015 that he was "suspending the resettlement of Syrian refugees in Indiana."[1] This was not an original action; at least fifteen other governors, mostly Republican, also proclaimed the same action after reports that one of the Paris bombers had posed as a Syrian refugee.

The state of Indiana usually takes in about 1,600 refugees a year from all countries, and a Syrian family had been scheduled to arrive that week in Indianapolis. Governor Pence refused to allow state support for this family so they were rerouted to a more supportive state, which turned out to be Connecticut.

This fear-filled political action infuriated me. Yes, we were upset with the terrorism in Paris. No, we do not take it out on the most vulnerable people, namely refugees from the region of conflict who had already lost so much.

The month before, in October 2015, I had given a paper at a conference at the University of Vienna and returned by way of Freiburg in Germany where I had a good friend. I had taken trains from Vienna to Freiburg and in every station had seen large groups of refugees. This was not a time for America to turn down Syrian refugees when Germany was taking in almost a million refugees. So I decided to volunteer to work in Refugee Transit Camps along the Balkan Migrant Trail. If Indiana would not take in Syrian refugees, I, as an American citizen with certain skills, including linguistic skills, would help them as best I could.

I have worked with refugees in the past. During the 1990s, I did all I could for Bosnian and then Kosovar refugees. I was living and working as a professor in my home state of Michigan then and helped resettlement of Balkan refugees, especially Kosovars since I have long worked in the Albanian immigrant community in Detroit and speak Albanian. As a linguistic anthropologist, I had done research in several countries in the Balkans including Macedonia. But more to the point, even earlier I had lived and worked in the Middle East. I speak a Levantine colloquial Arabic that I had learned when I served as a volunteer teacher in a village school in Lebanon in my twenties. I had lived in Syria and knew I could be especially useful to refugees from Syria and Iraq.

The question was where to serve along the Balkan Migrant Trail? Greece was full of volunteers. Hungary at the other end was brutal and closed to volunteers. I chose to work in Macedonia, a crucial link along the Balkan Migrant Trail, and one in which local people would be the ones who determined policies since Macedonia was not a member of NATO or the EU.

I knew that local non-governmental organizations, or NGOs, were most effective, and so I flew to Skopje and ended up working for Legis.mk, the Macedonian NGO that was the first organization in that country to work for the refugees. I worked in refugee transit camps on the northern and southern borders of Macedonia in the winter of 2015 and 2016. Almost all the refugees in Germany today came through the Balkan Migrant Trail that went through Macedonia. This route was closed in the spring of 2016.

I had been asked by a London publisher to write on the new refugees in Europe since at the time I was close to finishing a book on Muslim forced migrants from Europe.[2] At first I brushed this off because, if I did anything, I wanted to work with the refugees.

After the Balkan Migrant Trail closed in the spring of 2016, I went to Turkey, which has the greatest number of Syrian refugees, close to three million. There are critical problems of schooling and employment of these refugees. But something told me the political climate was not safe there. Indeed there was a coup in Turkey the following summer. I then moved on to Germany where so many of the refugees I had worked with in the refugee transit camps hoped to settle.

In Germany I found remarkable programs for refugees. It struck me that this should be documented. Why were we not hearing about these impressive initiatives, but only about occasional difficulties? So I proposed to that London publisher that I would write not on the new refugees, but on what people in Germany were doing with the refugees. This can be called "host reception" or how people are receiving the new refugees.

This is more important than the refugee stories alone.[3] Can we be receptive to people of significantly different backgrounds? Can we work to integrate new refugees into our societies? Can we be inclusive in this trying time? I say "we" here because questions of reception of refugees from wars in the Middle East are important for the entire Western world. Germany has just been brave enough to deal substantively with these questions first.

In Europe it is not easy. Events like the Paris terrorist attacks of November 2015, the Nice truck rampage of July 2016, and the Berlin Christmas market truck killings of December 2016 make it difficult for Europeans to think of new refugees from the Middle East without fear. We need to separate terrorists of French, Belgian, and North African origin from the new refugees. Can we allow ourselves to meet refugees as human beings and not categories?

After a short pilot study in the spring of 2016, I needed to return to Germany for a longer period to visit more towns and cities and talk with more people to document how different communities were working with the refugees, so I spent several months in Germany in the fall of 2016. I also needed to return home to support the efforts of my own university town of Bloomington in Indiana to receive refugees from Syria.

Later I found out I was not alone in countering Governor Pence and his stand against Syrian refugees. Exodus, the State Department organization that brings refugees to Indiana, sought an injunction against Pence's decree, saying that it was against federal laws to target individual nationality groups the way he had targeted "Syrians." The injunction was granted in February 2016, and Exodus continued to bring Syrian refugees into Indiana. Governor Pence got the State of Indiana to appeal the injunction. The Federal Appeals Court blocked this. On 3 October 2016 the Court decided against the appeal by the State of Indiana by a clear majority, finding that the State of Indiana had violated federal law.

Catholic Archbishop Joseph Tobin of Indianapolis also came out against Governor Pence's refusal to settle Syrian refugees in Indiana. As soon as the Archbishop learned of the Governor's stand, he spent several hours talking in private with Pence. They agreed to disagree. But it was stronger than that. Tobin, who comes from my hometown of Detroit, Michigan, was not to be ignored. Archbishop Tobin brought a Syrian refugee family to Indianapolis in December 2015 through Catholic Charities USA despite Governor Pence's decrees. The next year, in November 2016, Pope Francis made Archbishop Tobin a cardinal, and he is now Cardinal Tobin of Newark, New Jersey. I have no doubt his stand on refugees was approved by the Pope.

As for me, I have this book that resulted from my work in researching how Europeans responded to refugees in Macedonia, and in villages, towns, and cities across Germany. I bring out what I consider some of the finest initiatives for the new refugees with the hope that others can learn from them and be inspired by them, and that other researchers will work on host reception.

In all cases, it is the human element that matters. As Julia, a Macedonian worker in the mothers' and young children's shelter in the southern refugee transit camp said to me, "I put out one finger of love, and I get ten fingers back."

Postscript

In November 2016, Donald Trump was elected US President with Mike Pence as Vice-President. Trump issued his Executive Order of 27 January 2017[4] in which he cut in half the numbers of refugees allowed into the United States each year to a meager 50,000. He also prohibited entry of Syrian refugees to the United States indefinitely.

Airports across America spontaneously filled with thousands of protestors chanting, "Have no hate, have no fear, refugees are welcome here!" Our courts ruled that this travel ban was unconstitutional, and Syrian refugees have continued to enter. It looks as if they will continue to enter under a new order as well. But the limit on overall number of refugees officially permitted entry each year still stands and has recently been cut even lower to only 45,000.

As for myself, I left Indiana and now live and work with Syrian refugees in my hometown of Detroit.

INTRODUCTION

This book presents a rare human perspective on host and refugee interactions in contemporary Europe. Since those involved are not abstractions or categories, this should help to dispel fear. It counters news stories that focus on single negative incidents[1] and that build on negative assumptions about strangers. Refugees from Syria, northern Iraq, and other war-torn areas will not harm local communities in Europe or North America or any other country that welcomes them.[2] Instead, this book documents and analyses some of the most positive and constructive ways people have worked with refugees. Considering longer-term examples, rather than the common focus on knee-jerk reactions to refugees, this book offers a critical portrait of the ways refugees have and have not been welcomed – and most importantly what can be done better.

There is no other book that builds so tightly on fieldwork at a most crucial time – a year after the influx and initial responses when policy was being established. It is thus valuable to both researchers and to people working in practical situations. It exposes the essential directions on policy, personnel, and integration, and aims to inspire people to work with refugees in new ways.

The supportive evidence is what has been going on in the midst of European cities where new refugees were accepted. I traveled the length of Germany, a country of 80 million people, where almost one million refugees in a short period of time were taken in. There are new refugees all over Germany. They came in large numbers in 2015 leaving virtually no time for planning. People responded as best they could and adapted as they went along. They were creative and humane in different ways.

Focus

I focus primarily on two countries in this book in order to give depth. The first is Macedonia, a strategic country on the Balkan Migrant Trail between Greece and Serbia where refugees passed through on their way to Western Europe. The second country is Germany, which took in close to a million new refugees in 2015. Chancellor Angela Merkel required all towns and cities to take at least 1.5 per cent of their populations in refugees. As a result, the refugees are spread across the country.

Since communities of different sizes have different resources, and potentially different strategies for working with refugees, in Germany I made sure to study communities of different sizes. I studied three villages of fewer than 10,000 people. I studied three towns with populations from 40,000 to 70,000 people, and I also researched Nürnberg, a smaller city of half a million people. I studied three large cities: Cologne, a city of 1.2 million people; Munich, a city of 1.38 million people; and Hamburg, the second largest city in Germany with 1.8 million people. I also traveled from the south of Germany through the central region to the north.

Why did I focus on these two countries when Europe, which has a population of 500 million people, is made up of fifty countries? I chose Macedonia because it is on the Balkan Migrant Trail and refugees passed through it on an ongoing basis from 2013 to 2016, making it valuable for a case study for transit of refugees. It is also in Eastern Europe giving the trail and refugee journey an alternative perspective. The country is typical of Eastern European nations with its socialist past and new regime in 1991. And, like other Eastern European countries, Macedonia's transition to capitalism has not been easy.

As for Germany, it stands out, with Sweden,[3] as the most generous country in all Europe for accepting refugees, athough Austria and the Netherlands also took in some refugees. At this time an estimated 10,000 refugees gathered at Calais in France, hoping to go Britain. Britain, though, did not accept them; eventually they were spread out across different towns in France. Germany thus provided the best opportunity for a case study for the high numbers of refugees it allowed in – almost a million – and the variety of programs and responses it provided as a largely destination country. Moreover, Germany is similar to other countries in Western Europe in the level of its economic development and the services it provides to its citizens.

In both Macedonia and Germany, I sought out *positive* initiatives for dealing with the new refugees. But I did not neglect negative actions. In Macedonia I noted the long-term refusal of the government to allow refugees to use public transportation and its detention of refugees for months in a former nursery school in the capital. In a town in Germany I went to a demonstration against a community center for refugees, and in a large city I attended a Pegida[4] anti-Islam rally. I also talked with people of differing opinions. These experiences are noted as well as the contexts of the activities with refugees. Unfortunately, due to time constraints, I did not spend time in former East Germany where opinions are generally more negative toward new refugees.

I also sought out people who seemed to influence people's attitudes toward the refugees. This especially matters in organizations and smaller towns. When I found people in positions of leadership, I asked them how they had come to work with the refugees. For example, one man, an IT specialist, told me he had gone to a rally against the new refugees in a conservative part of his town. He noted what people were afraid of – that the kindergartens would be swamped with new refugee children, that they would bring illness with them, and that the refugees would bring crime. When none of these fears came to pass, he decided to work with the refugees. He became the coordinator of volunteers working with refugees in his town.

Researcher Quandaries and Stratagems

In talking with refugees, I realized that sometimes we were in similar quandaries. To begin with, we were both foreigners and we both had needs that often went counter to German bureaucracy, especially in Bavaria. "No, you may not visit any of the refugee accommodations in Munich," I was told, although there were fifteen large refugee accommodations all around the city, and I had visited refugee quarters in all the other German towns and cities I had been to.

Thanks to my habit of going to early church services on Sunday, contact with an Iraqi Assyrian priest, and the driving of a wily Uzbek taxi driver, I was able to get around this pronouncement. In what I came to see as a victory over Bavarian bureaucracy, I spent time in the largest and oldest refugee center in Munich. Accessing refugee accommodations was one matter. Getting interviews with German officials sometimes took even more determination on my part.

There is a basic problem of doing anthropological fieldwork in a highly bureaucratic country. Anthropological fieldwork has an intrinsic spontaneous quality to it. The researcher stays in a community as long as there are interesting programs and engaging people to talk with, both officials and others, and then moves on. Thus, it is hard to predict when interviews with officials should be set up in the next community. In Germany, for example, officials prefer interviews to be set up at least two weeks if not months in advance. However, I could not predict when I would be moving on to the next locality. It depended on what I found in the previous community. I would request interviews with officials as early as possible when I thought I would be in the next community.

Allow me to emphasize the value of this type of research and some of the features of it for researchers who are not fieldworkers. To understand what is going on in complex new social situations, like that of refugees passing through Macedonia or new refugees in Germany and Germany's responses to them, archival research at this time cannot begin to give the insights that good fieldwork can. Oral language skills, cultural knowledge, and the ability to work with different people are essential. There are multiple voices, many of which do not get written down, and the policies that exist are in flux. Only fieldwork can begin to reach these different voices and start to comprehend the impact of changing policies. To do fieldwork at such a time is both unpredictable and most valuable. Assumptions a researcher brings will be challenged. What is often revealed from fieldwork during this period is being able to identify who are important people and what are the directions of policies. Other research later on should then build on this knowledge.

Important Influences

There are scholars whose works I have long valued and who continue to affect how I work and think. I tend to reread their writing when I need inspiration, courage, insight, or just perseverance. Their influence is throughout this book.

One such scholar is Erving Goffman, originally from Canada, who was an early scholar of face-to-face interaction and a brilliant writer. His *Forms of Talk* (1981) and *Frame Analysis* (1974) affect how I think, analyze, and write about oral interaction. Every evening in Germany as I typed up my field notes of interviews and conversations of the day, I was aware of the influence of Goffman.

Another is Arjun Appadurai, a social anthropologist from Mumbai in India, who first helped me deal with the violence of the Yugoslav Wars of the 1990s. His compact book, *Fear of Small Numbers* (2006), looks at why majority peoples descend in violence on minorities in their midst. He explains the "anxiety of incompleteness and uncertainty" that dogs nationalism in our global world. Nation states create minorities who are often carriers of unwanted memories of previous failures, thus becoming natural scapegoats for displaying the anxieties of the state. This anxiety and violence appeared in Germany in ongoing subgroups of resistance in the fire-bombing of German Turks in the 1990s, and again most clearly in the fire-bombing of refugee hostels where asylum-seekers took the place of minorities.

In migration studies, James Hampshire's work, *The Politics of Immigration* (2013, 2016), is the clearest in bringing out the conflicting dynamics of exclusive and inclusive aspects of immigration policies in liberal societies. He notes that problems of integration in such societies pre-exist problems of integration with immigrants. In refugee studies, I have been most influenced by the work of the Finnish scholar Liisa Malkki. Her main fieldwork is reflected in her book, *Purity and Exile* (1995). It is an ethnography of displacement of two groups of Hutu refugees in Tanzania who had fled violence in Burundi after the 1972 massacres. Thus it predated the better-known genocide of 1993 in Burundi and 1994 in Rwanda. Malkki's work deals with questions of nationalist identity, memory, and exile from the framing experience of extreme violence and how this affects refugees in their future lives.

In migration studies in Germany, I look to the work of Friedrich Heckmann, a German sociologist who has been working on migration for his entire career. Modern Germany is especially complex. His recent book, *Integration von Migranten: Einwanderung und neue Nationenbildung* (2015) brings out much of his research. A different perspective on migration in Germany is anthropologist Ruth Mandel's several decades of study of Turks there. Her *Cosmopolitan Anxieties: Turkish Challenges to*

Citizenship and Belonging in Germany (2008) draws together her research. As Muslims, the Turks represent an important "prior text" for many Germans of Islam in their midst and a precursor of what the largely Muslim refugees might bring.

Still another scholar whose work affects my study is Keith Basso, an American linguistic anthropologist who spent his entire career studying and writing on the Western Apache, a Native American people whose stories were anchored linguistically and topographically in their rich understanding of their landscape as reflected in his book, *Wisdom Sits in Places* (1996). Basso had a rare ability to listen to people of a culture very different from his own. My difficulty was that Germany was too close to my own cultural background. I needed to listen carefully to make sure I was not making assumptions where they were not warranted. Sometimes I would try to picture myself on a distant Apache hillside to better respect the complexity of German history and cultures.

More obviously related to this book is the work of Hannah Arendt. She was a refugee from Nazi Germany to France and then moved to America. The importance of maintaining her relationship after the war with her teacher, Karl Jaspers, who stayed married to a Jew in Nazi Germany, always affected me. Of her writings, I have reread *On Violence* (1969) and *Men in Dark Times* (1955) several times. *Origins of Totalitarianism* (1951) has a long discussion on stateless people and how one aspect of such people is that they are hard to repatriate. We have found this to be true in recent days with false asylum-seekers like the criminal Tunisian in the Berlin Christmas market (2016) attack who had thrown away his documents so Tunisia more readily denied him. Arendt's insights into terror, isolation, and power are as pertinent today as ever.

Style

This book is written in a direct and personal manner. This draws from the genre of ethnographic writing in the discipline of anthropology in which the personal experience of careful fieldwork is the lens of legitimacy. As a linguistic anthropologist it was natural for me to write in direct voice, particularly in the sections on Macedonia and Germany where I conducted fieldwork. It should also make clearer the responses of the people, both Macedonian and German, as I present interactions with them. Notice that fieldwork has a narrative quality. Therefore, reading it, just as engaging in it, requires a different rhythm. The purpose will often become clearer at the end, not at the beginning, of a passage.

Organization

When the refugees left their homes in the Middle East, they embarked on a journey leading them along the Balkan Migrant Trail into Europe. Some refugees would talk about aspects of their journey in camps in Macedonia when I drank coffee with them in Germany, but more often they preferred to talk about the homes they had left. It was the journey that had defined them as "refugees." This journey is a backdrop to the book.

Yet the main focus of this book is on those who did *not* leave their homes: the Europeans who received the refugees. Therefore Chapter 1, by way of context, examines what affects European people's attitudes toward refugees. In recent times national leadership has been crucial. I present Angela Merkel, Chancellor of Germany, who has been the most positive of European leaders toward the new refugees, although it has caused her political difficulties within her own party. I also present Viktor Orbán, Prime Minister of Hungary, a very different sort of leader who has stood against receiving the refugees and even impeded their transit. The chapter also considers how Europe treated earlier European refugees. Continuing through the twentieth century, I consider postwar refugees-expelees, escapees from communism, "late settlers" and Russlanddeutsche, and those from "ethnic cleansing" in the Balkan Wars. Many people conflate migrants and refugees. I consider Turkish immigrants, the backlash of anti-immigrant violence, and the growth of a pro-immigrant consensus in the twenty-first century. This was met with the growth of Pegida, an anti-Islam group, and the new populist political party, Alternative for Germany (AfD). I conclude with a largely forgotten connection between Germany and Islam.

Part one is titled "Entry to Europe through Macedonia — Transit of Refugees." A major point here is that the refugees wanted to keep moving to arrive in some Western European country. This is fairly representative of Eastern European responses to Middle Eastern refugees as they traveled into Europe.

In Chapter 2, I present responses to refugees traveling in Macedonia along the Balkan Migrant Trail. Refugees began to pass through from 2013–14. Most people have read about refugees coming to the Greek islands, but they know less about their progress up the Balkan Peninsula. I discuss the Macedonian government's response to these refugees. I bring out the responses of several remarkable Macedonian individuals: the president of the NGO Legis.mk who is Muslim; his wife who was also a founder of Legis.mk; and a remarkable Slavic Christian woman who succored refugees as they went past her home.

With Chapter 3, I describe refugee transit camps in Macedonia where I worked in the winter of 2015 and 2016. There were personnel from government, police, international organizations, and NGOs, all with various goals, interacting with the refugees in different ways. Thousands of refugees passed through the camps irregularly, although they always seemed to be waiting. The experience of the camps and constant document checks was what made them into "refugees." They would be some of the last refugees to travel to Europe along the Balkan Migrant Trail.[5]

Part 2, titled "Inside Germany–Accommodation of Refugees," depicts a very different experience from transit. Germany took in close to one million asylum-seekers at one time, but it spread them across the entire country. As a society Germany is similar to other Western European societies.

In Chapter 4, I studied villages and how people in the smallest of communities reacted to the new refugees. Here individuals were able to set the tone of response across a village. I show differences between villages and similarities in the importance of volunteers.

In Chapter 5, I studied the responses to refugees in towns and smaller cities. Some of the early leaders I interviewed had profound insights into the broader context of refugees in Germany. Their responses framed questions I asked throughout my later research, such as why the response to Bosnian refugees in the early 1990s was so different from the response to new refugees between 2015–16. I began to study who were the people who made up the *Ehrenamtliche*, the dedicated volunteers who were so central to helping integrate the refugees. I visited refugee *Unterkünfte* and learned about the process of receiving the notification of residency. In many ways these towns and small cities were among the most interesting of communities. One town had been working on integration plans for immigrants and refugees for thirty years and had developed its own "community way" for doing so. The mayor here was deeply committed and his civic servants especially capable.

Chapter 6 takes an indepth look at programs for refugees in larger cities. Obviously there were problems of scale and especially problems of finding housing for refugees where housing was a problem for local people as well. Integration of services mattered. I describe a remarkable mentoring program for refugee children developed in a large northern city. I recommend it be adoped in schools wherever there are refugees. In contrast, most books on the recent Syrian refugee crisis, such as what is going on in Lebanon where there are a million Syrian refugees, discuss plans for schooling and integration, but never get to what actually works. In general their plans have been overwhelmed.[6]

An important part of the research is a question I posed to all people I considered knowledgeable about refugees. I asked each one, usually at the end of the interview, "What do you see as most difficult for the refugees in your area?" This may sound simple at first. The responses, however, were not simple. In essence, people were often telling me what they found difficult about the refugees, or what was most problematic about integration. There is much to be learned about German society here and attitudes to the new refugees.

In Chapter 7 I discuss the question of integration. This is crucial for Germans who do not want parallel societies of refugees developing like the ones around French cities. How can governments and people bring in large numbers of Middle Eastern refugees and integrate them into a skilled economy like that of Germany without creating ethnic districts cut off from the main society?

The conclusion brings the whole work together. I consider positive programs and strategies for success and emphasize the importance of local leadership and recount specific community personages who are making a difference. I finally return to the initial purposes of the book: to present a human perspective on host and refugee interaction and dispel fear, to encourage researchers to study host reception of refugees, and to inspire people in new initiatives in their work with refugees.

CHAPTER 1

WHAT AFFECTS ATTITUDES TOWARD REFUGEES

What affects people's attitudes toward refugees? Certainly if people know refugees personally it makes a difference. But what if people do not know any refugees? Where do their attitudes come from?

In my research I found that leaders, both national and local, made a difference. People heard the views of their national leaders through all manner of media. In Germany, Chancellor Merkel's words and actions stand out. They have affected not only her country but also the rest of Europe and the world. I present a speech she gave to her party after the major influx of refugees. I also present the context of her crucial decision to allow hundreds of thousands of refugees to enter Germany in the late summer of 2015. I also present a very different European leader, Prime Minister Viktor Orbán of Hungary. In his political speeches and public actions he has stood against EU programs to parcel out some of the new refugees to different countries of Europe. He has even made transit of refugees especially difficult through Hungary. His anti-migrant stance has gained popularity, particularly in Central Europe.

Attitudes to refugees also developed from knowledge of earlier refugees in Europe. I bring both historical background to bear as well as the experience with refugees from World War I, the interwar period, and World War II. In the postwar period there were refugees from three sources: Germans expelled from other countries in Europe, escapees from communist countries, and later refugees from "ethnic cleansing" in the Balkans.

However, often more salient was the experience with immigrants and especially the Turks in Germany and the rest of Europe. People often conflate immigrants and refugees. Here the fact that they were both Muslim and Middle Eastern added to the confusion. In the early 1990s negative attitudes toward migrants developed into violence in Germany. But surprisingly, beginning in 1998 a pro-immigrant consensus developed and grew in the new century as the German economy improved. At the same time other political movements also developed, including the AfD, an anti-immigrant populist party, and Pegida, an anti-Islam movement. Finally I note an often forgotten connection of Germany and Islam. I close with a short summary of attitudes toward refugees.

National Leadership

Angela Merkel

Angela Merkel stands out in multiple ways as a political leader. She was born in 1954 in Hamburg, Germany. Her father, a Lutheran pastor, soon moved the family to a rural area in the German Democratic Republic (GDR) north of East Berlin. She essentially grew up in East Germany. She studied physics at the University of Leipzig, worked as a research scientist, and has a doctorate in quantum chemistry.

Merkel entered politics in 1989 after the fall of the Berlin Wall as a member of a party that merged with the western Christian Democratic Union party (CDU). She was chosen party leader in 2000. In 2005, in coalition with the Social Democrats of Bavaria (CSU), Angela Merkel was declared Germany's first female chancellor and its youngest chancellor since the World War II. She was re-elected in 2009 with a greater majority. In 2013 there was another coalition and again Merkel was chancellor. Thus, she was chancellor of Germany through many major events, including the 2008 financial crisis, the European debt crisis, the Crimean conflict, and the refugee crisis. She agreed to run again in 2017 for a fourth term and her party won the greatest number of votes, but with 8 per cent fewer votes than in the previous election. As in other elections, her party would eventually rule as a coalition, but forming a coalition would be more difficult this time. Immigration policy was a major factor. I discuss it in the third chapter on the AfD, a new anti-immigrant populist party.

In researching Merkel's speeches, I found that eloquence was not a signal feature. Rather, in the build-up to the 2013 election where she was often referred to as *Mutti*, a colloquial term for "mother," analysts noted "Germans loved her because she is boring."[1] *The Economist* went a different direction at this time. It noted, "She is the world's most politically gifted democrat and a far safer bet than her leftist opponents." It added, "It is also partly because of what we believe she could still become – the great leader Germany and Europe so desperately need."[2]

The speech that Merkel gave to her Christian Democratic Union party members on 14 December 2015 is particularly revealing. *Time Magazine* had just named her as its "Person of the Year" showing her international acclaim. But there was dissension within her own center-right party due to her allowing so many refugees into Germany that year. For this reason, her speech is especially relevant for this book.

Major Speech by Merkel to CDU Party, 14 December 2015[3]

Chancellor Angela Merkel gave an hour-long speech to 1,000 Christian Democratic Union party members in Karlsruhe, Germany, on 14 December 2015. It was the annual party conference and especially important due to the events that had divided the party that year.

When Merkel took the stage, there was a small plaque in front of her on the platform stating, "for Germany, for Europe." She wore one of her usual pantsuits in the color black. As mentioned, the speech was about an hour in length and was interrupted multiple times by applause for which she did not pause.

Merkel began the speech with a list of events of the year 2015 month by month. January was the *Charlie Hebdo* newspaper killing in Paris. February was the Minsk negotiations for peace in Ukraine. March was the German Wings crash in the French Alps.[4] April was a special meeting of European leaders to discuss the hundreds of deaths in the Mediterranean. June and July were negotiations with the Greeks and a test of strength for Europe. By August it appeared there could be as many as 800,000 asylum-seekers for 2015, and in September Germany and Austria decided to allow all of them free entry. As Merkel put it, *"Das war nicht mehr und nicht weniger als ein humanitärer Imperativ."* "It was nothing more and nothing less than a humanitarian imperative." The CDU delegates applauded.

4 October 2015 marked twenty-five years of German reunification. On 13 November 2015 there were the attacks in Paris.[5] On 15 November there was cancellation of the German football match in Hannover[6] due to security reasons. Merkel is a football fan.

Merkel then proceeded to describe three Christian Democratic Union chancellors who had made promises that had all come out positively.[7] First she cited Konrad Adenauer, CDU chancellor in the 1950s. She quoted his speech in 1952 as asking not for "some sort of freedom," but for stating "We chose *the* freedom" when he sought support for the Paris treaty, the precursor of the European Union. There was applause after this.

Secondly, Merkel cited Ludwig Erhard. She noted that in 1957 he did not ask for prosperity "for some," but rather, "We seek prosperity *for all*," before he became the father of the German economic miracle. There was even more applause after this.

And lastly, Merkel brought up Helmet Kohl who as chancellor in the late 1980s did not speak of transforming "some regions" into flowering landscapes. "No," he said, "Through a joint effort we will bring Mecklenburg-Vorpommern, Sachsen-Anhalt, Brandenburg, Sachsen, and Thüringen [the five states of East Germany] into flowering landscapes." There was great applause here.

Merkel had thus given historical precedent to Germany's ability to accomplish difficult endeavors. As Merkel continued in her speech to weave the refugee crisis into these historical precedents, she emphasized that doing so was a moral imperative or, as she had earlier put it, "it was a humanitarian imperative," to once again persevere through trying times while aiding those in great need.

Merkel thanked the many volunteers who continued to serve all across the country though their work with the refugees. But then a surprise. Merkel said Germany could only do what it needed to do with the refugees if it reduced them in number. This would be "for the good of Germany, and for the good of the refugees."

It was not the cap to immigration some in her party had called for, particularly the Bavarian CSU party, and it was couched in terms of being for the good of all involved. Those who did not qualify for asylum would be sent back. These included those from countries not at war, such as refugees from the Western Balkans and Western Africa. Merkel claimed that only if they reduced the number of refugees could Germany integrate them. To do this Germany needed European help in sealing borders along with further support.

Merkel used again her famous phrase, *Wir schaffen das*, roughly, "We can do it," which she had used in August 2015 to explain how the German people would cope with so many new refugees coming into their land. But her new vision was based on the deeper understanding of what the German people had accomplished in the past seventy years. The understanding included *was in uns steckt*, 'what we are made of.'[8] Integration would be harder rather than welcoming.

Merkel explained that *multi-kulti* had not worked, as she had earlier declared in a speech in 2010, largely in reference to the Turkish population in Germany. This, though, was a midway feature on the way to a larger point. She continued that the refugees who remained in Germany all needed to learn German and integrate. By Germany taking in fewer refugees this would allow them to better integrate into Germany.

Merkel asked members to consider what Germany would be like in twenty-five years. It had been twenty-five years since German unification. Who could have expected for the time to pass so quickly, and yet so much had been accomplished. It was wise to step back and think in broader terms. Merkel then portrayed the CDU as the party that developed the European vision.

What would Germany be like then? They could only go forth and see, not remain closed. Merkel hoped Germany would still be Germany in 25 years. A country that preserved its loving qualities and strengths and passed them on. A nation with impressive cultural traditions.

At the end of her speech there was a sustained standing ovation of nine minutes. She finally told fellow party members, "We still have work to do." The speech was impressive and well received.

Context of Merkel's Opening Borders to Refugees

It was not in speeches though, but rather through a series of events and Merkel's responses to them in August and September 2015 that led Germany to open its borders to refugees.[9] The first event was a bureaucratic move from the Federal Office of Migration and Refugees in Nürnberg on 21 August 2015. It was decided that the Dublin procedures would be suspended for refugees from Syria, that is, they would not be sent back to the first European country they set foot in.

This inadvertently became public. Although it had not been enforced before this, the official nature of this was encouraging.

The next event was Merkel's visit on 26 August 2015 to a refugee hostel in Heidenau, south of Dresden, where rightwing extremists had rioted a few days before. Merkel announced, "There can be no tolerance of those who question the dignity of other people." She said this as she stood in front of placards accusing her of being a traitor. It was clear that the extremists were not appeased, as they screamed at her.

Following this, Merkel went to a conference in Vienna on 27 August 2015. While there, the news reported that 71 refugees were found dead, asphyxiated in an abandoned truck in Austria.

She continued to another meeting in Vienna on 31 August 2015 where she expressed how proud she was of the Germans who were helping the refugees. "People who are fleeing civil war will be welcome," she announced. "It won't be easy, *aber wir schaffen das*," "but we can do it."

By 4 September 2015, the situation in Hungary was getting worse. Over 2,000 refugees were stranded in Budapest. Merkel talked with the Austrian Chancellor Werner Faymann. She decided to welcome the refugees to Germany on special trains and informed her party members of her decision.

There was an early morning meeting of the CDU party the next day as the trains began to arrive in Munich. Not all party members were convinced of Merkel's decision to bring the refugees to Germany. But the welcome for the refugees in Munich was amazing as German "helpers" came out by the thousands and later in train stations across Germany.

A year later, in October 2016, there was a study from *Die Zeit* as to whether Merkel's comments and actions in the late summer and fall of 2015 could have so quickly triggered the large influx of refugees to Germany.[10] The researchers concluded that, contrary to Viktor Orbán's comments, the large influx of refugees could not have been caused by Merkel's actions. The refugees had to have left their home countries much earlier in order to arrive in Europe by late summer or fall of 2015.

Instead, it was circumstances in the home countries that led them to leave. International food sources were not making it to people in Syria in late spring of 2015 and it looked as though the situation was getting worse, especially for Palestinians in Yarmouk near Damascus. Lebanon had just instituted a visa for Syrian refugees and there was fear Turkey would do the same. Conditions in Afghanistan had deteriorated with more areas falling under Taliban control. The combination of these circumstances led people from these areas to leave their home countries and head to Europe during the summer of 2015.

Viktor Orbán, Prime Minister of Hungary

Viktor Orbán is head of a conservative center-right nationalist party. He was born in 1963 in Székesfehérvár to a middle-class rural family. He studied English in high school and then law at university in Budapest where he wrote his thesis on the Solidarity movement in Poland.

Politically he was a founding member of Fidisz (Alliance of Young Democrats) in 1988. As a radical student he spoke out against the communists in 1989. In the 1990s, as leader of Fidisz, he moved to the right and also moved Fidisz from a liberal student party to a central-right one. Ruling in a coalition government from 1998–2002, he became one of the youngest prime ministers. During this time he weakened parliamentary control and strengthened executive rule.

Orbán lost in a close fought election in 2004 and became head of the opposition. During this time political analysts came to see him as a populist, to the extent that in 2007 the UK's *Economist* awarded him its "politics of the gutter award," citing his "cynical populism and mystifyingly authoritarian socialist-style policies."[11] In 2010 he regained power and again became prime minister, an office he has held ever since. He further centralized power by cutting the number of parliamentary seats from 386 to 199. It is during this second period as Hungary's prime minister that his public speeches have become more widely known for their conservative nature.

Orbán's Recent Rhetoric

Orbán is most famous for a speech he gave in a Hungarian ethnic region of Rumania in July 2014, known as the "Tusnádfürdő" speech.[12] It is not as relevant to this book so I will only summarize it. In this speech Orbán called for abandoning liberal democracy in favor of what he calls the "illiberal state." His "illiberal state" should be most concerned with preserving national sovereignty, self-sufficiency, cultural heritage, and full employment, but not traditional liberal values like individual civil rights. The states he admires as models are Turkey, Singapore, China, and Russia. He also gave the vote to Hungarian minorities outside Hungary, helping assure his ongoing re-election.

The following year, in 2015, Orbán consistently linked migration to terrorism and blamed EU policies for the influx of refugees.[13] Internal political considerations played a part in his view. At this time, his Fidisz party was competing with the even further right Jobbik party.

Although Orbán's anti-migrant policies are extreme, he has become the voice of other Central European countries including Poland, the Czech Republic, and Slovakia who also reject the EU plan for migrant quotas promoted by Germany, France, and Italy. Orbán directly states that whereas Western Europeans may host Muslims, Eastern Europeans are free to reject them.[14]

Orbán's actions in Hungary have consistently been in line with his rhetoric against refugees.

Actions of Orbán against Refugees

Hungary is at the far end of the Balkan Migrant Trail. The most direct route for refugees is from Serbia into Hungary, then onto Austria, and finally to Germany. Due to Hungary's location, the country's refugee policies mattered a great deal.

Orbán had a tall razor wire fence built all along the 175 km Hungarian border with Serbia to impede arrivals of refugees from the Balkan Migrant Trail. Hungarian police were known for their brutality in their treatment of refugees as they tried to cross into Hungary on their way to Western Europe. This came to a head in the summer of 2015 when thousands of refugees, mostly from Syria, were blocked from trains in Budapest's Keleti station where they had gathered. They had been told that they were to be transported further west, but this was not in fact the case. Eventually the most refugees passed on to Austria and then to Germany.

Hungary has since made it even more difficult for refugees to cross, with new restrictive laws. Only those who seek asylum in Hungary are allowed to enter. Others who enter will be considered as breaking the law and could face imprisonment.

In the fall of 2016 Orbán initiated a referendum asking Hungarians to stand with him against EU quotas of refugees. Despite a massive campaign, the referendum just failed to reach the requisite 50 per cent of registered voters to pass.

As for local leaders, I will describe them in Parts I and II in the sections on Macedonia and Germany in the context of their communities. Their attitudes and actions toward refugees are especially important in their regions but, as with many positive actions, often do not gain broader media coverage.

Earlier Refugees in Europe

Previous attitudes toward refugees potentially affected Europeans' initial responses to the new refugees. During the twentieth century with the two world wars, Europe had more refugees than any other continent.

Before the nineteenth century, all mass groups of people expelled from some country in Europe appeared to be religious minorities.[15] There were the Jews expelled from Spain beginning in 1492. A century later there were the Muslims expelled from Spain. Then there were the Protestants in France who, after the revocation of the Edict of Nantes in 1685, left in large numbers to be able to practice their religion.

What is interesting about these groups is that they were all welcomed in other places. The Jews from Spain and Portugal were formally invited to settle in the Ottoman Empire by Sultan Bayezit II, who mocked King Ferdinand for his foolish action to give up such valuable citizens. The Muslims of Spain sailed across to North Africa to fellow Muslims. The Ottomans also sent ships to assist them. Many Spanish Jews settled in the Ottoman Balkans in Salonika, in Monastir, which later became Macedonia, and up to Sarajevo. The French Protestants, or Huguenots as they came to be called, traveled to various lands where they could practice their faith: Holland, Switzerland, East Prussia, and the American colonies.

In the American colonies many American patriots including Paul Revere, James Monroe, John Jay, and Francis Marion were descended from Huguenots. The Huguenots also settled in many areas of what is now unified Germany. Thomas de Maizière, the current Minister of the Interior, is of Huguenot descent.

The term "refugee" was first used to refer to these Protestants from France in the *Encyclopedia Britannica* in 1796, as "those who leave their country in distress."[16] But it did not move into general usage until after World War I.

Refugees and World War I

The millions of refugees from World War I were the first ones generally referred to as such and came largely from the east with the dissolution of the Romanov, Hohenzollern, Hapsburg, and Ottoman Empires. The sheer numbers of refugees – some estimate nine million–were daunting as new nation states arose and masses of people who had been dispossessed in the fighting found that new national borders and ideologies left them with no place to return.

From Russia alone there were about one million refugees. Many were anti-Bolshevik. Initially Germany and France took most of these refugees. Indeed the White Russians were even seen as welcome in France.[17] They did not, though, arrive directly. Their transit was circuitous, often by way of Odessa, the Black Sea, and Constantinople where they languished for several years. Utter poverty and diseases such as typhus and typhoid came with them.

In 1921 there were still some 800,000 Russian refugees scattered across Europe, many still in Constantinople. Fridtjof Nansen, the famous Norwegian explorer, was asked to lead this refugee work through a League of Nations commission. Thus he became the first High Commissioner for Refugees. He was to negotiate settlement of the refugees or their return where possible. The time frame for the commission was limited to ten years after which the "refugee problem" would have been taken care of for good.

France took the largest number of refugees at this time, about 400,000. France needed migrants. Russia and Germany had lost the greatest numbers of men in the war, but France had lost the highest per capita of men of any country in the war.[18]

Refugees and the 1930s

But the flow of refugees did not stop. This was now largely a problem for Europe to solve within itself since America had passed a restrictive quota system for immigration in the Johnson Act of 1924. The growth of fascist nation states, including Italy in the 1920s and Germany and Spain in the 1930s, led to the production of more refugees. These refugees mostly went to France where they were accepted openly at first. But as the world economy shrank, France began to impose more restrictions on new foreigners. Work permits became harder to obtain.

The question of Jewish refugees from Germany was addressed in 1933 by the League of Nations. A new High Commissioner for Refugees, James G. McDonald, was named. He was an American who would attempt to do for Jewish refugees what Nansen had done for Russian refugees in the early 1920s. But after two years, he resigned in frustration. He said that with current economic problems, few European states could absorb refugees. The problem must be tackled at its source if disaster was to be averted.[19]

It did get worse. When Germany invaded Austria in March 1938, the Jews there tried to flee, but had no where to go. To top this off, in 1939 there were 450,000 refugees from the Spanish Civil War who entered France from the south. France was in no mood to keep them and repatriated as many as possible.

Refugees and World War II

In the west, the German invasion of the Low Countries in 1940 led to a massive movement of refugees as six to eight million people tried to escape to the south. The more personal story from Arendt's *Men in Dark Times*[20] makes this clearer.

Walter Benjamin, the German literary critic, was an emigrant in France at this time. He was from Berlin and had come to Paris in 1933 to escape the Nazis after the Reichstag fire. In 1938 the Nazi regime stripped German Jews of their German citizenship so he was considered stateless. The French arrested him and put him in a prison camp in Burgundy for three months.

Benjamin left Paris with his sister the day before the Germans entered and traveled south. To avoid the threat of being sent back to Germany, he obtained a visa in Marseilles to travel to the United States and a ticket to leave on a ship from Lisbon. Benjamin only lacked a French exit visa which the Vichy French, to please the Gestapo, refused to give to German refugees.

When he finally arrived at the border town with a small group of refugees, they found that Spain had closed the border that day and the border officials would not honor visas made out in Marseilles. That night, on 25 September 1940, fearing he would be repatriated to France and into Nazi hands, Walter Benjamin killed himself. This upset the border guards so they let the small group through the next day where they safely reached Portugal.

His brother Georg was killed at Mauthausen, the slave-labor concentration camp near Linz in Austria in 1942. It was known for its abject brutality and as a place where intellectuals were sent.

And, yet, there is also a positive story. This I know from my long association with immigrant Albanians in Detroit. Getting into Albania secured safety for Jews from Greece and Italy, and even Austria and Yugoslavia. This did not come out until after communism fell there in 1991,[21] and then slowly it became known that Albania, the only majority Muslim country in Europe, had protected Jews throughout World War II.

There is a traditional concept in Albanian culture known as *besa*, one's honor or oath. When a stranger asks for hospitality, it must be given. This is also related to Muslim values of hospitality. When a person gives his or her *besa* to protect a stranger, that stranger becomes more precious than the person's own child.

Jews who made it to Albania, one of the poorest countries in Europe, were given Muslim names, local clothing, and absorbed into the communities. Though integrated into the local society, everyone knew who the strangers were. When Germans, who took over Albania from the Italians in 1943, insisted on the Jews being given over to them, not a single Albanian complied. Families were threatened but no one conceded. All the Jews in Albania before the war, about 200, and all those who had escaped to Albania during the war survived. Thus Albania was the only country in Europe to have more Jews at the end of the war, about 2,000, than at the beginning, as documented by Yad Vashem. My teacher's sister in Tirana, the capital of Albania, hid Jews from Greece for several years.

When, Norman Gershman, a Jewish-American photographer, learned of this in the late 1990s, he went to Albania to photograph and interview the remaining Albanians, now very old, who had protected Jews. The result is a remarkable book[22] and a movie, *Besa: The Promise*. The people responded to Gershman's questions by saying that all Albanians would have done the same. It was *besa*.

By the end of World War II, the destruction was unimaginable. Some estimated there were as many as 30 million refugees or displaced Europeans. Both the Allies and the Soviets claimed they cared for seven million displaced persons. These included prisoners of war, forced laborers, concentration camp survivors, expelled Germans, and people who could not return for political reasons.

After World War I, medical epidemics became a main problem. The Spanish flu had ravaged in two waves and there was also famine and typhus in the east. However, after World War II, the main problem was continuing political conflicts. This affected refugee groups who feared returning home and, therefore, tried to refuse repatriation. The Soviets forced repatriation. The Allies went along with this at first, but when they learned of subsequent executions of Ukrainian refugees, they relented and allowed half a million refugees to remain outside Soviet and East European lands.

Postwar Refugees: Expulsions, Escapees, to "Ethnic Cleansing"

The largest numbers of displaced persons after World War II were Germans. Certainly many Germans had fled the Red Army advances. But the main source of German displaced persons came from forced expulsions after the war.

In Germany people know of this because a quarter of the people are descended from people from these forced expulsions. It is estimated there were from 12–14 million Germans who were expelled from their lands in the Sudetenland of Czechoslovakia, from East Prussia in what is now in Poland, from Hungary, former Yugoslavia, and Rumania between 1945 and 1947. Most were women, children, and the elderly.

The main instigator of this was Edvard Beneš of Czechoslovakia. Before the war, in 1938, Beneš proposed to give Hitler 6,000 square km of Czech territory if Hitler would take 1.5–2 million Sudeten Germans.[23] Hitler did not take him seriously. Throughout the war, while Beneš was in the United States, he continued to lobby for the Sudeten Germans' expulsion from Czechoslovakia.

The executors of the expulsions were Stalin and Polish leaders. Germany would lose territory and Germans would have to be expelled for this to work. Churchill and Roosevelt went along with it. This agreement was finalized in the Potsdam Agreement of 1945. The program would begin in 1945 in Czechoslovakia, Poland, and Hungary, with the expulsions in Yugoslavia and Rumania to be conducted more informally. These "transfers of population" were to take place in "an orderly and humane manner" according to the Potsdam Agreement.

Many Germans had fled in terror before the advance of the Red Army. It had been truly chaotic. These expulsions were to be different.

The Sudeten Germans were the first to be expelled and there was even a public demonstration for the press to show how humane it was. But this soon disintegrated when it became clear that people had been given little warning, some only ten minutes prior to their impending expulsion, and soon led to much local looting.

When the first trains of Germans from Hungary arrived in Germany the British military in the British-occupied sector of Germany found that the refugees all bore the marks of systematic mistreatment over a long period. "Most of the women had been violated,"[24] noted the British medical examiner, "including the girls." The Americans however managed to slow down the expulsions from Hungary, which in the long run was the wisest tactic in this inhumane exercise.

The worst were the expulsions and transit from the former German lands now in the hands of the Poles. Along the way people were kept in former concentration camps. The Red Cross was not permitted into the camps. Little food was provided and the refugees were beaten, robbed, and assaulted by guards and bandits as they slowly progressed over frozen terrain. Conditions were brutal. Estimates of mortality throughout the process range from 500,000 to 1.5 million,[25] with the greatest numbers coming from those sent from Poland and Russia.

By the end of 1946, the American and British militaries were looking for ways to close down the programs. They were appalled by the physical condition of the refugees upon their arrival. The purpose of the program had been "to stabilize the continent." The explusions were not contributing to this in any conceivable way.[26]

In 1947 when the organized expulsions were ending, the US officials who had administered their part of the program "recommend that the Control Council declare its opposition to all future compulsory population transfers, in particular the forcible removal of persons from places which have been their homes for generations."[27] The Sudeten Germans had been in their homes since the twelfth century. It is important to reflect on this.

To expel people as nationalist punishment constitutes "ethnic cleansing." It is a sort of bureaucratic warfare that tarnishes those who propose it, who carry it out, and who "profit from it." It creates great suffering in those expelled that lingers for generations. Mass population transfers imply mass human rights abuses.

The Cold War to Wars in Former Yugoslavia

Just as fascism in Italy and Germany in the inter-war period had created new refugees, so communism in the post-World War II period also created new refugees. These refugees were generally individuals rather than masses of people who escaped from behind the Iron Curtain, and they were generally welcomed in Western Europe and North America. Their numbers were generally not high, their escape was a positive symbol to the West, and the economies in the West were able to absorb them.

An exception in scale was the Hungarian Uprising of 1956 when 180,000 refugees escaped through Austria. They were understood as "freedom fighters" and taken in by different Western countries. In 1968 during the Prague Spring numbers of refugees from Czechoslovakia were welcomed in the West.

In the 1990s however, 3.5 million people from former Yugoslavia became homeless. This included 2.7 million from Bosnia and Croatia in 1991–95, and 800,000 from Kosovo in 1998–99 – the greatest number of European refugees since World War II.

"Ethnic cleansing" is a form of terrorism, practiced especially by Bosnian Serb paramilitary and military, and also by Bosnian Croats to establish ethnic exclusivity in regions that had long been ethnically mixed with Bosnian Muslims. It involved raping Muslim women and girls of all ages. Prison camps were established for Muslim military prisoners and civilians where inmates were beaten, starved, and killed. The purpose of "ethnic cleansing" was to destroy the multiethnic society of Bosnia.[28]

Understandably people fled. Half of the population of Bosnia became refugees in the first year of the war. However there was a lack of consensus among the European Community (EC) on how to deal with the situation or even with the refugees. Germany took half the refugees and wanted a quota system, but Great Britain and France who had only accepted a few, argued the refugees should stay as close to their place of origin as possible. They pledged more relief and winter housing inside Bosnia. They did agree on the granting of "temporary protection" to all refugees from former Yugoslavia but not on the granting of asylum.[29]

Someone came up with the idea of "safe havens" to keep the refugees in their homelands.

Finally, with the massacre of close to 8,000 Bosnian Muslim men and boys from the UN "safe haven" of Srebrenica that was inadequately protected by a small UN Dutch contingent in July 1995, there was an impetus for the US-led NATO bombing of Bosnian Serb targets. In the second half of 1995 the Serbs were pushed back. This led to Holbrook's Dayton Peace Accords.

The new UN Secretary General, Kofi Annan, in a report critical of the UN, condemned the organization's tendency to remain neutral in civil conflicts. "Through error, misjudgment, and the inability to recognize the scope of evil confronting us, we failed to do our part to save the people of Srebrenica from the Serb campaign of mass murder."[30]

The EC made no such comment on its problems in dealing constructively with refugees and security in Europe. Clearly it had not seen refugees as a major concern for Europe. The error in this would become clearer in the new century.

Postwar Immigrants

Another potential influence on people's attitudes toward the refugees is their attitude toward immigrants and immigration. Until 1998, Germany continued to assert that it was "not an immigrant nation." Nevertheless, Germany took in expellees, groups of guest-workers who became immigrants, and asylum-seekers, along with other immigrants like the "late settlers" or Germans from other parts of Europe and especially from Russia.

Expellees from the East

People do not generally think today of the 12–14 million German displaced persons from the massive postwar expulsions as immigrants. Yet they posed many of the same problems as immigrants and had the misfortune to come at an inauspicious time. Germany was in dire condition without enough food or housing right after World War II. And here came these impoverished people in huge numbers, with their own needs and the added trauma of expulsion. No preparation had been made to receive them. Moreover, Germany had lost twice as much land as in 1919.

The top priority was to have the expellees spread out across the land and to find accommodations – in barracks, in former camps, and in forced billeting. The local Germans saw them as Poles or Hungarians, and many of the expellees did not consider themselves principally German. The relations with the expellees were so bad that in 1947 85 per cent reported they would return to countries of origin if at all possible.[31]

I learned much about this from my friend Erika who herself was expelled from the Sudetenland at age six with her grandparents and her aunt. They rode in trains in cattle cars for several days and were fortunate enough to end up in the American sector in Germany, but still in a small town where the people greeted them with insults like "Rifraff, gypsies! Go back to where you came from!"[32] They were put in the schoolhouse, and then billeted with different families. Food and fuel were in short supply. No one had money. The refugee families hired out to local farmers in exchange for food. And still more refugee families from the east arrived.

They formed *Landsmannschaften*, or homeland associations, as immigrants had in America for generations. But there was fear that the expellees would eventually prove a separate and disruptive group in German society.

Konrad Adenauer, the Christian Democrat Union chancellor of the early 1950s, was able to get passed crucial legislation for the expellees. This included making them eligible for compensation on a sliding scale, housing loans, and job training, and in 1953 making them eligible for social insurance as if they had always lived in the Federal Republic. He also was empathetic to their longing for their homelands, no matter how futile. The Marshall Plan and the upturn in the West German economy helped greatly. Still some say that second only to the economic miracle of Germany after World War II was the integration of the expellees.[33] Certainly the two are related.

In the Soviet sector the expellees were also unwelcome. Various approaches were tried, including combining their resettlement with new land redistribution. This proved a dismal failure as the expellees lacked animals, basic farming equipment, and even seed. They left the farmsteads and fled to the West. In 1950 East Germany and Poland formally recognized the Oder-Neisse Rivers as the permanent border between their two countries further upsetting the expellees, many of whom had been staying in the East in hopes of returning home. East Germany then provided them loans for household goods, but was unable to keep up with the demand. They still had the option of leaving for the West, which 830,000 of them took until 1961 when the Berlin Wall was built.[34] From then on they could not leave and the government in the East forbade talk of the expulsions.

Gastarbeiter: Italians, Greeks, and Turks

When Germans think of immigrants in the second half of the twentieth century, they think of the *Gastarbeiter*, the "guest-workers" who initially came in the 1950s and 1960s to work temporarily, some of who then stayed. The term, "guest-worker," is used because the term "foreign-worker" was used by the Nazis to designate slave laborer.

With its economic boom beginning in the 1950s, Germany had a labor shortage and so it signed recruitment agreements with Italy in 1955, and with Spain in 1960.

With the building of the Berlin Wall in 1961, there was an even greater need for migrant labor since East Germany was effectively closed as a source of labor. Germany signed a recruitment contract with Turkey in 1961, and subsequently with Morocco in 1963, with Portugal in 1964, with Tunisia in 1965, and with Yugoslavia in 1968. The Turks soon became the largest group, making up about half of the country's guest-workers.

The program was designed to work in cycles of two to three years at which point the workers were to return to their home countries. Some Spanish, Italians, and Portuguese did just that, although there was high inter-marriage of Spanish with Germans. However, industries lobbied to have the "rotation clause" removed from the German–Turkish contracts in 1964 since they appreciated the workers whom they had trained and did not want to have to retrain new ones. The Turks were dependable workers. Many of the Turks also began to stay after a coup in Turkey in 1971, since there was more security for them in Germany at that time.

The program ended in 1973 when the oil embargo stalled the economy. By then Turks had begun to bring their families. Initially they had lived in factory dormitories where there was no need to learn German. Translators were provided in the factory. When their families came they moved out to cheap apartments in the area of the factory. Ethnic communities began to form like Kreuzberg in Berlin and Kalk in

Cologne. The children went to school, but did not receive adequate instruction. The result was few Turks graduating from high school or going on to higher learning. The official policy from the 1970s until the late 1990s was to promote the desire to return home.

Meanwhile German industry changed and required more skilled workers. There began to be unemployment among former Gastarbeiter. The earlier recruitment of Turks from uneducated classes along with the subsequent lack of interest by the government in the education of their children and their integration once they and their families arrived, was now seen as deeply unwise.[35] The tendency, however, has been to blame the Turks.

Relations between Turks and Germans came to a head on 22 November 1992 with an arson attack on a Turkish home in which a grandmother and two granddaughters died. It took place on a Sunday evening in Mölln in Schleswig-Holstein in northern Germany. The grandmother, and her fourteen-year-old and ten-year-old granddaughters died, while others were seriously injured. The Arslan family had been living in Mölln for more than twenty years. An elderly disabled neighbor reported that they were nice and courteous. She said the Turkish neighbors always helped her by shoveling snow. She added, "This hate has got to stop."[36]

Two right-wing extremists, nineteen-year-old Lars Christiansen and twenty-five-year-old Michael Peters, had thrown Molotov cocktails at two homes of Turks and Kurds. In the first home nine people were seriously injured but no one died. In the second home, some were able to jump out of the upper windows, but the grandmother and the two granddaughters burned to death. The murderers called the police after the attacks and screamed, "Heil Hitler." They were arrested, tried, and sentenced to ten years and life in prison respectively. They are both out of prison now.

The attack in Mölln, a town of 17,000 people and about 700 Turks, shocked people throughout Germany. Before this the clamour had been against immigrants and asylum-seekers, that there were too many "foreigners" in Germany, and "that the boat was overfull." Now attention finally turned to right-wing violence as Germans confronted the racism and prejudice their anti-immigrant anti-refugee stands had encouraged. People demonstrated in different cities in Germany against this violence. It began to wake people up. The violence, though, was only just starting.

Asylum-seekers to "Late Settlers," the Germans from Russia

Germany did not have coherent immigration regulations for the last decades of the twentieth century as it continued to see itself as "not a country for immigrants." As a result, political asylum functioned as an immigration institution from 1970.[37] This helps explain why asylum became such a political issue by 1990 when the numbers of people applying for asylum increased greatly.

After World War II, Germany had the most generous asylum policy in Europe. Specifically, the policy encouraged "persons persecuted for political reasons enjoy the right of asylum." The Geneva Convention was also in force in Germany guaranteeing rights for refugees with race, religion, nationality, and membership in particular groups as additional reasons for protection from persecution.

The problem for Germany was the increase in the numbers of people applying for asylum, beginning in the mid-1970s. Many Kurds applied then after the coup in Turkey in 1971. Iranians followed them after the revolution in 1979, and then the Afghans in the 1980s. During the application process they were not allowed to work, but they did receive federal support funds from the German government. When turned down, many were allowed to remain under the Geneva Convention as refugees.

Meanwhile there was another group of migrants who had been coming into Germany but who increased significantly in number in the early 1990s. The term *"Aussiedler"* or sometimes *"Spätaussiedler,"* "late-settler," refers to "ethnic Germans" from countries outside Germany, as opposed to Germans from East Germany. Chancellor Helmut Kohn offered "late-settlers" automatic citizenship and other benefits should they come to West Germany to settle. *Aussiedlers* principally from Poland (848,00) and Romania (206,000) came to Germany in the 1980s, while only some 110,000 came from the Soviet Union in the 1970s and the 1980s.[38]

But when communism fell, so did travel restrictions. The "Russian Germans" or *Russlanddeutsche* came to Germany in much greater numbers. Between 1988 and 1994, one million people came to Germany from Russia. This number peaked in 1993 when over 400,000 entered. Eventually 2.5 million *Aussiedler* from Russia would come. The German government realized immediately it had to control the flow and set a quota in place, first to 225,000 a year, and then down to 100,000 a year from Russia. Recall this was the time that many Germans were coming from former East Germany as well and there was not a labor shortage. From other Eastern European countries, ethnic Germans who wanted to come then had to prove discrimination.[39]

The background to these "Russian Germans" goes back to the time of Catherine the Great, herself a German princess. She invited Europeans in 1762 to settle in Russia to farm Russian lands where they would be allowed to maintain their language and customs. German farmers, including Mennonites, took up her offer and settled principally in the Volga region of Russia. However, in the nineteenth century conditions worsened in Russia and promises that had been made to these settlers, including freedom from military conscription, were broken. In response, most of the pacifist Mennonites among the Germans in Russia then emigrated to North America.

Thus there are descendants of the Volga Germans across the northern Great Plains of the United States – land that is similar to the Russian plain. They were expert in dry farming and settled similar lands in the Dakotas, Kansas, Nebraska, and on into Canada in Manitoba and Saskatchewan. People like politician Tom Daschle, musician and singer John Denver (John Deutschendorf), actress Angie Dickinson (originally Angelina Braun from North Dakota), and popular music conductor Lawrence Welk, with his English accent that was flavored by German from his German-speaking community in North Dakota, are all of Russian German descent.

Returning to Russia, in the twentieth century in 1941 Stalin took what he termed a "preventive" measure and expelled all the Volga Germans, along with other Russian Germans to Kazakhstan and other eastern regions. This was estimated at half a million people. The able-bodied ones were sent to labor camps where a third died.

After the war, many of these Russian Germans had to remain in Kazakhstan, Siberia, and the Ural Mountains. Presumably that is where the man I met the first day in the Frankfurt train station had come from. They never were able to return to the Volga region. There was discrimination against them and they were limited in what they could study in the Soviet Union.

People sought to fit in and some began to deny their Germany origin. There was also intermarriage with Russians in the east. With Glasnost in the 1980s however, some sought a way to go to

Germany as *Aussiedlers*. The qualifications for entry from Russia included: being known as German, confirmed by descent, language, education, culture; being descended from at least one German parent; and ability to lead at least a simple conversation in German with family members.[40] This last qualification soon became the most problematic.

Back in the Soviet Union, due to intermarriage, by 1989 only 48 per cent of the *Russelanddeusche* had preserved German as the mother tongue. Lack of fluency in German turned out to be the main problem. And it got worse over time. A simple language test was instituted that many failed. By the 2000s, of those who were coming, only 20 per cent were of German ancestry; the rest were non-German family members but were still admitted.

The seriousness of the lack of German language ability of the "late-settlers" from Russia should not be underrated. The German government provided two years of full support for the new citizens, as well as housing and health care, along with first a nine-month, then a six-month language course. Nearly half a billion DM per year in the 1990s were spent as part of their integration policy.[41] Still not a lot of progress was made. In 1996, after two to five years in the country, 45 per cent of the families spoke Russian as the main language in their homes, 47 per cent spoke a mixture of Russian and German, but only 8 per cent used German extensively.[42]

Lack of knowledge of German led to problems in education and problems in employment. The young people had difficulty completing high school as might be expected, and there were problems with drugs and alcohol. Some saw drug addiction as having been imported from Russia for Kazakhstan was not far from Afghanistan and drugs were a major problem in Russia. Others saw drug and alcohol addiction as responses to the depression the young *Russlanddeutsche* experienced from being uprooted. Russian German youth began to develop negative associations in the German media with violence and crime.[43] These were made more problematic by the tendency to live in colonies. Despite all the assistance, many Russian Germans continued to speak Russian as their main language, live in Russian colonies, and function culturally as Russians with many Russian-language newspapers.

Anti-Immigrant Violence to Pro-Immigrant Consensus

Before the attack in Mölln, there were many acts of violence immediately following unification in 1990. Between 1990 and 1992, there was an over 800 per cent increase in the number of attacks on foreigners.[44] Racially motivated attacks on foreigners increased from 2,426 in 1991 to 6,336 in 1992.[45] Hostility against foreigners was linked to new right-wing and neo-Nazi groups. In 1991, the government reported that there were thirty neo-Nazi groups and forty-six other right-wing groups, plus over 4,000 militant skinheads who were not members of any group.[46]

It was not a simple phenomenon. Leaders of the neo-Nazis often came from the West. Many of the new skinheads however were from the East where people had been isolated and there had been very few foreigners. During communist times contract workers in East Germany from other communist states like Poland, Vietnam, and Cuba were kept separate from the rest of the people, and reportedly looked down on. People did not know foreigners as people. So after 1990 when the federal government in Berlin began to send asylum-seekers from the Middle East or Africa to former East Germany to live in buildings that would be used as hostels, the local people did not react well. The local police did not feel called to protect these "foreigners."

Besides the many attacks on foreigners, two riots in the East give a picture of many of the problems. The first was in Saxony in Hoyerswerda where skinheads attacked a hostel of about 150 Vietnamese and Mozambique contract workers with petrol bombs. The rioting continued for four days with local people encouraging the skinheads until the foreigners were finally expelled. The second riot was in Rostock, also in the East. Again skinheads attacked a hostel, this time with about 200 Roma asylum-seekers from Romania, but with a shelter for Vietnamese contract workers next door. The local police were not at all effective and the hostel was partially burned, while the local people cheered on the skinheads.

In reading about the skinheads in Germany in the period of the early 1990s, I found that what was most important to them was their music.[47] They had around fifty bands, shared tapes, and went to underground concerts. The lyrics were overtly racist and anti-Semitic, with some inspired by the American White-Power movement rhetoric, grounded in a sort of Nazi machismo. When this was coupled with alcohol and gang behavior, the result could often be local violence against whatever vulnerable people were available – foreigners or sometimes even handicapped people.

In general the police were very slow to respond and often arrested the foreigners rather than the local skinhead assailants. Holidays became opportunities to "hunt the foreigners." When Human Rights Watch did a study on the increase in violent attacks against foreigners from 1990 to 1992 in Germany, it concluded that "Germany is currently confronted with a political and social crisis that has profound consequences for German citizens, as well as for the foreigners who seek refuge within its borders ... Physical injury, fear and humiliation have become a daily experience for foreigners in unified Germany."[48]

It was not just the police who were lax, although they were a major problem in that 70 per cent of the cases that actually made it to court in the early 1990s were dismissed for insufficient evidence. The police had not bothered to collect evidence. The judiciary was also at fault in giving lenient sentences – "disturbing the peace" instead of "attempted manslaughter" for fire-bombing, or probation instead of jail terms.

The politicians were seen as initially at fault for setting the framework for anti-foreigner attitudes. Instead of calling the right-wing violence what it was and condemning it, they focused on the asylum debate, and limiting the numbers of asylum-seekers, thereby shifting the blame to the foreigners themselves. There did need to be a change in the asylum law. It was, however, deeply unwise to do this in the context of the racist violence and not also call out the violence.

The murders in Mölln occurred in late 1992 just after the first Human Rights Report came out. They shocked the country. They not only took place in the West, but the victims had lived 20 years in Mölln in their own home. The grandmother died saving her grandson. The two young girls who also died were fluent in German and missed in their German school. Despite all this, reported in the media, they were viewed as foreign by the perpetrators and died because of this.[49] However this case was treated differently in the courts than earlier cases. Instead of local prosecutors, for the first time a federal prosecutor took the case. And the two perpetrators were appropriately charged with murder.

The response in Germany was also significantly different. There were marches and demonstrations in twenty cities across Germany against violence and racism. In Berlin 350,000 people marched, in Dresden

10,000 marched, and in Bonn 100,000. There were more demonstrations in December with 350,000 people in Munich; 450,000 in Hamburg; 150,000 in Frankfurt am Main; 120,000 in Hannover; 100,000 in Stuttgart; 10,000 in Dresden; and many more people in other towns. On Christmas Day 1992, 200,000 people demonstrated against xenophobia in Berlin. On New Year's Day 1993, 300,000 people gathered in Essen to protest violence against foreigners. Almost three million people joined in at least fifty different demonstrations against xenophobia and racism in late 1992 and early 1993.[50] Unfortunately, these public demonstrations did not stop the attacks.

Over the next year there were more attacks on foreigners, mostly arson attacks and more people were killed. The next spring, only three days after the Bundestag had voted to restrict the right of asylum, on 29 May 1993, in Solingen near Cologne, four skinheads aged 19–23 set fire to the house of a large Turkish family. The family had lived there for fifteen years and owned the home. This time five people died including four sisters and a friend. Eight others were injured in the fire, including two small children hospitalized in critical condition. Fourteen others inside the building barely escaped injury. Outside the house there were swastikas painted on nearby buildings. Those who committed the murders were found guilty and given prison sentences of ten to fifteen years.

Later that fall in October 1993, the American Olympic luge team was at an athletic training camp in the eastern German city of Oberhof. They were celebrating the birthday of a teammate at a local bar when an African-American team member became the object of skinhead insults. Fifteen skinheads gathered and began to yell, "Nigger out! Nigger out!" The owner of the bar told the Americans to leave and they did, but the skinheads chased after them. As the Americans ran up the stairs of their hotel, one team member stayed back to block the stairs where he was kicked and beaten and ended up with a concussion and bruised ribs.

On 25 March 1994, the eve of Passover, four young men, aged 19–24, threw two Molotov cocktails at the synagogue in Lübeck, a port city in Schleshwig-Holstein. Since the cantor and his family were asleep in their apartment above the synagogue, this could have been fatal had neighbors not awakened the family from the sound of breaking glass. They awoke to find the fire in its early stages. Two years later there would be another case of arson in Lübeck, this time in a refugee hostel on 18 January 1996 in which ten people died and thirty-eight were injured. There were three suspects with burn marks on their bodies, but due to continued police incompetence they were never charged.

These attacks took place in cities and towns in the east and in the west of Germany. Although there were more attacks in the west, per capita there were more in the east where anti-foreigner talk was more open. In addition the police in the east were less well trained and continued to not have a tradition of protecting individuals from human rights violations. The commissioner for foreigners' affairs of the state of Mecklenburg-Vorpommern in the east, Jochen Rössler, stated in no uncertain terms that there was a real need for political leadership. "The youth are responding to the xenophobic tone set by adult politicians."[51]

Human Rights Watch produced a second report in 1995 as follow-up on its 1992 report. Among its recommendations were updating the old 1913 citizenship laws in Germany and providing a path to citizenship for permanent residents.

Maryellen Fullerton, who wrote the report, asserted that tying citizenship to ethnic descent had played a role in anti-foreigner feeling. She also criticized politicians who said Germany was not a country of immigration since that led the population to think that the 6.5 million foreigners who then lived there must be illegal. She recommended acknowledging Germany was indeed an immigrant country, recognizing it needed immigrants due to a declining population, and should therefore set up systematic quotas. She also noted the need for an anti-discrimination statute in Germany since foreigners, including long-time permanent residents, were confronted with discrimination on a daily basis.[52]

In the 1995 Human Rights Report there was also a short section on positive things that German people had done for foreigners. In Mölln neighbors tried to rescue the Aslan family and cried when they could not. Others sought to rescue the Vietnamese who were trapped in Rostock from rioters. There are names of Germans who worked full time to protect foreigners in Schwerin, in Berlin, in Potsdam, and in Brandenburg. There is mention of people who help tutor foreigners to learn German, who establish community programs where foreigners and Germans can meet or work on anti-racist telephone chains and other educational or political activities. Despite the anti-foreigner violence that was then occurring in Germany, the report added, "the number of private citizens in Germany actively engaged in supporting foreigners is remarkable and generally unreported."

For this book and my research in 2016, I too found that the support of foreigners by German people was truly remarkable, and at least in the American press, had generally gone unreported.

Gradual Growth of a Pro-Immigrant Consensus

All through his long time in office Chancellor Helmut Kohl had declared, *Deutschland ist kein Einwanderungsland*, "Germany is not a country of immigration." In the election in 1998, Kohl ran again as head of his CDU party with the slogan, "Safety not risks." A major issue of the campaign was unemployment, which stood at 9 per cent, and especially in the east where it was 20 per cent. Many blamed Kohl for this. The polls showed that the SPD, the more left-leaning Social Democrats with their coalition party the Greens, were in a dead heat with the CDU and its coalition partner the CSU. But the polls were wrong.

To the surprise of everyone, the SPD won by over 5 per cent and, for the first time, there was a left-wing party in power in postwar Germany. Kohl stepped down.

Several important policy initiatives related directly to immigration were finally passed in Germany in 2000, in 2005, and in 2012. These were long overdue and helped change the public discourse around immigration in the twenty-first century. They allowed Germany to take a different path than the rest of Europe in this time. Great Britain, for example, became more negative to immigration, Germany became more positive. The strength of the German economy was linked to immigration in a positive way. Leaders in industry, politics, and media all contributed.[53] But the path to this more positive consensus regarding immigration was not smooth.

In 2000 there was reform of citizenship laws making naturalization of permanent residency easier to secure. Recall that unlike in America, being born in Germany had meant virtually nothing for citizenship in the past. Rather German descent or "blood," was what was culturally meaningful. That was how so many people from the former Soviet Union with one parent of German descent had gained immediate German citizenship in 1992, while Turks who had lived and worked in Germany for three generations had not.

The new law hammered out in 2000 stated that people born in Germany, with one parent who had worked in Germany for eight years, and had a residency permit to prove it, could receive German citizenship. The problem here was many "third country nationals" (a term for people not from the EU who were mostly of Turkish descent) had lived and worked in Germany much longer than eight years, but had not needed the residency permit until 1997. As a result, they did not have one.[54]

But the main debate that made the whole discussion of citizenship and loyalty messy was the question of dual citizenship. The SPD and Green parties wanted the new citizens to be able to maintain dual citizenship if they so wanted. The CDU/CSD did not. It is a somewhat hypocritical issue in Germany since people born of parents of two nationalities there automatically retain both nationalities. Further, the *Russlanddeutsche* were all allowed to retain their Russian citizenship when they came to Germany.[55] In Western Europe, the tendency had been toward retention of dual citizenship.[56] The citizenship reforms in 2000 were passed without the possibility of dual citizenship, but in 2014 these were changed to allow it in limited circumstances.

More central to German bureaucracy was the change in 2005 that led to an actual immigration system and a formal legal framework for permanent settlement of foreign workers. Here, the office that had previously worked with asylum, the BAMF (Bundesamt für Migration und Flüchtlinge), began to work with implementing migration and immigration policy. In addition it organized language courses, integration courses, and a large research department as well. In 2006 there was a General Equal Treatment Act and a federal anti-discrimination agency created in the same year[57] to support anti-racism work.

Positive initiatives were occurring across German society. Basic to these were Germany's now strong economy, with reforms of its social welfare policies in 2005 and expansion of employment. Industry and employers' associations eventually came to link immigration to economic competitiveness.[58] Since fertility had remained low at 1.4 children per woman, there was a growing need for immigration to replace the aging population and thereby support the social system in Germany, or by 2030 there would be significant problems. In 2012 there were new laws to encourage the immigration of highly skilled people and more industry-driven hiring.

Media also became somewhat more positive toward immigrants, especially at the local levels. There were efforts, including by major media outlets, to hire journalists with *Migrationshintergrund*, that is,

Figure 1.1   Poster "Must the next generation work for two [in German]" that supports the prediction of the severe lack of workers in coming decades and, therefore, the need for immigrants now. Produced by the German government.

with "a migration background."[59] This meant either "immigrants or people who had an immigrant parent." In either case it suggested people were more informed at a personal level about immigrant issues.

This descriptor came into general use as people began to realize how many people in Germany fit into this category.

Yet in the largely positive climate, the bestseller book by banker Theo Sarrazin in 2010 asserting that Muslims had dumbed down Germany[60] was a highly negative contribution. In response, Chancellor Merkel announced that, "multiculturalism had failed." Clearly the times were ripe to consider what Germany should do with its cultural diversity.

Two ideas came forth. One was the *Willkommenskultur* or "Welcoming Culture," to try to present the positive aspects that new people of different cultures could bring to Germany. The other idea was the *Anerkennungskultur* or "Culture of Recognition" of what contributions immigrants already residing in Germany can bring to society. These penetrated into the general society in ways to become apparent when the refugees came in great numbers in 2015. The positive attitude toward immigrants continued.

Why had Germany become more positive toward immigrants when most of Europe had gone the other direction in the same time period? Some saw this as the way the new EU workers were allowed into different countries. Britain and Sweden allowed them in directly in 2004 so they came in large numbers. Germany had a more measured approach and new EU workers came more slowly. Also the German economy was stronger during this period and there was less unemployment in general. But the confluence of political, industrial, and media made all the difference here as well.

A study on societal attitudes to immigrants conducted in 2008–11 shows the differences in different European countries. In contrast to other European countries at the time, anti-immigrant sentiment was lower in Germany. In this time period, each year about 28 per cent of Germans agreed with the statement "there are too many immigrants in the country." In contrast, in the same time period, about 57 per cent of British supported that opinion. The French, Spanish, and Italians were in the middle, with the French closest to the German position, and the Italians closest to the British one.[61]

Politically no party with an anti-immigrant agenda in Germany was able to gain significant political influence for the years 2005–15.[62] The remarkable positive responses to refugees, beginning in 2014, and in cities all across Germany in 2015 must be taken as evidence of German societal changes as well. Even in the most recent election, the anti-immigrant party, the AfD, only received 12.6 per cent of the vote and it was skewed with the highest per centages of votes coming from states in former East Germany. Although the AfD did receive 15 per cent of the votes in the west in Baden-Württemberg, these were presumably from the many *Russlanddeutsche* in smaller towns there.

The "Alternative for Germany:" Pegida and AfD

At the same time as positive consensus had grown, there were other forces at work. In late 2014 Pegida, which was said to have started on Facebook in October, was also growing. I was in Berlin in December of that year, and every Monday evening, the crowds in nearby Dresden would gather. They were getting bigger and by December they were in the thousands.

Pegida from Dresden

Pegida stands for *Patriotische Europäer gegen die Islamisierung des Abendlandes*, that is, "Patriotic Europeans against the Islamisation of the Occident." By January 2015, they drew 25,000 for their Monday stroll turning out to be their peak number. After that the numbers declined. Just what they stood for was not always clear, but it included more selective immigration, expulsion of religious extremists, tighter security, and the duty of migrants to integrate. It was not so much the specific points as much as the negativity that the crowds engendered toward migrants in general and Muslims in particular. It was also strange because there are relatively few Muslims in Saxony, the state in which Dresden lies. But maybe that made it easier – people did not know any Muslims so it was easier to fear and disparage them.

The founder of Pegida, Lutz Bachmann, is himself from Dresden and was born in 1972. It was suggested the main reason he founded the group was because he was against the locating of sixteen refugee shelters in Dresden. Due to his background, he has been less than a credit to the group. Bachmann had been convicted of sixteen burglaries, drunk driving, dealing in cocaine, and failure to pay child-support. He left Germany for South Africa in the 1990s to avoid prison and several years later was extradited back to Germany where he finally served his jail sentence. He can hardly preach against immigrants as problematic citizens.

In January 2015, Bachmann was accused of using hate speech on Facebook in referring to immigrants as "animals," "scumbags," and "trash." At the end of January 2015, Bachmann resigned from the leadership of Pegida. With other former Pegida members he founded a new political party, Direkte Demokratie für Europe. Soon after, however, he was re-elected as head of Pegida. He was tried in court for hate speech and fined. He then migrated to the Canary Islands where he was not welcome and returned.

There have been many counter-demonstrations to Pegida rallies whose participants, like those in Cologne where 35,000 gathered in January 2015, or those in Berlin, easily outnumbered those at Pegida rallies. Meanwhile, researchers have studied participants at Pegida rallies. They have found that the participants are overwhelmingly male, include people who have no confidence in institutions, and who are focused on enmity and racism.

Another study, this one by the Forsa Institute, asked more generally of the German people if they thought Islamisation was a danger. They found that 67 per cent of the people felt this was exaggerated. There continue to be Pegida rallies in Germany and offshoots in other countries in Europe. The most recent one of significant size was on Unification Day in Dresden, 3 October 2016, when some 5,000 gathered and demonstrated.

Chancellor Angela Merkel went to Dresden on this day where she was treated with some disrespect. Chancellor Merkel had earlier criticized Pegida in her New Year's message on 30 December 2014, saying, "their leaders have prejudice, coldness, even hatred in their hearts." Two weeks earlier, on 12 December 2014, the Federal Minister of the Interior, Thomas de Maizière had said "the participants of the mass rallies were many ordinary people who expressed their concerns about today's society."[63] Germany's Muslims are made fearful by Pegida. De Maizière clearly does not include them when he speaks of "ordinary people in today's society." Germany's Muslims need to hear clear, unequivocal words such as those from Chancellor Merkel. What is very much at stake here though is the CDU political base. The fear is that actions of Pegida will push the CDU further to the right. This is even more the case with the AfD.

AfD, the "Alternative for Germany" and Its Changing Leadership
More politically astute than Pegida, but also right-wing and anti-immigrant is the populist political party, the AfD, Alternative für Deutschland, "the Alternative for Germany." But it did not start out that way. The origins of the AfD were as a political group in 2012 made up of economists, editors, business leaders, and academics who did not think Germany taxpayers should pay for southern Europe's and especially Greece's economic woes. They came to be against the euro and the legality of various eurozone policies. They called themselves the "Electoral Alternative 2013," and that year decided to try to get into federal politics in Germany where some referred to them as the "professors' party" for all their academic degrees. Economist Bernd Lucke was an initial founder. The party, though, did not reach the necessary 5 per cent of the vote to get into the Bundestag that year.

By 2014, they were doing better. They won seats in the east in Saxony, Thuringia, and Brandenburg, In 2015 they won seats for the first time in the west in Hamburg. The focus of the party had been changing, however, and there was infighting in the leadership. In July 2015 the founding leader, economist Bernd Lucke of Berlin, was replaced by chemist Frauke Petry of Dresden. Petry represented the faction of people who were less interested in eurozone policies and more interested in countering migration and Islam.

Petry has a degree in chemistry from the University of Reading and a doctorate from Göttingen. But she had been forced to go through bankruptcy in 2013 due to her small business of polyurethane tire fillers being unprofitable. Her mother then called her attention to the new political party and she had jumped at the chance. Lucke understandably referred to her not as an ideologue but as an opportunist. Lucke claimed that Petry was turning the party into a "Pegida Party." There is overlap, and like Pegida participants, 85 per cent of AfD members are male. To emphasize the change, five other founding members left the AfD as did Lucke, citing the growth of xenophobic and pro-Russian sentiments.

By 2016 the main focus of the AfD was the question of migrants. At the party congress in May 2016, Petry added strong anti-Islam elements to the platform. She called for opposition to Islam, a ban on Muslim symbols including burkas, minarets, and the call to prayer. She publicly stated, "Islam is not part of Germany."

This last remark was a direct strike at the CDU and Merkel. Christian Wulff, a liberal member of the CDU, had said that Islam belongs to Europe. Angela Merkel had reiterated this several times in 2015. After Petry had declared that Islam is not part of Germany, the head of the Muslim Central Council, Aiman Mazyek, invited Petry to discuss this at a meeting in Berlin in the Regent Hotel. Petry accepted. With the press corps around them, Petry accused Mazyek of wanting to impose Sharia law in Germany, a false claim. Mazyek then brought out what he said was a gift for Petry – a large copy of the German Basic Law. Mazyek had his signature written next to Article 4 stating the guarantee of religious freedom.[64]

What could Petry do? If she did not accept the gift, she would be disrespecting the German constitution. If she accepted, she would be capitulating to a Muslim, albeit one born in Germany of Syrian and German parentage. She got up and rushed out of the room to head downstairs to the hotel lobby where she would continue the press conference. Mazyek held his own press conference where he was.

Afterwards, when asked, Mazyek said he had wanted to raise awareness of the unconstitutional agenda of the AfD, and to show that the AfD is not capable of having democratic discussions. He added,

> The AfD uses the refugee crisis to foment a propaganda of fear in the minds of its followers. Insults and daily Islamophobia have led to the desecration of houses of worship, and bullying in the streets.[65]

In April 2017 there was another change in leadership of the AfD. Petry, who had been trying to lead the party in what she called a more realistic and pragmatic approach so it would have a chance to be part of a coalition in a future government, found her ideas rejected. Instead the party saw as its goal to remain in strong opposition to the politics of Merkel.[66] Petry stepped aside and the two new co-leaders of the AfD became 76-year old Alexander Gauland and 38-year old Alice Weidel. Petry subsequently, just after the September 2017 election and to the surprise of everyone, announced she would serve only as an independent member from her constituency, not from the party. Four other party members followed in her path.

As for the two new leaders of the AfD, Alexander Gauland is a conservative who formerly served in the CDU for many years before moving to the right and the AfD. He is known for his racist statements about a famous German football player whose father was from Ghana, and his suggestion that the current Minister of Integration, whose ancestry is Turkish, return to Anatolia. Alice Weidel is a trained economist and investment banker who lives in Switzerland with her female partner from Sri Lanka and two sons. She is publicly less problematic than Gauland although emails have come out where she refers to Merkel's government as "pigs who were nothing more than puppets of WWII allies."

In the 24 September 2017 election the AfD garnered 12.6 per cent of the vote. It was the first time a far right party had gotten above the 5 per cent minimum required to have seats in the Parliament. As such it was seen as a success.

How important will this be in German politics? Analysis from the polls show 60 per cent of AfD voters voted against all other parties, and only 34 per cent voted out of conviction for AfD. Thus, the relationship between AfD and its voters is alleged to be weak. Moreover, only 12 per cent of Germans were satisfied with the political work of Alice Weidel and Alexander Gauland. This was the lowest for political leaders of all political parties. What people see is that the election shows de-alignment from the mainstream parties, both the CDU/CSD and the SPD, rather than re-alignment to the AfD. It is far more likely the internal struggles of the AfD will prevent any re-alignment.[67]

When asked about influence of the AfD, Merkel responded that the AfD would have no influence on Germany's foreign, European, and refugee policies.[68]

However, after the election, Merkel did agree to a long-standing request of the CSU, the Bavarian part of her own party, that there be a limit of 200,000 on the number of asylum-seekers allowed to enter Germany each year, although this number will be allowed to fluctuate depending on circumstances.[69]

Forgotten Connections of Germany and Islam

Before leaving the question of Germany and Islam, however, I cannot help but remember the Kaiser. Yes, Kaiser Wilhem II worked to maintain a positive relationship with Muslims and the Ottoman Empire in the late nineteenth century. Sometimes it helps to step back.

The German Empire under the Kaiser worked to maintain good relations with the Muslim world and the Ottomans as a way to thwart the British, the French, and the Russians. The Berlin–Baghdad Railway was part of this design. As a symbol of this, the elegant train station on the Asian side of Constantinople, Haydarpaşa, was a gift from the Kaiser. From their side, the Ottomans valued the Germans as the only power that did not have territorial designs on the Middle East. Kaiser Wilhem II took a formal trip to Ottoman lands in the 1890s. There is a beautiful fountain at the north end of the Hippodrome in Istanbul to commemorate the Kaiser's visit in 1898.

But much more important is the role of German scholars of Islam. It began with Biblical studies and spread to studies of Islam. Here though I cannot leave out the romantic influence of Goethe and his *West-östlicher Divan* (1819, 1827) that was inspired by translations of the great Persian poet Hafez. At the end of his life, Goethe studied Persian and Oriental literature so he could poetically come into dialogue with fourteenth century poet Hafez of Shiraz, despite the cultural and historic distance. To understand the spiritual love in Hafez' lyric poetry Goethe had to study Islam as well. Goethe's *West-östlicher Divan* inspired German scholars to pursue studies of the Islamic world.

There is Theodor Nöldeke (1836–1930), born in Harburg, now part of Hamburg, who studied in Göttingen, Vienna, Leiden, and Berlin. He is most famous for his French-language history of the Qur'an (1857) which won prizes in Paris, and which he then translated into German the next year.

There is Ignac Goldziher (1850–1921), born in Hungary in Székesfehérvár, the same hometown as the prime minister of Hungary, Viktor Orbán, but educated at the universities of Budapest, Berlin, Leipzig, and Leiden. He traveled in Syria, Palestine, and Egypt, and studied at al-Azhar, in Cairo, the oldest university in the world. He wrote on pre-Islamic and Islamic law, as well as religion and poetry. Together with Nöldeke, Goldziher founded Islamic studies in Europe.

Carl Brockelmann (1868–1956) was from Rostock. He studied in Rostock, Breslau, and Strasbourg under Nöldeke. He is best known for his remarkable five-volume *Geschichte der arabischen Literatur*, "History of Arabic Literature."

Then there is Franz Rosenthal (1914–2003) from Berlin. He translated the *Muqaddimah* of Ibn Khaldun, the great Muslim traveler and historiographer who journeyed across North Africa in the fourteenth century, and who is seen as a forerunner of the modern disciplines of sociology and demography. Rosenthal was an expert on Semitic languages and also wrote on the concept of knowledge in medieval Islam.

Annemarie Schimmel (1922–2003) from Erfurt in central Germany studied at the University of Berlin. She spoke Arabic, Farsi, Turkish, Sindhi, Urdu, and Punjabi, and knew extensive poetry and numerous writings in all these languages. She was especially known for her profound understanding of mystical aspects of Islam or Sufism as it is called.

What these scholars show is that there has long been great appreciation of the Islamic world by Germans. These scholars clearly brought Islam into their minds and have given much to the world in return. Through their work I do think Islam most certainly belongs in Germany.

Reflection on Attitudes Toward Refugees

It is clear that Europeans in general and Germans in particular have had varying attitudes toward refugees. It is interesting to note that historically, in earlier times in Europe, refugees like the Jews and Muslims from Spain, and the Huguenots from France were seen to a certain extent as "desirable citizens." Even after World War I, Germany and especially France absorbed many refugees from Russia. However the Jews from Germany in the 1930s and the Bosnians in the 1990s were not seen positively in Europe.

At the end of the 1990s and into the twenty-first century, the attitude to immigrants in Germany became more positive and this transferred to refugees. The economy became stronger, and the demographic need became clearer. The media became more sensitive as people with a migration background were hired. Employment from other EU countries was phased in gradually. There was national leadership as well. Chancellor Merkel's words and actions toward the new refugees and welcoming them in Germany in the late summer of 2015 were reflected in the reception they received in Munich and many cities in Germany that fall.

In contrast Prime Minister Orbán opposed the refugees and spoke of them as if they were terrorists. Refugee accounts of the difficulties they faced trying to cross Hungary document police brutality and local people's distance from them. Indeed, as the attitudes had become more positive in Germany toward immigrants and then refugees, feelings had become more negative toward refugees in many other countries in Europe.

PART I

ENTRY TO EUROPE THROUGH MACEDONIA – TRANSIT OF REFUGEES

CHAPTER 2

NGOs AND LOCAL RESPONSES

Macedonia as a modern country is not well known. During most of the twentieth century, it was part of former Yugoslavia. Before that it was an important province in the European territories of the Ottoman Empire for 500 years (1392–1912). Located in the central Balkans, it was known for trade and its commercial cities like Skopje, which had the largest Turkish market or bazaar in the entire Balkans.

When former Yugoslavia erupted in war in the 1990s, Macedonia, the southern-most republic and one of the poorest, declared its independence in 1991, and stayed out of the fray. Macedonia today is thus a small country of an estimated 2.1 million inhabitants. Its population is made up of a Christian majority, an estimated 63 per cent, including Macedonian Slavs, Serbs, and Vlachs; with a large Albanian Muslim minority and other smaller Muslim minorities,[1] including Turks, Bosnians, Roma, and Torbach, bringing the Muslim population to an estimated 37 per cent of the country.

Its economy is not strong. It has unemployment of 28 per cent with some figures much higher. Its economy has been held back by its neighbor Greece's unwillingness to recognize its name and, therefore, continual blocking of its membership in international organizations such as the EU or NATO. In the UN, Macedonia is known by the unwieldy "the former Yugoslav Republic of Macedonia." Greece contends it can only use the name "Macedonia" for historic reasons. With the Macedonian government of Zoran Zaev however, there have been new discussions in 2018 between Macedonia and Greece on the name issue.

Macedonia has also been constrained by political polarization, weak institutions, media censorship, and problems of corruption. The division between the two largest ethnic groups of Macedonian Slavs and Muslim Albanians has never been healed since the Slavic Macedonians set up the Constitution in 1991 without any local Albanian input.

Macedonia and Refugees

Macedonia's Earlier Experiences with Refugees

Macedonia has had multiple experiences with refugees despite its young age. As recently as the spring of 1999 from its northern border 377,500 Kosovar Albanian refugees entered Macedonia, pushed out of their homes in adjacent Kosovo by Serbian military and paramilitary forces. The Kosovar Albanian refugees entered Macedonia in a nine-week period. This was a large number of refugees for a small country and was potentially destabilizing for a country that already had a minority problem with Albanians. That was Serbian President Milošević's intention. What he had not counted on was the remarkable hospitality of Albanian families living in Macedonia.

The West realized Milošević's intentions so the UN set up two camps there; however, Albanian families in Macedonia in the western cities of Tetovo, Gostivar, Skopje, Debar, and Struga, and the northern city of Kumanovo hosted most of the refugees. For example in May 1999, the UN camps took in 130,000 refugees while host Albanian families took in 170,000 refugees.[2] The refugees did not stay long in Macedonia; instead, most returned to Kosovo that summer.

Over a generation earlier, refugees had entered Macedonia from its southern border. These were ethnic Slavic Macedonians in the late 1940s who fled Greece in the Greek Civil War. They had fought with the Greek Communists, hoping for more ethnic rights within Greece. These refugees included tens of thousands of Macedonian refugee children, who now gather internationally as part of ARCAM (Association of Refugee Children from the Aegean part of Macedonia).

Yet earlier still, the Ottoman province of Macedonia had been deluged with Muslim refugees in the First Balkan War (1912–13). There was a battle by Kumanovo in 1912 and much killing of Muslims there and in and around Skopje.[3] Further south, 80 per cent of the

Muslim villages around Manastir were burned.[4] What was worse for the Muslim refugees was that their natural exit to Turkey was blocked by Bulgarian troops who sought to take Istanbul.

All this suggests that Macedonia would not take kindly to new refugees of largely Muslim backgrounds entering their territory.

The Balkan Migrant Trail

Macedonia and Greece share a somewhat porous border of 228 kilometers. In 2013 refugees began to cross this border in increasing numbers. Greece is part of the European Union and Macedonia is not. However Greece has had major economic difficulties for the past ten years. In any case the border was not well policed.

As refugees entered from Greece, Macedonian police and border guards would beat them and send them back to Greece again and again.[5] They considered them illegal migrants and aliens. The numbers increased in 2014 as the war in Syria got worse and other desperate people joined. The route the refugees followed from the south to the north in Macedonia went through largely Slavic Christian agricultural lands. It was far from areas where the minority Muslims live in the northwest of Macedonia. I should add that the Muslims in Macedonia are among the poorest of its citizens. But generosity is not linked to wealth.[6]

Initially the refugees followed the age-old route along the Vardar River up from northern Greece into Macedonia. At least they tried to follow it. If border guards or police caught them, they were beaten and forced back into Greece. If they made it past them, they continued, often following the train tracks that also took this route, north 200 kilometers toward Serbia. They would walk at night, hide, and try to sleep during the day.

There were several towns and cities to avoid by the tracks and the river. The border town in the south was Gevgelija with its train station and border guards. It has 15,000 people. Then along to the northwest, is Demir Kapija, a town whose name means "Iron Gate" in Turkish, referring to the gorge in the mountains the Vardar passes through. The town has has only 3,700 people. Two more towns are along the way, and then the larger central Macedonian city of Veles, with 55,000 people.

By the time they reached Veles, the refugees were famished. They had to be careful because the train forked to the west to Skopje, and then to the east just beyond there. But they wanted to follow the tracks that kept going directly north to Kumanovo, a city of 76,000, where they could stay in the large mosque before continuing to the border. At that border again they had to avoid border guards on both sides, both Macedonian and Serbian. If they were most fortunate, they might make the journey in ten days.

In 2014, an estimated 21,000 refugees traveled through Macedonia on their way to Western Europe.[7] Macedonia had become a strategic part of the Balkan Migrant Trail. See Map 1. Balkan Trail into Europe, but note that Hungary essentially closed the route that went through its country in 2016.

Not Macedonia's Finest Hour

As mentioned, the first response of Macedonian police and border guards to refugees, who attempted to cross at the southern border from Greece into Macedonia on their way to Western Europe, was to beat them and

Map 1   Balkan Trail into Europe.

force them back into Greece. This is well attested to in an Amnesty International report.[8] They were considered "illegal aliens."

The other main response, if refugees were found with a taxi driver or someone who could be considered a smuggler, is that they were taken to Gazi Baba Detention Centre for Foreigners, named for the neighborhood in which it is located in Skopje. It was a former nursery that originally housed forty children. Amnesty International notes that the Government said it could house 120 people. Refugees reported that 450 refugees were detained there with one shower and two working toilets.[9] The alleged purpose was to keep them there until the "smugglers" could be tried, but Macedonian law does not allow for witnesses to be detained. Many refugees were kept in these inhuman conditions for several months while the "smugglers" were long gone.

Meanwhile, there were some tragedies for those who followed the railroad tracks on foot. On 6 November 2014, a train near Gevgelija hit an Afghan father and his infant killing both. The mother watched this and was then taken to the detention center. Later that November, eight refugees were killed along the tracks between Veles and Skopje in central Macedonia. And on 24 April 2015, fourteen people were killed by trains in the same area.[10] These were on bridges and in tunnels where the refugees could not escape the oncoming train.[11] This last incident would help mobilize people to change government policy.

In between there were other dangers of attacks, theft, and kidnapping for funds from local villagers and criminal gangs, as well as constant hunger and thirst, exhaustion, and medical problems from the long journey. Despite all these difficulties, refugees continued to cross the border from Idomeni, the last town in northern Greece, into Macedonia, and on to the border with Serbia. In the first half of 2015, an estimated 30,000 refugees made this journey, although many had to make multiple attempts to cross the southern Macedonian border since they were often beaten and sent back by the police.

How did the Macedonian people respond to the refugees? As mentioned, Macedonia is a poor country and divided by religion and ethnicity. Many people are unemployed or underemployed. To have strange foreigners walking through their land was not taken well by most. The press was not positive and suggested crime was a possibility, although no crimes by refugees were reported.

Culturally the Muslims in Macedonia had little in common with the refugees, but during Ramadan they would donate to help them. Geographically the Muslims lived far from the Balkan Migrant Trail, except in the far north by Kumanovo, a mixed city about half Slavic, half Muslim, with some Albanian Muslim villages in the north as well. Not all the Muslim villagers were helpful, although they were reportedly more so than Christian villagers.

The real difficulty for Macedonia was that it was caught in the middle of ill-defined EU policies for migration. Should refugees be sent back to Greece since that was the first place they had touched ground in Europe as suggested by the Dublin Accords? Macedonia was a new country and did not have experience with transiting refugees. This did not excuse detaining people for indefinite periods in inhuman conditions.

Ultimately it was citizens of Macedonia who came to the rescue.

Jasmin Redjepi's Response: Establish an NGO with Friends

Before I went to Macedonia in December 2015, I researched NGOs and determined that Legis.mk was the best local NGO for my purposes. It had been the first local organization to work with refugees in Macedonia and its work was expanding. I could tell it was held in high regard by other NGOs, which was a good sign. For example, the Helsinki Foundation was represented on its executive board.

The location of the headquarters of Legis.mk in Çair, a largely Muslim municipality within Skopje, also encouraged me to work for it. Most international organizations had their headquarters on the other side of the city. I assumed the officials of Legis were also from Çair. I knew Çair well and knew it included the old city of Skopje.

When I say "old city," I mean old in the Roman, Byzantine, Bulgarian, and Ottoman sense. A main mosque there, Sultan Murat Mosque, dated back to 1463. The Turkish school, Tefeyyüz, along the street the first Legis warehouse was on, had been founded in 1884. Between it and the warehouse was the Rufa'i Sufi brotherhood headquarters. All these had meaning for me with my Albanian connections back in Detroit. I do not like fly-by night operations. I prefer to work with people who are rooted in their cultures.

So I flew to Skopje and went to the Super 8 Hotel on the Muslim side of town by the entry to the old Turkish Bazaar and the university, in Çair of course. Its owner is an Albanian from Kirçevo and he had worked in Alaska where he had earned the funds for the hotel and presumably derived the name. He hires staff from different ethnic groups – Macedonian, Albanian, and Turkish, who all work well together.

Communication had to come first. The first morning I got a Macedonian chip in my phone and, on the way out of the T-Mobile store, I caught the eye of an older man, clearly Albanian. Just outside the store I asked him in Albanian about Legis. He nodded and we walked together to the street of its warehouse, over a main thoroughfare of the city, past some elegant old mosques, and down a road to the street with the Turkish school.

Now the NGO Legis has a better warehouse, but the one I went to on that cold morning in December was a typical one of the region – unadorned concrete block and red brick. The steps up had no bannister. One floor up and inside, it was full of boxes on all sides, and the windows did not have glass in them.

There were two young women working there: Emineh who spoke Macedonian, Bosnian, and English, and Sara who spoke Albanian and English, and who had dark curly hair. Both had university degrees, both were very welcoming and attractive, and both were wisely wearing their winter coats. There was a small table with coke and water bottles. Would I like some? Water please. Emineh went and got me a bottle of water from a large storage of water bottles against the wall – maybe a thousand such bottles were in storage ready to take to the refugee transit camps.

There were two plastic chairs and a very unsteady seat from a van. They told me they had a van in which they transported things to the border. They explained that they would take out the seat so they could carry more. They were packing bags of things for the children, toys and cookies, and warm clothing to take to the refugees in Tabanovce in the north and Gevgelia in the south.

I asked about Legis. Emineh said Hadis knew more since he has been working much longer. "When he comes he can tell you." I would learn that Hadis was an important man in the organization, one of the founders. I would meet him soon enough.

Still Emineh knew a lot. She said that Legis had started helping with food for the refugees before the new law. They had distributed food along the train route from their van. Wherever they saw refugees, they would pass out bags of food. It was illegal for refugees to stop in anyone's home.

Figure 2.1   Sara, author, and Emineh by Balkan Relief poster in Legis warehouse, Skopje, Macedonia, 2015.

If the police caught the refugees doing something wrong they took them to Gazi Baba.

She explained that Gazi Baba was a kindergarten that had been made for forty children. However, now it was being used as a detention center for 400 refugees. Sara added that they had four refugees to a bed.

Emineh said that "the new law" dated from 18 June 2015. It allowed refugees to use public transportation. After that Legis took food to the two border stations. I asked how they got the law changed. Emineh sought an English word. "Pressure?" I asked. "Yes, many put pressure. Especially Jasmin and others. So finally the law changed so the refugees could ride the train. Before that they could not even take a taxi."

I asked about the financing of the food and toys and clothing. "You better ask Jasmin. He knows all that," they answered. Not long after a man in a suit with a reddish beard came in. He was Jasmin Redzepi. I was introduced to him as, "This is Jasmin." In effect, everyone should know who he was already. I gave him my business card showing I had been a professor at Indiana University with my email address. I had written my new Macedonian phone number on it. He gave me his business card too. But only later when I looked at his card did I realize that he was the President of Legis. The exchange of cards was more a ritual than a time for careful reading.

Instead we started talking. Since he was dressed more formally than the young women I asked him different questions. He said he had much experience with media since 2003. He said he had worked for other NGOs. Then he told me he was on the Mavi Marmara.[12] Ahh. That impressed me. I said, "So you were in Israel." He nodded, but he did not elaborate.

We sat on the van seat and some boxes and talked. Jasmin has a gentle manner and a clear way of talking. I asked him about his family. His father is Albanian, originally from Gilan in Kosovo, an intellectual center, and his mother is Bosnian from the Montenegrin Sancak. So he knows both cultures. He was raised in Macedonia in Macedonian schools and speaks very good Macedonian, which matters for the media. I later listened to interviews he gave on Macedonian television. His manner is especially good – he is appealing and knows how to use humor. Despite having a Muslim last name, he has no discernible accent, which matters in Macedonia.

He asked me what I thought about orientalism. It looked like he had read my business card. I told him that Palestinian Edward Said, who proposed the theory of orientalism,[13] could not read Arabic. He also did not deal at all with the whole field of German orientalists who were most important. I have a lot of respect for many orientalists and their scholarship. I told him I thought Said was a good man, but one skilled in literature, not history or philology.

I said while I agreed with Said's idea that outsiders could bring stereotypes and prejudices to bear, so too could local people. For example nationalists in the Balkans had many false ideas about the Ottomans who had ruled here for many centuries. I knew this well because I taught a university course on "Islam in the Balkans" that dealt with the history of the Ottomans in the Balkans. Balkan nationalists had twisted much of Balkan history to support their myths.

Then he asked me about books on Islam. What did I think of John Esposito? Karen Armstrong? I told him among foreign scholars I preferred people of faith like Karen Armstrong.[14] Martin Lings? Yes. I also liked the German Annemarie Schimmel. We talked about the spread of Islam. I said the Balkans were very important for understanding the spread of Islam since the sources were so good.[15] And I mentioned why in the past women might have chosen to convert here too. Historically Muslim women had the right to divorce and could inherit property. Christian women lacked both these rights until recent times.

He talked about his translation work. He has translated many books. He said when he was younger he could not find the books he wanted to read on Islam. So he sees his work as making sure there are these books now. He has also translated the Qur'an into Macedonian. He asked Emineh to bring over a copy. He showed it to me; it is beautifully done. It is a remarkable feat to translate the Qur'an which was first recited in Arabic in the seventh century.[16] The language is powerful poetic Arabic, very different from the modern standard Arabic of today.

Jasmin said it was the second time the Qur'an had been translated into Macedonian. He gave me a copy. I am honored. I asked him to sign it, and to write the year of publication. Jasmin added that he feels his contribution is to translate works into Macedonian. He recently translated a life of the Prophet Muhammad. Clearly Jasmin is a scholar.

Changing the topic some, I asked more about media experience. Jasmin said that he had been on the media just the night before. He said that whenever the media wants to know about what is going on with the refugees, they come to Legis. "We know," he said.

Earlier, when his wife, Mersiha Smailović, was still working on her law decree, he noted with pride that she was the one who fought against the regulation stating Muslim women had to have the photos on their ID cards taken without their headscarves. She was successful in this in 2007, and they got some notoriety for this. The implication was that this helped cement the media's coming to them.

I then asked Jasmin about the financial backing of Legis. "Where does the money come from?" I asked. "From the banks," he answered with a smile. I smiled too. "Did it come mostly from Muslims?" "No, from all Macedonians," he said. "We are not limited by religion. And corporations too." The implication was that these too were various. He later implied media coverage helped them get contributions. But this did not imply the Macedonian government was behind them. He gave an example of when they had a German donor who wanted to build facilities at Tabanovce in the north. The government had refused multiple times for fear that if there were a camp there, people would stay. And at that time they only had a few tents and one toilet. They needed facilities. No refugees wanted to stay in Macedonia. There were no prospects for work. They all wanted to go on to Germany or Sweden. But the government would not listen. I began to understand more the difficulty of working in Macedonia.

Back to Jasmin's own background, I mentioned that there had been many Turkish speakers in Gilan where he had told me his father's family had come from. Yes, his grandmother there was Turkish and they had been aghas. But in 1945 when the Serbs came back to power in Kosovo after World War II, they had killed his grandfather. He had not been against them. Still they had killed all intellectuals and leaders and people of wealth to make sure the Albanians would not have any chance of rising up. I said he looked like a Turkish aristocrat. He laughed and said people had always chided him for the way he ate.

At that time many box loads of clothing and boots were coming in. I took photos of the young women by bags of toys and cookies, and of Jasmin Redjepi by the water bottles.

Questions not Asked

When I got back to my hotel, I realized that Jasmin Redjepi had been interviewing me. Clearly he was a professional. There were questions that I had wanted to ask and somehow had forgotten. One was how Legis

Figure 2.2 Jasmin Redjepi, NGO President Legis.mk in Legis.mk warehouse in Skopje, Macedonia, 2015.

came into the refugee work in Macedonia. The other was how Legis had lobbied to get the law changed. Eventually I did learn that several of the six founders of Legis.mk had worked for other NGOs before the founding of Legis in 2009. In their mission statement they noted there was a need for a local Macedonian organization to be "a dignified spoken voice of community needs and necessities." According to their website, it was to be:

> The organized will of the people where its founders lived, in order to promote the basic human values in helping vulnerable people in need, to increase the level of social awareness, as well as to give the best social response."[17]

So what projects had they engaged in early on? They listed six international projects on their website including: solidarity with Gaza, aid to the Dadaab camp of Somali refugees in Kenya, fund raising for Muslims in Myanmar, donation of three ambulance cars to the refugee camp in the Syrian border town of Bab al-Hawa, and aid for a flood in Bosnia and Herzegovina. At least three of these relate to refugees.

Their seventh listed project was within Macedonia and was ongoing. It was providing humanitarian help during the refugee crises along the Balkan route and in both refugee transit camps in Macedonia. On their website they noted that they currently helped refugees who transit Macedonia with food packets, hygiene products, necessary clothing, and first aid items. They had helped thousands of refugees by handing out at least 200,000 food packets since the winter of 2014.

Finally, and I think most importantly, they noted they were advocates to change the refugee law in Macedonia that resulted in their "dignified lawful treatment by providing them legal public transport to Serbia." They explained that before June 2015 refugees had to walk across Macedonia by foot or by bicycle, as they were not permitted to use public transport. Criminal gangs would attack them on their way and steal their money and Syrian passports. They had no recourse since they were afraid to call the police as they were considered "illegal aliens."

Legis lobbied through media and with members of Parliament to change the law to make it easier for refugees to transit Macedonia. I see it as their most important contribution.

Changing the Law so Refugees Could Use Public Transport
The best account of this change comes from Mersiha Smailović, one of the founders of Legis.mk and the wife of Jasmin Redjepi. She has a law degree from the Faculty of Law, Saints Cyril and Methodius University

Skopje and, as her husband mentioned, when she was still a law student, she was able to get the regulation changed regarding photo IDs and headscarves that had been on the books for fifty years. Clearly she knows how to navigate complex legal matters, and is also both attractive and highly intelligent.

As for her background in refugee affairs, as a founding member of Legis, she had visited the enormous refugee camp in Kenya at Dabaab in 2011. This camp, which was one of their international projects, has some 300,000 people living there.[18] On a more personal level, she was a little girl in Macedonia during the time of the Bosnian war. Her family had taken in refugees from Bosnia, and later refugees from Kosovo. She said these were not relatives but complete strangers. She learned early on to help those in need.

Mersiha explained how Legis had gotten involved in working with refugees in Macedonia in the first place and how Legis worked to change the law on refugee transport. Much of this is also in a published interview.[19]

As mentioned earlier, Legis had been working with human rights since its founding in 2009. In early 2014, they were called into a public hospital to help translate for a Syrian patient who had been thrown out of a moving vehicle by an Egyptian trafficker. Clearly this was a smuggler dealing with a refugee. Legis became involved.

Later in the fall of that year they were at the northern border of Macedonia with Serbia where they saw Syrian families waiting for traffickers. They could recognize the traffickers by the quality of their clothing. They also met Lence Zdravkin, a Slavic Macedonian woman who had been working with refugees passing through Veles.

Mersiha explained that they started to collect aid for the refugees. Legis would bring aid to Lence in Veles on Saturdays and Sundays in their van. They would bring water bottles, clothing, and other items to refurbish her supplies for Lence was on the main refugee trail, and the refugees were in need of these by the time they got to Veles.

Mersiha noted that when Legis found out about the Gazi Baba Detention Centre in Skopje, they requested authorization to enter it. There they found a deplorable situation of detainees, including women and children with no way to get out. She described these conditions to Human Rights Watch and this came out in their September 2015 report. Again her legal background was most valuable. She knew

Macedonia had no asylum policy and no right to detain "witnesses" in this way.

She brought up the number of deaths of refugees in Macedonia caused by trains – thirty – and contrasted this to Serbia where there were none because Serbia permitted refugees to travel through the country legally for seventy-two hours. This of course implied refugees were able to use public transportation there. "We applied pressure for the same law to be applied in Macedonia."[20] But the Macedonian government was not convinced.

Finally, on 18 June 2015 the Macedonian Parliament came up with a new law, called "Intention for Asylum" that would allow refugees to circulate in the country for 72 hours and use public transportation.

They finally allowed transport for refugees and migrants around the country in a legal way. The pressure came as well from various countries and organizations, and on June 28 the Parliament gave its consent to the new law.[21]

What the new law amounted to was that refugees, when they entered Macedonia, should register at the border control, and receive the intention paper allowing them to spend seventy-two hours in the country. This permitted them to use any kind of transport. After seventy-two hours, they should leave Macedonia or seek asylum.

In effect, the most practical transport was the train. The government then increased the price of the train, from five euros to twenty-five euros per person, allowing them to make a healthy profit on the refugees. Still it was a distinct improvement for the refugees to be able to ride the train for four hours, instead of spending ten or more days, ducking border police and thieves, and walking the 200-kilometer length of Macedonia.

By the time I came in December 2015, hundreds of thousands of refugees had ridden the train across Macedonia from the southern border to the northern border. This was the year Germany would take in about a million asylum-seekers and almost all came through Macedonia. They could not imagine walking this distance. This also allowed many more women and children to come who would not have been able to handle the earlier dangers of trying to do this distance walking.

There is another outcome from the refugee crisis in Macedonia noted by that Mersiha, namely a new solidarity had developed in a country that has ethnic, religious, and political divisions. The network of volunteers

Legis built included Macedonians of Slavic, Albanian, and Bosnian backgrounds, and international volunteers. They came together to work for the refugees – something that seemed almost impossible for other causes in Macedonia. There was even aid from the Macedonian Orthodox Church, which gave five tons of water, and aid from the Islamic Community that donated twenty tons of water and 5,000 packets of food. The Islamic Community recognized Legis as an organization. It also recognized Lence Zdravkin and two others for humanitarian activity – three non-Muslims. Both Protestant and Catholic international organizations also sent aid.[22]

Again on a personal level, Mersiha Smailović noted that, as a woman and a mother, she empathized with the refugee women. At the height of the refugee crisis she was pregnant with her second child. She would see refugee women who were also pregnant, some who were exhausted and miscarried, and some who delivered new babies and then, two days later, continued on the Balkan Migrant Trail.

Lence Zdravkin's Response: Feed Those Who Pass By

To work in the refugee transit camp in the north, I needed to bring a copy of my passport to Legis. In the morning on the way, I stopped at the Mosque of Sultan Murat. I had to take a circuitous pathway past rubble and waste leading up to the higher ground where the mosque is built. I came up to the gateway to the mosque. I walked in. There were still roses blooming despite the cold. How Ottoman this felt. It was very clean and neat. I sat down and savored the peace above the noisy city. There are five perfect arches and a handsome minaret off to the right. By the main gate is a tall hexagonal clock tower.

The caretaker came out. He was an older man in a blue over-garment. We spoke first in Turkish and then in Albanian. "Yes, Sultan Murat was built in 1463," he said. "It withstood earthquakes." "And wars," I added. "And the clock tower?" I asked. "A century later," he said, "from the time of Sultan Suleyman." "They have lasted so long," I remarked. He nodded. "Communism came and went," I said. He nodded. "Now we have democracy," he said with irony.

"How is life in Macedonia?" I asked. "It is not easy," he said. "There are not enough jobs, and salaries and pensions are too low." "Was it better during the time of Yugoslavia?" "Much better," he said. "But,"

I added, "even if Yugoslavia had stayed together, the factories would have been in trouble. The whole world economy changed." Still it is harder for small countries. He said his pension was only 100 euros a month. And water and heat cost so much. It is important to realize how poor Macedonia is to understand the situation of refugees coming through here.

I went on to the Legis warehouse where there was a man from Secours Islamique France, a French Muslim Aid organization that donates funds used to buy clothing for refugees. That day boots, socks, and jackets for men, women, and children arrived. What is especially good about the French organization is that it sends funds. Then goods are purchased in Macedonia creating a win-win situation. It is also the only way. If goods were bought outside they would be charged heavy customs duties.

Emineh and Hadis started immediately taking inventory and organizing the new items. Meanwhile Dr Sabena, the member who would get me officially registered, had arrived. She called me over to do the contract. It was finished in five minutes. How efficient.

I asked her how she got involved in Legis. She said it was through her sister. I asked if she were older or younger. "Younger," she said and smiled. "She is a second sister. Don't you know that second sisters are always revolutionaries?" I laughed and told her that I was a second sister. She said, "Napoleon and Florence Nightingale were both second siblings. They did not get enough attention." I allowed as how it was true, adding that I had a younger brother. "Is he spoiled some?" I told her that he was deeply loved. "Yes, see," she said. Families are not that different.

I asked her to tell me about Legis. She said:

Legis was the first group to work with the refugees when it was still illegal. You could be put in jail for doing so. For example if you took refugees in your car or your taxi. There was a woman in Veles who helped on the way of the train. We got clothes to her. We got food to the refugees on the way.

Hadis is a mountain biker. He went along on his bike. Then we had our van and gave out food bags. It was all volunteer. We worked through enthusiasm. That is very different from major organizations. Now we appreciate them more.

But we were the first. And we worked from the start. It was only us. We were the first people at Tabanovce and at Gevgelija. We had been working before then. There were only six men at Tabanovce, thanks to Legis.

That night I would see what changes and how many staff and volunteers there were now at Tabanovce on the northern border.

But who was this woman who "helped on the way of the train?" Legis had assisted her too, but it sounded as if she had worked on her own at first. After I had been in Macedonia a few days, working in the refugee transit camp in the north, I became more curious. We tended to work in the warehouse during the day and in the northern transit camp at night. One late afternoon when we were traveling at breakneck speed over highways on the way to the refugee transit camp in Tabanovce I thought, "Now I can ask." So I did.

I asked who was the woman who fed the refugees that people talked about. "You mean Lence Zdravkin," said one. "She lives in Veles, in central Macedonia, and her house is next to the train tracks. Probably she is in her late 40s."

"When did she start helping the refugees?" I asked. By her name I could tell she was not Muslim like most of the people in our van, but of a Slavic Christian background. "We started in 2014, and she had been helping earlier."

I knew Legis had a connection with her work, so I asked how Legis worked with her. "Legis got clothing to her. And we got water and food to her," people said. "We have a van, and Hadis has his mountain bike. Legis would take water to people along the trail as well." And then they talked of other things.

On another van trip the following week, this time to Gevgelija, the refugee transit camp in the south, again I asked about the woman in Veles who had helped the refugees. This time Jasmin said:

You mean Lence Zdravkin. Her house was near where they walked and she helped them from her house. We delivered food and clothing to her every Saturday and Sunday.

"Did the police know about it?" I asked. "They knew, but they did not do anything," answered Jasmin.

She was in a truly strategic location along the Balkan Migrant Trail. Veles is about halfway from south to north. I learned that her house was right above the train tracks. She could look down and see refugees walking along the tracks in the night. Apparently she even let them into her garage or house if they had medical problems.

Some told me she would hang bags of food and water along walls by the tracks for the refugees. That is what Legis did to help the refugees all along the tracks. But with Lence, her house was right above the tracks. The refugees, as they walked along the tracks, came to her. It is my understanding that she also took food and water out to them.

I wondered why the police ignored her activities. Maybe they could not believe that a Slavic Christian woman would help Muslim refugees. Or maybe, since Veles was so far from the border, they were not so concerned with refugees.

The next time I got to my laptop computer, I went on the web and looked for information on Lence Zdravkin. At least I had her name now. I found a photograph of her. She was slender and fair-haired. She looked like many other Macedonian women. I even found an interview in Macedonian from July 2015, portions of which I translate below.[23]

According to the interview, the first refugees that Lence Zdravkin saw passing her home in Veles were young men from Syria, Somalia, and Afghanistan. As they were the age of her own children, she said she had no trouble giving them tea, bread, and water. When spring came, and other refugees came by, she would give them fruit too.

I must note what an unusual response this was in Macedonia at that time – late winter of 2013. The refugees were foreigners, young Muslim males who were poor and dark. Her response to see them as similar to her own children was unique among Christians.

Returning to the interview, she added that, over time, she increased the amount of food she gave. The groups grew in size.

By 2014, she noted she was getting help from others, including Legis.mk, to aid the "migrants." By the winter of 2015 there could be 200 to 300 people in a group at a time. She did not always know how she would provide for the "migrants" as she called them.

When asked how she coped, she said she bought more flour and made bread. Her husband got her a dough mixer. She also bought potatoes and heated them and gave them to the migrants.

The reporter asked how her family took to all this extra work and expense. She and her husband had a television station in Veles. She responded that they helped her, including her little grandson. She said, he would sit on the balcony, and when he saw migrants, he would say, "Grandmother, the refugees are coming. Quickly, hurry."[24]

The reporter asked her how she was affected by the news of the migrants who were killed by the trains. She responded that the fourteen young men (killed in April 2015) are buried there in Veles and that she attended their funeral.

"They were young men, between the ages of 20 and 27." She added that somewhere a mother waits for them. She said, "It is hard for her since she knows they went from a country at war and died in a country at peace. That is life."

The reporter then asked if she was ever afraid of the migrants or of the law that said it was illegal to aid the illegal migrants. She answered that she never feared. She said she could not imagine a law that would forbid her to help someone who needed it.

The reporter said that media call you "the new Mother Teresa"[25] and your house, "the house of salvation." "What is your reaction to this?" She said that whoever found themselves in her place would do the same. She said she felt there needed to be a solution for these people. But then she turned the tables on the reporter. She said,

> We should all be grateful for what we have. Human life is precious. I thank that my children have beds. Today they are refugees. Tomorrow it could be us.

Earlier she had said how much the migrants had changed her. She was not the same person she had been when she began putting out bread and tea.

I kept hoping that I would meet Lence Zdravkin. Of course things changed for her when the new law went into effect. With the new law the refugees no longer walked past her house. Instead they took the train from the south to the north. Instead of ten or more days, it took four hours to travel through Macedonia. But often they could be stuck at the southern or northern borders for different reasons, so their time in Macedonia extended to several days.

The Macedonian interview of Lence Zdravkin that I found said that now she always had her cell phone in her hand in case anyone called her from either of the borders in need of help. She cared deeply about the "migrants," and was especially effective in working with them and Macedonian authorities. She probably reminded the authorities of their mothers, or of what they wished their mothers were like.

I just missed meeting Lence Zdravkin one day in Gevgelija. She came during midday, and my shift was later and into the night. But I kept asking about her and her work for the refugees. I found another interview with her.[26] In this interview, she mentioned that before the new law she used to sit in her garden waiting for the migrants. Sometimes she would go to bed at 9 pm, sleep until midnight, and then sit outside waiting again.

She described a particular migrant from Syria who had passed through the previous year. His name was Ferdi and he was over six feet tall. She said that when she saw him on the tracks, he was wearing plastic slippers of size seven, a size much smaller than his feet. She took care of the wounds on his feet and made him coffee.

Ferdi had left his wife and two children in Turkey. His plan was to get to the Netherlands and then try to get his family there. Lence stayed in touch with him when he got to the Netherlands. He would become depressed if he did not hear from them for a few days.

Then last April, Lence's family paid for tickets for his wife and children to join him in the Netherlands. He could not believe it when she told him. He told her, "I will marry her a second time, and you will be my godmother."

Lence added:

My life has become simpler since the crisis. I don't worry about the little things I used to, like what detergent to buy. I have seen what it means for people to have nothing. I have seen children walking on stones, hungry. The entire perspective shifts.

CHAPTER 3

REFUGEE TRANSIT CAMPS

Later, when talking to refugees in Germany, I would mention that I had worked in refugee transit camps in Macedonia. This would bring a look of recognition to their faces. They all remembered these camps for almost all the refugees in Germany had come along the Balkan Migrant Trail through Macedonia. Most had come on the train after the new law was passed. They were however more interested in my time in Syria. It was true respite for them to talk of peaceful times before the war. I had stayed in a truly quiet place in Syria in Jebel Druze. But the memory of the refugee transit camps was also a connection to the refugees in Germany. I knew without their telling me some of what they had been through on their way to Germany.

The process that turns people into refugees, that makes them feel as if they do not belong anywhere, comes from experiences like passing through the Balkan Migrant Trail. Putting aside the actual departure from home, with the sadness and guilt for all who must be left behind, there is the journey to the border with Turkey. Once inside Turkey travelers must journey to the coast. There they need to locate smugglers to find small boats to cross the Aegean Sea. No one ever knew how long this would take. Some waited weeks in Turkey, some days. It often took multiple tries. And of course the outcome was unknown.

The experience on the sea was unforgettable and horrifying, especially for parents with small children, for almost none of them could swim. Time lost meaning in the over-crowded boats as they drifted and started to sink, far from shore. Some rolled out and tried to kick the boats along, others drowned in the boat itself. Eventually a ship might come along and they would be saved or they would not. On a rocky island someone would pull them out or they would clamber ashore. They were taken to some camp, and then by ship to the mainland.

With the sea passage, many thought the worst must be over. They had not heard of the Hungarian police, or the unpredictable combinations of waiting and alienating directives they had to follow as "new refugees" from then on, for they were no longer just "travelers." By their pathway they had entered a net of suspicion.

There would be group travel with other strangers on buses or trains for periods of up to eight hours punctuated by document checks. There would be walking between borders, followed again by document checks. They would need to wait in large tents on hard wooden benches for unpredictable periods of time.

Women had to be especially careful because there were so many men, not just other refugees, but police and border guards as well. As they waited in groups they could be groped, propositioned, or assaulted. Was it safe to go to the facilities? It was a risk. In summer it was hot, in winter, frightfully cold. They learned to look down at all times. They were truly refugees now.

Hopefully there would be food and water after document checks. Did it matter who they were? No, only that they were not of the groups who were no longer permitted to cross the borders. It was an alienating process, but one that hopefully would allow them to reach a secure country in the West.

So anything that could give a slight human touch was welcome. A group called "Clouds" tried to play games with the children in the southern transit camp, but the Macedonian authorities put a stop to that. They feared it might make people want to remain. I saw no danger of that.

I did end up spending both Christmases in refugee camps – the Latin one on the northern border and the Orthodox one on the southern border. The refugees and many volunteers were mostly Muslim. Would Christmas have any meaning for the staff or others in the camps? Holidays are special in part because they break ordinary patterns. But what patterns could holidays break in refugee transit camps where thousands of refugees passed through irregularly? What usually broke patterns in the camps was the weather, which might get worse. Or a train or bus might malfunction. Or, heaven forbid, there might be political closure of some important border further up the Balkan Migrant Trail.

Hungary's talk of high, electrified fences made everyone nervous. Eventually in March 2016 there was closure of the border up north with unfortunate refugees stuck in the different countries – in Slovenia, Croatia, Serbia, Macedonia, and Greece. Fully 1,500 people would be caught in Tabanovce in the north and Gevgelija in the south of Macedonia, not to mention the over 60,000 eventually trapped in Greece.

In the following field narratives, notice how the Macedonian government officials, police, and volunteer groups made up of different locals and internationals interact around refugees in the winter months on the Balkan Trail. At the same time the refugees always seem to be waiting for the trains to arrive, and then in long lines for their documents to be checked. Still, thereby hundreds of thousands of refugees slowly moved north across international borders of many states toward a safer life.

Tabanovce on the Northern Border

The First Night on the High Plateau
The first time I went to Tabanovce, I went in the Legis van late in the afternoon. Hadis drove, with Jasmin in the front seat, as we hurtled over the highway. We whizzed along to Kumanovo and talked first about packaging of socks, and then Islamic law. I could see the lights of the large city below the highway. As we drove on through and went north, I realized that the terrain had been rising. We were on a high plateau as we headed down toward the little village of Tabanovce. Only then did I see one police car at a turn-off from the highway, but no one stopped.

The village of Tabanovce, a Slavic Christian village, is small and dreary. We passed through the narrow road without seeing a soul and continued out across fields. Eventually we crossed the railroad tracks and arrived at the camp where there were some white buildings that Jasmin said were IKEA-made. There was a parking lot and some lights, thank goodness. It was pitch black by then.

We walked around to an area that had different volunteers who had soup bowls ready, a tea area, and an area for used clothing that looked much picked over. Across from this complex were the train tracks where the trains come in.

I met Mare Bojkovska, a Legis volunteer from Kumanovo whom I had been trying to reach on the phone all afternoon. She is Slavic Macedonian. I also met Driton Maliqi. He is Albanian of Macedonia and speaks good standard Arabic. His family worked in the Gulf and he had gone to high school there. We talked while standing around a heater in the middle of the food area. Apparently Driton and Mare had been talking together late that afternoon. Driton had been defending his dissertation on multi-cultural education. I asked her with a smile if he passed. "Very well," she said.

This sort of discussion, between a Slavic Christian and an Albanian Muslim, might not have occurred if they had not both been working for the refugees. Driton has international experience in the Gulf and he is a respected activist. Mare served for two years in a private American company in Afghanistan. Mare told me that her friends chide her for "working for terrorists." So she took photos of refugees with crosses on their sleeves. There are some Christian refugees, although only a minority. I told her Syria was about 10 per cent Christian, but most of the refugees are not Christian. Many Syrian Christians had stayed in the Middle East.

I later learned she had been working with Legis since July 2015. But she had started working for the refugees from her hometown of Kumanovo earlier in May 2015[1] even before the law was changed.

The refugees would rest in the large mosque in her city, exhausted from the days of walking. One day she went in to see what was going on with them. This took courage for a Slavic Christian. She found a family with two small children. She went out and bought milk for them and returned with it. She found herself going back each day to see what they needed. Eventually she became part of a group with Albanians who were seeing to the material needs of the refugees in the mosque. When the law changed at the end of June, the refugees moved to the new transit camp in Tabanovce. She then became involved with Legis.mk.

But where were the refugees? Earlier in the day I was told 5,000 people had come and gone through the camp. I spoke with two young Norwegian women who were working in the tea area. They were there for a week with the mother and husband of one. Eventually refugees began to arrive and we gave them bowls of soup, pieces of bread, and oranges. The children were crying from the cold as they got out of taxis, not the train. It was bitterly cold. I helped people find certain clothing in the piles of clothes. They came in smaller groups than usual because there had been a strike of taxi drivers in the south. The taxi drivers had driven their taxis over the train tracks to protest not getting any customers. So the authorities in the south had let them take some refugees at 200–400 euros a car. That was why there were so few new refugees my first night.

Then I met Valentina. She is the Macedonian staff person in charge of the area where the refugees get food and rest. I asked her what I could do to help since the numbers of refugees were not high. "Perhaps go to the tents with the people," she suggested. These were large tents, lined up perpendicular to the train tracks beyond the soup area. She showed me the first one that already had people in it. There were long wooden benches with blankets on them. There was a heater at the front, clearly insufficient for the size of the tent. There were people in the tents who had come in on earlier trains.

It was a good suggestion. People needed to talk at night. Here my language skills could be especially valuable. And as I knew little about how the camp actually functioned, it seemed wise.

In the first large tent, when my eyes got used to the lack of light, I saw a man lying alone by the front bench closest to the heater. He did not look healthy. I began to talk with him in Arabic. He answered, but I could not understand his Arabic. I asked him where he was from. "Algeria." "Algeria? I thought they were not letting people from North Africa through," I said. "No, they let all through now," he said. Later someone told me someone must have made a mistake. He could understand my Arabic, but I could not understand his North African dialect. So we spoke in French. We talked about French and this and that. Later it struck me that he was very lonely.

I asked where he wanted to go. He said France since he knew French. I said that made sense, but the French were not so welcoming at this time.[2] He mentioned America. I said Canada was better now. He said it was difficult to know how the Canadians chose their immigrants. I said I had no idea. They came by plane, I said. But Canada is a good country. I needed to talk to others. I told him to sleep. He said he had a cold and took a pill. I hope he made it through.

I went to a big family down the line. They were from Mosul. They had come from Izmir in Turkey a week before. "And we saw death," said the man in Arabic. He repeated this several times and made motions with his hands. "How are the children?" I asked. He had four of them. They shook their heads. The children were small. The wife looked up and said that they trust in God, that is the only way. I cannot imagine what the sea must have been for a mother with such young children. Some in their boat had not made it, the father told me. "And how long from Mosul?" I asked. "Twenty-five days," the man said.

Next I met a woman whose husband had left four months before with their seven-year-old daughter. And now the wife was coming with their two-year-old daughter. She was traveling with her sister and her sister's husband and their three children. They asked about me. I said I was an American and my country should never have gone into Iraq. The man nodded. Much suffering had come from that. The least I can do is try to help now.

Nearby a young couple with a child listened. The man asked me in Arabic where he could plug his phone in. I went out, found where he could recharge the battery, and came back and told him. Truly my Arabic is useful for different things.

I went outside the tent to a heater where local men were who had done the necessary job of cleaning up after so many refugees had passed through. One had been in Afghanistan for six years. I told him my stepson who had served in Afghanistan had said the Macedonians were good there. He was pleased.

I looked north. The land was high and stark and cold. It was 500 meters to the border. Across was Serbia, and then a longer two to three kilometer walk to the next transit camp inside Serbia. Macedonia

Figure 3.1 Refugees inside tent at the refugee transit camp in Tabanovce.

had been kind to build the transit camp close to the border. An Albanian man came by and said if I wanted to go back that night he could take me to Kumanovo. So I went. By then I was tired and beginning to confuse languages. And so ended my first night at the refugee transit camp.

Christmas at Tabanovce

On 25 December I had to remind myself it was Christmas. When I went to Tabanovce that afternoon for the late shift, a Sikh volunteer who worked the soup counter for a Muslim charity told me about how nearly a thousand refugees had come through on trains earlier in the day. That was good. It was better for people to come earlier when it was so cold. But not all had gone directly on to Serbia.

I spoke with the Norwegian volunteer mother in the tea area. She told me she had been invited by her daughter, her daughter's husband, and her daughter's friend to come to Macedonia for Christmas. She thought it was good for the young people to actually do something. They had a small Christmas tree by the tea counter as a reminder of the holiday.

Just then a train arrived full of people from the south. There were young men hanging out the windows. One asked what we had. Soup, tea, some clothes. He asked for a jacket. I went and found him one. It was for a young teen but it fit him and had a hood. I asked where he was from. He told me Baghdad. He had a friend who needed a jacket too, but I could not find one for him.

Then I went into the first big tent. What a chaotic situation! People were gathering there. It had heaters, but it was not peaceful. In the next tent it was not as chaotic, but the heaters were not working. I asked a staff man in a special vest about them. He said these heaters were almost done heating. He told me to tell the people in that tent if they wanted to spend the night, to wait and go to the first tent when the others left. The heaters there still worked.

Halebi Family

Meanwhile, next to the heater that was on its last legs, there was an older man, probably in his 50s. I started talking with him. He was from Aleppo. I asked him how he was. He said he was fine, but he was tired. He was with his wife and his youngest son, a young man of about twenty years old. I asked the older man how long he had been on the

Figure 3.2   Refugees arriving in Tabanovce on train from the south.

road. He asked what day it was. "Friday," I said. He thought. "Ten days," he said. "Ten days! That is fast," I said. "Fast, hmmm," he thought. It must have seemed long to him. "Where are you going?" I asked. "To Sweden." Ahh. From the wife it came out slowly that they had two sons who had gone to Sweden two years ago. They would join them there. It was good that they were expecting them.

I was able to ask them why they had left. I rarely asked this since it invariably brought up memories of hardship and loss. In this case I could ask since they knew where they were going and would be taken in by their sons in Sweden. The father answered first. "Our house is gone. Our shop is gone. We have no *fulouse*, that is, no money," with the implication that there is no way to make money anymore. Then the mother answered. "Every time my son went to university, I worried, 'Would he return?'" I reached out my hand to her and told her that a mother understands that.

It was time for them to leave. I looked at the son and then said to the parents in the typical Arabic phrase,"May God keep him safe for you." Then I asked the son, "And you will care for them?" He nodded.

But they have two daughters still there, in Aleppo, probably married. They could not come. The cost of 600–1,700 euros each at the Aegean

Sea crossing was too much for them That is an enormous sum for people who have been at war for five years. And this family had already saved enough for three people. God help them. I wished them well.

Problem on the Serbian Border

Then I went back to the tea area. There was a problem. The Norwegian woman's daughter, a blond woman in her late twenties, a volunteer, had helped some handicapped refugees in wheelchairs cross the Serbian border. But then the Serbian police had not let her return to the Macedonian side. It is not an official border — only for asylum seekers. Allegedly they thought she was a journalist. I am sure they could see exactly what was going on. The Serbian border guards must have been bored.

The mother was deeply distraught. Why did her daughter have to do this alone? She should have stayed in the tea area doing what they were supposed to do. I said we needed help. I found a Macedonian volunteer who talked with the Macedonian police who were polite but not helpful. The Macedonian police said they had no contact with the Serbian police who are one minute across the border. So much for professional courtesy.

We walked back to the tea area. Meanwhile the young Norwegian husband was in touch with his wife by cell phone. It sounded as if the Serbian police were being somewhat reasonable and wanted to take her to the regular border area where her husband could pick her up.

Then to add to the problems along came a Macedonian staff person who said we should contact the Norwegian ambassador. It was almost midnight. "No," I said. Then she said that the volunteer could be imprisoned for five years. The mother by then was totally upset.

Meanwhile the first Macedonian volunteer who had tried to help with the police had found a lawyer who said the Norwegian volunteer had done nothing wrong and could be kept at most for twenty-four hours. Off went the husband and a friend in a car to the regular border crossing. When they came back, they did not have the wife with them. It turned out the Serbs kept her. When at last they had decided she was not a journalist, the judge had gone to bed and would not sign the paper to let her return to Macedonia. Apparently she had had her passport, thank goodness, but the power in her phone was almost out. She was texting and seemed OK, he said.

While this was interesting, I had earlier made the mistake of asking for a ride back to Skopje with the Norwegians. Usually the most dependable group, only not that night. I got back very late. So this was Christmas in the refugee transit camp on the northern border of Macedonia.

But I thought again of the handicapped refugees that the Norwegian volunteer had been helping cross the border. The first time I had seen refugees in wheelchairs I had thought they were crazy. How could they possibly make it along the Balkan Migrant Trail? But then I thought, how could families leave them in Syria or Iraq? Who would take care of them? Better to bring them and hopefully they could get prostheses or better medical care in Western Europe.

These handicapped refugees were often young. Were they victims of bomb attacks? Most likely. Buildings had probably fallen on them. Mercy Corps International, one of the international NGOs that I respected, had a white van that would take handicapped refugees over the border, but at Christmas they were not operating.

Gevgelija on the Southern Border

Traveling South to a Different Camp

I had long wanted to work in the refugee transit camp on the southern border as well. I had heard it was different from the northern camp in Tabanovce. People, though, did not say how it was different.

It was certainly more strategic. When new regulations were put in place by the countries along the Balkan Migrant Trail – for example when North Africans were no longer permitted passage as occurred in late November 2015 – this was enforced at the border crossing with Greece at Idomeni and Macedonia at Gevgelja. So by the time I came to work in the refugee transit camps in Macedonia, the only refugees who were permitted legal passage on the Balkan Migrant Trail were Syrians, Iraqis, and Afghans. That was why I had been so surprised to find an Algerian in a tent the first night in Tabanovce.

I was excited when one day at the Legis warehouse where Hadis said Emineh's brother Sabit would be driving down to Gevgelja in the afternoon. My permission to work in the southern camp had been approved a week before. Sabit agreed to take me. On the way he stopped and picked up Jasmin and we took off.

As we drove south it was raining and foggy. I asked what Legis had done in the south after the law changed the previous summer in late June and refugees were finally allowed to use public transportation. Jasmin explained how they had still delivered food and clothing to the refugees as they waited for the train at the train station in Gevgelija. Apparently there was no other place to go. There was no camp for several months. The UN had waited until they had donors. He explained that people would put plastic bags on their heads when it rained. They did not build a camp in the south until September.

Eventually we arrived in Gevgelja. We drove into the town and Jasmin pointed out the train station where the refugees would gather by the thousands. It was an attractive station from Ottoman times. I wondered how many people remembered that Sultan Reşad, one of the last Ottoman sultans, had traveled through here in 1911. Times had certainly changed.

We drove through the small town, over a river, and out past a vineyard. Jasmin explained that the town had not wanted the camp in the town. This caused problems because with the camp outside the town there was no source of water or electricity in the camp.

After we got our police passes, we drove into the camp. Beyond the police station there were white square prefabricated buildings on both sides, placed in an orderly fashion down a center way. "UNHCR" was imprinted on their sides, but there were no UN staff in sight. We drove down the center way. I later learned that after the UN had set up the camp, they had wanted to manage it. However the Macedonian government Crisis Center had also wanted to run it and they had won out. The only UN-run unit was a UNICEF building for mothers and small children near the three reception tents.

There were two very large white tents at the far end near the train tracks, but there were not many refugees in sight. The train had recently left. Still there could be refugees in the tents. It had rained all day long.

They introduced me to Nazife. I liked her immediately. She is a Legis staff person, an Albanian from Skopje. I would later learn that she had started out by making 1,000 food packets for the refugees for Ramadan one year. She wanted to make sure they got to the refugees. So she took the packets to the refugees and never stopped working for them.

Sabit parked the Legis van to the side of a white square container booth – originally intended for goods on ships but which we used to store clothing. It was near the large tents in front of the tracks. Immediately we made a chain to bring in clothing and boxes that we had packed in the van from the Skopje warehouse. Our booth had clothing and footware for men, women, and children, all piled on shelves, in boxes, or hanging against the walls. Some were new and some used. The people had to stay outside and ask for what they wanted. We would look for it and, if we had it, bring it out for them to try on outside. The booth itself, a white IKEA container, was too small to hold people other than us, along with the garments and boxes inside.

The Importance of Culture

It had started raining again. Some men wanted boots. In this rain I did not wonder. What size? One man said forty-eight. Forty-eight? That is high. No, his friend wears forty-eight pants, I wear forty-three shoes, said another. I found him forty-three boots. He was lucky. Soon the boots were almost gone. And they were decent.

Then several young men came to our container booth, maybe four, standing next to each other, all wanting size forty. I only had one pair of size forty boots left. I could see they all needed boots. They only had shoes and they were wet. What could I do? And then off to the side there was also an older man. "What size do you need sir?" I asked in Arabic. He also needed size forty boots.

I looked at the young men and paused. Then I told them the older man was the one I was giving the single pair of size forty boots to. "He is longer in the tooth"–I used a formal Arabic phrase. They all listened respectfully. "I must do this," I said. "You understand." They nodded. In Arabic culture, there is clear respect for age. Then I said to the older man, "And you will care for these young men?" He nodded.

It was dark out. I had the older man put on the boots. I put his old shoes in a plastic bag. I think the others appreciated their values being reiterated to them in this strange place of white square prefabricated booths and mud and darkness. It was a sort of home returning. The men waited and then quietly melted away.

Days in Gevgelija

The days working in the camp in the south were exhausting. I heard early that staff there worked three days on and three days off. At first I thought that was too easy, but by the end I realized it was wise. It was emotionally taxing. Refugees would arrive with no notice, a thousand at a time from Greece. And we never knew when the train would come to take them to the north.

We would do our best to find them the clothing they needed. I learned a valuable lesson early on. I learned that I could joke with them. I also thanked my lucky stars that I had sons. It made life easier since most of the refugees were young men. There would be thirty young men out front of the container booth, all asking for some sort of item. Since I was fluent in Arabic, I had the front duty. Nazife would be back inside trying to find things. Yes, they wanted the item, but they wanted to be treated like humans. And they wanted some fun too sometimes.

One day a strapping young man came with plastic clogs on his feet and asked for boots. His other clothing was too good for the clogs. Behind him were some of his friends as well as a Macedonian policeman. I took one look at the young man and his friends and knew something was afoot. So I started to curse him in Arabic. I had learned to swear like a fourteen-year-old boy when I had taught in Lebanon years ago. I told him I would not waste good boots on him when he already had them in the tent. What kind of fool did he think I was? The policeman enjoyed it

Figure 3.3   Refugees waiting to register in Gevgelija Camp. December 2015.

thoroughly as did the friends. The young man backed away. It was the talk of the morning.

I also learned to say when we had had enough. I would put the side of my hand to my forehead, bend down, tell them how tired I was, and saying, "There are so many of you, and only one of me. Enough!" They actually seemed to enjoy the drama. And then Nazife and I would close up shop and go have coffee.

An Older Iraqi Woman Alone

When we got word that new refugees had come, we would go to the reception tents to see if there were any special needs. One day I saw an older woman sitting alone in one of our reception tents. I went to her and asked how she was. "*Allah Kerim*, God is Generous," she said. She looked all right but alone. An older person should not be alone. I asked where in Iraq she was from. She told me but I did not recognize it – some place in the north. I told her I would see her later.

Then when I went back to the booth, Jasmin and Sabit were there from Skopje. I worked giving out some clothing. "How are you doing?" they asked. "Just fine," I said. A little later, when I needed a break, I went to find them. I found them near the front of the main reception tent. They wanted to see the French toilets. A donor from France had sent funds for toilets that were then purchased and brought to the camp.

We went back to the container booth. Again, we worked with men's sweaters, hats, scarves, socks, and the occasional boots. It was getting late and dark. We walked over to the big tents at the far end in front of the tracks. There were some Syrians who were dancing in a circular line dance. "All we need is music," they said. Jasmin picked up a baby and joined in. Gabi, a Legis volunteer from Demir Kapija joined, and eventually I did too.

The older Iraqi woman, whom I had seen alone earlier in the reception tent, must have come out of the big tent to watch. I had not seen her at first. But she was there too standing alone watching the dancing. Gabi wanted to know how old she was. She did look very old. Gabi asked me to ask her. So I went over, put my arm around her, and I asked her age. When she told me, I looked up surprised. I told them, "She is my age!" Then I asked her how many children she had. "Six girls and four boys." That must account for some of the aging. But then it came out.

One of her sons had been killed. She had cried so much for him. He was only thirty-two and he had small children. "And the father?" I asked, meaning her husband. She was all in black so I assumed she was a widow and there was no man with her. "He died a year and four months ago," she said. I guessed she had been living with the son who had recently been killed. How tragic.

Jasmin had someone bring out warm coats from the Legis booth for her. She would only consider the black one. I told her she must take it because it would be much colder up north. She asked me to go to Germany with her. She has a son there whom she would join. Her other two sons are in Canada. I told her she was strong and she would be fine. I hugged her again. I would think of her again and again. It was not easy – an older mother alone on the Balkan Migrant Trail, with so much grief.

Yezidis and Pink Coats

The next day when I arrived there were already incoming refugees in the reception tent. All of the volunteers waited with boxes of boots in hand as they went through the documentation checks.

There was a tall man with a great white moustache in a white headdress and a long dark cloak. "Amazing. Who is he?" someone asked. "I do not know," I said.

We went inside the tents to give boots to the women who had rubber clogs on their feet instead of decent shoes or boots. One person said that they were Yezidis. Ahh, Yezidis, from Mt Sinjar in northern Iraq. There was a family with a baby who was only twenty-seven days old.

The Yezidis were targeted by ISIS in genocidal murder in August 2014 in northern Iraq where they have lived for millennia. They are ancient gnostic monotheists. The men were executed outright and the women and girls sold into slavery. Those who escaped fled north and west. I had never seen Yezidis before. It was the Kurds who went to Mt Sinjar to try to save them, including units made up of Kurdish women fighters.

Some men from the Red Cross came and dumped several large boxes of coats in our booth. How wonderful! They were men's coats in black and dark brown, and women's coats in bright fluorescent pink. It was an awful color but the coats were very warm. The older women did not like the pink. I do not blame them. But I cannot put men in bright pink.

Who decided on bright pink for women? Did they not think of older women too? Some fool who only thinks of women as little girls.

Brocade and Toilets and an Unaccompanied Minor

Then a man of medium height and gentle demeanor came by. I found a brown coat for him that fit and gloves, a hat, and a scarf. He was grateful. "Where are you from?" I asked. He was from Damascus. Then he told me he had worked in brocade of silk with silk embroidery. "There are only three of us in the world who do this. It has been in my family for generations." But who will do this now? I wondered. "Perhaps in Germany you can get work in a museum," I suggested. That is so specialized, so remarkable. What a loss for people who have such special skills. I would see him later with other people from Damascus in one of the big tents.

Then Nazife and I went for a break. We had a coffee and talked. Nazife was going to meet with the solidarity man who donated the French toilets. I said I would like to meet him too. So when they came, I went with Nazife to meet him. He asked me in French if the toilets had fallen over in the wind. I did not think so, but they had the day before.

A woman came and asked me to "tell the Arabs not to put clothing on the heaters." So I went to the large tent that had the most people. There was no clothing on the heaters. Instead I found a group of people from Damascus. We started talking. There was the man who did silk brocade, and several of the young men whom I had dressed in winter coats and who liked to take photos with the volunteers. We talked.

We were having a good time when we heard that the train was coming. All the people had to line up outside in their groups. I went outside and saw the police getting people to line up. It included Hungarian police. Slowly they let families go through. I spoke in English to a Hungarian policeman. "Why did you treat the refugees so poorly in Hungary?" I asked. "We did not want them," he said. "But they did not want to stay in Hungary," I said. "They wanted to pass through to Austria and Germany."

I told him, "We have many Hungarians in Detroit. The famous fencing coach at Wayne State University in Detroit was Hungarian." "Ahh," he said. "We used to be very good in that."

"Can I go toward the train?" I asked. I was concerned for the two families that did not have enough funds for the train tickets. One had

Figure 3.4   Refugees in line for train. Gevgelija, Macedonia.

nine family members, and the other six. He let me go forward. I was walking back when a young man came off the train crying. "What is wrong?" "He is an unaccompanied minor," said an officer.

"Is this true?" I tried to ask him. He was sobbing. "How old are you?" I asked in Arabic. He was sixteen. It turned out he had his sister and his brother with him. "So he is not unaccompanied if he has a sister and a brother," I stated. Actually, he needed a parent. Now he was missing a special Macedonian paper. I explained in Arabic to the young man that it was better to go and get the right document in Gevgelija. "Tabanovce is smaller. You must get the right document here." "Will they hold the train?" I asked. "We hope so." We walked quickly to the UNHCR booth and a translator I had never seen met us and talked to the young man. Poor child.

My Last Day at Gevgelija

On my last day at the camp, I arrived early in the morning and announced in my best Macedonian that it was "мојот последен ден", that is, "my last day." The policeman at security wrote out my name, the time of entry, and gave me back my paper and passport with no problem. No fuss with hours on this day.

I could see that many refugees had come in the night. I walked down the main path and saw the soup area. It was manned by people from AGAPE, evangelicals from Skopje. I asked for some hot soup and asked them where they were from. Grand Rapids, Michigan. I almost fell over. Fellow Michiganders. If it were not for these good people, we would have had no hot soup for the refugees, staff, or volunteers. Reportedly the EU had given the Macedonian government funds for a kitchen for hot food like soup, but it had never been built. It was good nutritious soup.

Police Asking Me for Assistance

I walked over toward the reception tent. A policeman asked me to read an ID card in Arabic. It was from Syria. "What is the young man's name?" asked the policeman. I read it and then wrote out the young man's name in Latin letters for the policeman. "And his birth date?" I wrote these out too in western numbers. The policeman did not explain why. This was the first time the police had come to me, and on my last day. I smiled to myself.

Then about 15 minutes later a young man came up to me, telling me that a policeman had kept his ID card. He did not know why. I told him the policeman had asked me to transliterate his card. But all I could remember about the policeman was that he was wearing blue. All the police wore blue. They all looked the same. I said, "Stay with me. We will find him."

Eventually we went back there and his friend waved to him. The policeman was inside. He read the young man's name. The policeman said, "Do not lie again." I looked at him and said to him in Arabic "Did you not tell the truth?" He nodded. "I said a man was my uncle. I am here alone. I was afraid they would keep me here." "No," I said. "No one wants to keep people here. They want to keep people moving on. Do not worry about that. It is good you are over eighteen. That is the only concern. But the policeman was right. Do not lie."

Waiting to Leave on a Train with 800 Others

Time was passing slowly with this very large group of refugees. Finally around 1 pm the train came. I had thought there were only 600 places on the train, but some Danish refugee workers told me there were different trains. One train had room for 1,000 refugees. I hoped it was this train. There were clearly over 600 refugees waiting.

The police insisted on lines of refugees. All documents had to be checked one by one. I did not think people from the unapproved groups would try to slip through during broad daylight. But still they had to check each document, one by one. It turned out there were over 800 refugees. So people stood waiting a long time.

The waiting was difficult. The police had the first group lined up in front of us so slowly each line seemed to go at a snail's pace. Would there be enough room on the train? That was everyone's worry. "Yes," I said. "There would be, hopefully."

I would go and ask people how they were. It was so hard to wait. It made me understand more what it was like. The refugees, though, would make it. They were fortunate. It was harder and harder to get out of Syria. Turkey now required visas. I mentioned this to some people and they nodded. "You are fortunate," I said. "We know," they said. "We just got out in time." Still it was hard waiting for the train.

Finally all boarded and the train left. It was 2:40 pm. Not a bad time to depart. They would arrive around 6:40 pm. They would be able to stay half an hour to an hour in Tabanovce. Then they could walk the 500 meters to the border, and the two to three kilometers to the bus to the larger camp in Preshevo, Serbia.

Yezidis and the Path to the Border and Back

There was a new group of refugees coming. Tara, a volunteer from Ohrid, went to meet them with hats and scarves. She asked me if I wanted to walk to the Greek border. I agreed. I had never walked that way before.

As we walked to the reception tents, a group of Jezidis came from the other direction toward us. They kept coming and went into the back of the tent. They were given food. This time it was yellow rice. A young boy helped me get hats and scarves distributed to those who needed them. I asked if I could take his picture. He agreed.

Then I went the opposite direction of the refugees, walking back to the Greek border. To one side were vineyards and in the distance the mountains of central Macedonia. The path was beaten down. To the other side was the train track. The refugees had to walk this. It took Tara and me about twenty minutes to get to the border with Greece. It was the back of Idomeni Camp in Greece. There were police there. That is where they checked their documents. They must have had to wait at that border as well. All the waiting and walking. It is not easy, but it is better in daylight. That must have meant that the Yezidis had gotten on their bus from Athens at 7 am. This was not a bad time. It let them arrive in daylight. So much the better.

Then we walked back. The sun was setting over the vineyards. How many refugees had walked this way? Thousands and hundreds of thousands. It was lovely, but I do not know if they could appreciate the beauty. There were so many unknowns on their paths.

I went back to the container booth. I was exhausted. I had had a ten-hour day and no lunch or dinner. I said goodbye to my fellow volunteers and to the camp. The next day I would return to Skopje.

A Final Visit to Tabanovce

Back in Skopje, I visited the new warehouse, which was an improvement on the old one. It was good to see Sara and Emineh again. I even went out to Tabanovce one more time. It was smaller and more relaxed than the camp in Gevgelija. At the police entry, the policeman wanted my official pass. I said I knew Valentina. That sealed it when she recognized me. She was the Macedonian in charge of much of the camp. I had a good long talk with her. Then we heard that the train had come in early.

Figure 3.5   Refugees waiting for the train at the refugee transit camp in Gevgelija, Macedonia.

People were already coming fast out of the train. There were bags of food piled on top of the counter, but the soup was not ready yet. The young men were first in line of course. The train had pulled too far forward so many carriages were ahead of the food area. People had to backtrack to get food. There was an older man who asked me where the men's toilets were. I led him quickly to the area of the toilets at the far end of the camp. There was a group from Damascus.

By then the soup was ready. Then the grey blankets came out. It was so cold that we were giving out grey blankets to everyone to put over them as they walked. The Damascus group got one for each person it seemed. I wished them well.

Then I went along to the tents. There was a problem in one tent. A young boy was crying. "Help here," said Valentina to me. I went over. "What is wrong?" I asked the boy as I sat down next to him on the long bench. It seemed a problem with a game. But I was sure it was the stress he was feeling as well. I asked his mother where they were from. "Idlib," she said. Idlib is an ancient city in northwest Syria.

I reached in my long purse for a tissue. It was so cold. The young boy asked for one too. I held out the small package of tissues to him. "Take one," I said. He took one. I looked again at the young boy.

"Do you have a pocket?" I asked in Arabic. He nodded and showed me with his hand in his winter coat. "But do not let any other children see this. I have only one left." I reached into my purse again and pulled out my last Spiderman toy. It was round and just the size of a child's palm. I put it straight into his hand and he put it into his pocket quickly and smiled. Then we all got up. They went to the other bench. I looked at some other people to see how they were. Then I looked across at the young boy. I wished his family well.

Out into the cold again. It was getting dark. I knew I needed to get back. I went with Albanians from Kumanovo who worked for the NGO Merhamet, a Muslim group, who were returning to their city. They had been working for the refugees every day for eight months. I got back to Skopje. I was glad I had been able to say goodbye to the good people at Tabanovce one last time.

Within a matter of weeks the countries along its path would close the Balkan Migrant Trail. The refugees I had been working with in Macedonia that winter were some of the last ones to get through. They were fortunate and they knew it.

Reflection on Refugee Transit Camps

The different personnel in the refugee transit camps had different purposes. Government officials and police were concerned with

Figure 3.6   Refugees in winter just after coming from train in Tabanovce.

controlling who passed through and who was excluded. Hence the
document checks and regulations of numbers of hours allowed in each
country. There were also official translators and some medical personnel.
International organizations like the UN sent officials if they had agencies
to run, like the "mother and young child center." NGOs, both local and
international volunteer groups like the one I worked for, filled in the

gaps in providing hot food, other food, medical aid, sanitary supplies, and clothing, both new and used. This was especially important during the winter months.

How the refugees were treated depended on the personnel involved. Few people spoke the languages of the refugees. The sheer numbers of the refugees did not encourage time for personal involvement. Many of the refugees had been through fearful times and kept to themselves. Illness was a threat. There were no female medical staff where I was and women were unlikely to ask strange males for medical help. This was a problem for women and I know of one woman who died as a result of this.

The design of the camps could have been much better. There should have been separate tents for families and for single men. Ideally there should have been facilities for women close to where they had to sleep. There should have been at least some female staff. There needed to be more people who spoke their languages.

Meanwhile kindness was never out of place. The young children were still children and wanted to play, although many picked up on the stress of their parents. Overall there should be ways to make this experience safer for women and children and less alienating.

PART II

INSIDE GERMANY –
ACCOMMODATION
OF REFUGEES

CHAPTER 4

RESPONSES OF VILLAGES

The First Village and First Refugee

The first village I researched in Germany was south of Freiburg. It was quite small with approximately 1,700 inhabitants.

My first full day, after breakfast, I visited a wine store on the edge of the village and struck up a conversation with the owner. He had lovingly taken out a large book published in 1914 on the village to show me when the sausage seller came in to resupply the front display. While the wine merchant was dealing with the sausage seller, I carefully paged through the book of the village.

The book chronicled German emigration through the nineteenth century. Many villagers had left in the 1850s or 1870s for North America or other destinations unknown. There were lists of family names of people who had left. I later asked why so many people had then left the region. The wine merchant said there had been famine. At the end of the book there was also a photograph of all the young men of the village who had gone to fight in 1914. Later, when I brought this to the wine merchant's attention, he said, "They all died, well over a hundred." I just looked at the young faces in their photographic ovals and felt sad. No wonder the village was so small now, not just from emigration, but also from the young dying in the war.

Then I asked if they had refugees in the village. "Not here, but in Bad Krozingen, my wife worked with them." Since the villages were so small, they grouped three small villages together for refugee numbers. I asked if I could talk with her. He said he would see.

His wife was working in the back room. When she came out, I asked her what she thought about the refugees. She said it was not simple. It turned out she had been helping with accommodations for refugees. There had been a large "family" and the possibility of a good accommodation in Bad Krozingen. The one member of the group who was acting as a translator knew some English. The "translator" had explained to the rest in such a way that three members had walked out. There had been shouting and the wine merchant's wife had gotten upset. She said it had been a very good plan and there were refugees living in much worse situations in containers elsewhere. Later the "translator" had wanted an accommodation for his smaller group. Truly there is a need for translators to be unrelated to the refugees. The upshot was that people who were trying to help became discouraged.

We began to talk politics. She said:

> Europe has not listened to Merkel. Merkel is right that the refugees must be spread out. That is the only way. What is Poland doing? There are Poles all over. Why will Poland not take some? And Hungary is worse. If Merkel does not get re-elected it will be a catastrophe.

I told her that in America we knew that Trump was just an entertainer, someone without character. I said, "We fear him too. I want America to take many more refugees." I told her what I was doing in Germany and that I wanted to learn the positive and share it with American people. I would write what I learned.

After the wine store, I walked up into the village. Across from the church was a bench with an older man sitting on it in the shade. We sat and talked for a while. He was a distributor for a regional newspaper of southern Baden-Württemberg. We talked about religion in the region. He was a member of the Lutheran Free Church. I had thought the region was mostly Catholic. He assured me there were some Protestants too. He explained how the city of Freiburg had everything, even Muslims, and that their religious center was full all the time. When I asked if they were refugees or Turkish immigrants, he said that he did not know. After a while he looked down. "It is good not to be alone," he said. "I enjoyed it too," I said. We smiled and said goodbye.

Talk of the Wars, a Turkish Taxi Driver,
and the Problem of a Foreign Name

After spending the rest of the day wandering the village, I had an interesting evening talking in German about what I had learned with a German guest in the hotel. I told her about all the young men of the village who had died in World War I. She said that once she had visited Belgium and it was clear people there had not forgotten that war. We also talked about World War II.

She said young people asked the older ones why they did not just say no, but they could not say no at the time. I said I knew of one book I had read in German called *Die Weisse Rose, "The White Rose,"* of young people in Munich who did resist.[1] But they were killed. I said it was impossible to resist and remain alive. People needed to resist earlier in the 1930s. But they did not know that then. I told her that we see now with Trump how easy it is for people to get caught up. I added. "One of the reasons I am writing my book is to show how good the German people can be. But I would do it for whoever was doing what they are doing for refugees now."

The next morning I had a long taxi ride to Freiburg. The young taxi driver drove through the small towns that were linked together for helping refugees. When I asked about Freiburg and its people, he mentioned that he was a Turk. I started speaking Turkish and he was flabbergasted. I do not know if it was my northern features or my fluent Turkish, all topped off with my grey hair. In any case I was able to ask him in Turkish what he thought of the refugees in Freiburg and how they were getting along.

He said he understood the refugees more than the German people did because he understood their culture. "They expected more here," he said. "They thought it would be better. Now they want to go to Turkey or Lebanon or Jordan." Over-expectation is a common problem of refugees.

I had been to Turkey that year and had seen that there was little work and few schools for them there. The culture was closer though, he was right. Then he added, "But there is no system there. Here there is system, but the German people do not understand the refugees." He said he had tried to explain to the German people that the refugees were like their parents who had lived through conditions in the 1940s of war, of bombing, of lack of food.

He began to speak of his own experience in Germany. "My family came twenty years ago. And only now they begin to accept us." I said that the German people take time to get to know you. "Yes," he said. I said they do not move around like Americans. "And they are afraid of Islam," he said. "Ahh," I said, "Paris and Brussels, and the incidents here last July did not help."

"Don't the refugees know they are fortunate to be here?" I asked. He answered, "At least the children do. But in school, it is not easy. They see your foreign name. I have been here twenty years," he reiterated. "Ahh, they know you are foreign from your name," I repeated.

The relation of the Germans and the Turks is truly complex. It was not my main concern. But it would continue to hit me in the face. I would find myself speaking for both groups. It did not seem as if there was much real dialogue between them.

When I arrived back at the train station in Freiburg I thanked the taxi driver and paid him extra for his conversation. I went to buy my ticket for Elzach, a village at the far end of the Valley of Elz. Then I went out on the platform to wait for the train.

A Man with a Big Beard

At the far end of the platform there was a bench and on it was a young man with bushy beard. Why such a big beard? Was he making a statement with the beard? I am sure it scared people away. But I have sons and so am not easily put off.

I walked down the platform and asked him in German if he were waiting for the train to Elzach. He answered in German that he did not know where Elzach was. I sat down on the same bench to wait.

"Where are you from?" I asked in German. "Syria," he said. Ahh, I started speaking colloquial Arabic. He was amazed. I asked him where he was from in Syria, again in Arabic. "Dar'aa," he answered. Then I asked him how long he had been here. "A year." I told him it was good he spoke German.

"Where did you learn Arabic?" he asked me. I told him I had learned in Lebanon where I had been a teacher and had learned from the children. I told him that earlier I had studied *fusha*, the formal Arabic at university, but everyone laughed when I had tried to speak it. He smiled. Then I told him I had lived in Syria too, in Jebel Druze, al-Suwaida, but not in Dar'aa.

"How are you doing here?" I asked. "So so," he said. "I go to school here," he motioned to one side, "and live there," he motioned to another side. I asked if he had family here. "No," he said. I asked if they were back in Syria. "Yes," he said. "My mother and family. I am not married." I told him that was hard. "I am studying for the MA." I told him that was good.

"You know English?" he asked. I told him it was my home language, and that I was from America. "Ohh," he said. "I thought you were German." I let him know that I was still working on German, and that it was important. "Yes," he said. "Patience," I said, "patience is the key to knowledge." He finished the proverb with me. We both smiled.

Then my train came, but at the other end of the station. I started hurrying with my big suitcase. He helped me run with it. Without his help I might not have made it. He lifted it onto the train too. "God give you strength," I said to him in Arabic. "Thank you so much." I shook his hand. I had just met my first refugee in Germany.

The Second Village of Elzach: Whose People Made Wise Decisions

I got on the train but most of the seats were taken. I found a place on the aisle by two older men who were next to the window. I sat down and pulled my big suitcase in front of me. The man across from me asked me where I was going. "To Elzach." He nodded.

It took us 20 minutes to reach Waldkirch and that was only part way up the valley. Waldkirch is where my friend Siglind lives. I had first heard of Elzach and the refugees there when I had been visiting my friend Siglind in Waldkirch.

It had been the previous May when Siglind and I were sitting in the market square in Waldkirch. All the chairs at the tables were occupied and so Siglind asked a woman if we could join her. It turned out she was from the north, but she had moved to the south. That day she had come to Waldkirch on her bicycle from Elzach, a small town at the end of the valley where she lived, to buy half a baby goat!

When my friend had gone to buy bread from the bakery before it closed on Saturday, I had stayed at the table with the woman. She asked me in German how long I was would be in Waldkirch. I said a few days in Waldkirch, but for longer in Germany. I wanted to visit programs for the *Flüchtlinge*, the refugees.

The woman then excitedly told me that they had *Flüchtlinge* in Elzach! She explained that Elzach only had 4,000 people and was very Catholic. But it was humanitarian Catholic. There was a concert of Catholic music that night and people would bring refugees to the concert. Mostly, though, she spoke about a *Bioladen*, that is, an organic food store in Elzach. The owner of the store regularly bought four passes for public transport for the refugees so they could go to Freiburg on the trains. The woman traced the initiative and positive spirit in Elzach to the owner of the store as a model for humanistic spirit for the town.

She then explained how at first the refugees had lived in a center for poor people outside the town. They were going to enlarge it, but the town decided against this. They did not want to have a center only for poor people. Instead they bought a building for the refugees to live in above an information center, an apartment above a second-hand clothing store, and a small house. It was better to have them in three locations, not just in one. They also had a main hall where retired people came to help the refugees learn German. Then she said goodbye and went off on her bicycle.

How impressive! When my friend came back I told her what I had learned and that I needed to visit Elzach the next day. We did go by train the next day, but it was Sunday and so the store was closed. I met some refugees on the street, Kurds who had come two months earlier from northern Syria. They knew they had come to a good place. But I also knew I needed to come back to Elzach.

By this time, with all my musing, the train had come into the small station of Elzach, the end of the line. As I got out, the older man who had been sitting next to me asked where I was going. When I told him I was going to a hotel and needed to find a taxi, he said he would help. It was raining and as we walked down a long staircase from the station, it occurred to me there might not be taxis in this village. He helped by carrying my big suitcase. He told me to wait as he went to get his car. He took me all the way to my hotel, which turned out to be a pension, up outside Elzach. I thanked him profusely. I was most grateful for so much kindness from a stranger.

In the pension, I asked the older owner if there was a hotel in the town. She explained that they were only two kilometers from the town, not a far distance. I later found out that there used to be a guesthouse in town, but now it was converted into a home for the elderly.

The Social Worker

A good way to begin to research a town is to visit the *Rathaus*, the city hall. I had earlier emailed the mayor, asking for an appointment to meet with him. He had replied, saying his staff would let me know when he would be available.

That first morning I went to the Elzach City Hall and explained what I was interested in. I hoped there would be someone knowledgeable I could speak with. I was told I should see a particular woman who would soon return. I waited. She turned out to be the village social worker. I told her that I had heard that Elzach was good with refugees, and that we in America needed to learn from the German experience. She described how the local Catholic and Evangelical churches, and the *Ehrenamtliche*, a traditional term for "volunteers," all worked together in Elzach. They had developed an "Asylum Working Circle" that met regularly.

In the 1990s people in the small town had worked with refugees from Yugoslavia. "They must be helped," they had said. I found it most interesting that this was not the first time this small town had worked with refugees.

She explained more specifically what different people did. For example, Caritas, the Catholic charity, had two staff women who worked with the refugees. They had a kindergarten and a school. She looked for places for the refugees to live. The volunteers took families to doctors, helped them when they had problems, and took care of incidentals, like difficulties with a washing machine. There was self-help too which was considered important. She added that people donated clothing and shoes. Indeed, while I was in her office a man came in to give school bags and shoes for those in need. She told me there was a second-hand store on the main street that was open three days a week for refugees and for local poor people too.

The refugees came from Syria, Iraq, Afghanistan, Gambia, Pakistan, and Algeria. They were both single men as well as families. She counted in her head – "There are eight families and thirty single men." Many volunteers helped with language learning. There were also six-month language courses in Freiburg, Waldkirch, Emmendingen, and Winden im Elztal for the course on integration.

I was truly impressed. I then asked her what she saw as the greatest problem for the refugees. She answered, "Language." She continued.

And then for integration, I especially see this as a problem for the women. The women stay home with the children and never get to the language and integration course. They sit at home. We must all be tolerant. But there is a problem with the women.

I tried to explain to her more about Middle Eastern culture and gender separation. I suggested food and handwork as a natural means of coming together in Germany. A weekly meeting of women with older German women might work. It was good for them to learn German, and always to encourage it by saying that it was useful for their children. I told her that the women were intelligent, but I do not think she believed me.

On another note, I asked how many people there were in Elzach. She responded immediately, "7,000." This number includes the town and the surrounding small towns as well. I asked her if she was from Elzach. She said she was. I told her I grew up on an island where everyone knew everyone else. But the island was flat land in the Detroit River, whereas Elzach had such beautiful mountains. She smiled. I could tell how much she valued her hometown. She mentioned that she had thought about living elsewhere but had never done so.

I asked about problems with culture. She answered in a way I had not expected. She said, "There are some who say 'refugees' – and a curse word. But mostly, given half a chance, especially with the children it will work with sports, music, and things like that. But it is harder with the women."

As I looked at her I wondered, how could I bring German women like her, who probably related better to hiking and mountains, to understanding of Middle Eastern women whose lives had such different parameters? I thanked her for her time and insights.

A Refugee Family

I walked down the street from the *Rathaus*, in search of the organic food store. The name of the store was *Sünnewirbili*, an Alemanic[2] term for a "field lettuce." It was not far away but then nothing in the small town was distant.

As I entered the organic store I was greeted by fresh produce up front. It was homey with its wooden shelves and welcoming atmosphere. At the counter I told the young woman I was interested in refugees. She told me to come back the next day, on Saturday morning at eight o'clock. It was the owner, Rita Andris, I should talk with and she would be there then.

Meanwhile, I hoped to meet some of the refugee families in Elzach. After a while I saw a young woman hurrying along, carrying a cake with powdered sugar on it. She looked Middle Eastern. I asked in Arabic where she was from. She told me she was from Mt Sinjar and she had been in Elzach for five months. I asked if I could meet her family. She took me back behind the row of stores that front on the main street.

We went upstairs where I took off my shoes. Her father and mother came out and greeted me. She introduced me as "an American who speaks Arabic." I greeted them appropriately and we went into the living room. There was also another Arab man there from a news source.

The family spoke Kurdish, a Zaza dialect, and of course Arabic. I learned that they had come through Turkey where they had spent a year in Niğde. They had come by boat to Greece, along the Balkan Trail, and finally arrived in Heidelberg.

The Arab man from the news source, a photographer, explained why he was there. One of the younger sons had a medical condition, a liver disease that was serious. The German medical services had been most helpful. The mother had donated an organ from her body for her son. I looked over at her with respect. She smiled at me. It must have been terrifying to be a refugee with a very sick child and not know if care was possible. He had had an operation in Heidelberg and the photographer had covered it for the press. He was there that day to see how they were doing.

The family had four sons and two daughters. I asked the eldest son if he were studying German. He replied by telling me what day his German classes began that month. He explained how each of his younger brothers went to a school in a different town with only the youngest going to school in Elzach. He said he would go by bus to his course every day when it began.

I asked about their extended family. They still have family in Iraq. And the battle for Mosul was just beginning. Where will their relatives go?

The young woman whom I had seen on the street brought us all tea and cake. We talked some more. The children moved to another room and I was with the parents in the front room. I told them in Arabic that I knew from immigrants and refugees in America that they would suffer the most. It was for their children that they did this. They nodded.

It is hardest on them. They lose their other relatives and friends. I had their total attention.

But why was I telling them this? I think I mirrored their special pain. The medical problem of the son had made it even more difficult. I wanted to let them know I felt their suffering. I had seen this most recently in the refugee transit camps in Macedonia as well. The incredible loneliness of the adult refugees.

I told them their children would not know what they had given up. Maybe later they would come to understand. Probably the daughters first. But that they would give so much. The mother started to cry. I put my arms around her. It is truly incredibly hard to be in a strange country where you do not know the language and are far from the family and friends when you need them almost as much as you need air. That is Middle Eastern culture.

The mother wanted me to go to Freiburg with her. I thanked her but I needed to go back to the pension. I stood up to leave. I thanked them. I would come back to see them again. I had never talked like this before so early with a family. I hoped I was doing right by them.

Later on the way back to the pension I thought about the father and especially the mother of the refugee family. She had given an organ to her son. She now would probably become the mediator in the family of eight people, a role that others might have played back home. How could I explain to the social worker the stresses and loneliness of her life in Germany? There was so much she had to contend with before any thought of learning a new language. How could I help the social worker begin to respect her courage?

The Treasure Trove

On the way back I passed the used clothing store. I was emotionally tired from visiting the refugee family, but I figured I should check out the store since it had limited hours. On the door was written, "*Elzacher Fundgrube*," that is, the "Treasure Trove of Elzach."

The store had a good feel to it and was brightly lit. It had two main rooms with a back area and a place for trying on clothing. Up front there was a checkout counter where customers were charged nominal fees for each item. The clothing was hanging or neatly folded. There were children's clothing and shoes on the left side, as well as toys and baby strollers, and bedroom and bathroom supplies like towels. On the right side were more adult goods including women's and men's clothing and shoes, along with purses. Clothing and shoes in Germany are quite expensive so there was real value here.

While I was visiting, a man was carefully vacuuming. It turned out that he too was an older refugee and this work was a way he contributed. A tall handsome woman in a light colored dress greeted me. I told her I was a visitor from America who wanted to learn about her store. She told me right off the store was run by thirty women. "Thirty!" I said. "Yes," she said. "*Frauen* power," she added with a gesture of both arms, and a big smile. She told me they collected the clothing and items and made sure they were in good condition. They would hang them up and appropriately display the clothes. I noticed the hours the store was open for business. They were Mondays from nine o'clock to noon, Wednesdays from three to six o'clock, and Fridays from three to six o'clock. These were most reasonable hours for customers and working hours for women with families.

I asked her how the store had evolved. She said it was about three years old. Before people had collected clothing for those in need and taken them to Emmendingen, a nearby town bigger than Elzach. But then the Asylum Circle said they had a need of them here. Why not keep them here? So they did. First they just had a small room. Then the mayor helped them get this place. Originally it had been a drug store that had been empty for a while. The mayor thought it would be a good use of the place. The city would pay the rent and the utilities.

I thanked her and said I would tell others about this. It was not just for refugees, but also for those on limited budgets and others who needed it as well. What felt different from the American thrift shops I was accustomed to was the level of community involvement and pride in the shop. Perhaps American thrift shops had been that way at the outset.

How One Person Can Set the Tone

On Saturday I was careful to wake up early and have breakfast early too. I wanted to be sure I was at *Sünnewirbili*, the organic store, by eight o'clock in the morning. Punctuality in Germany matters.

I entered *Sünnewirbili* and looked around. A woman asked me who I was meeting. When I told her it was Rita Andris, she said Rita would be late that morning because she had to take her elderly mother to the doctor. So I ended up in the back room of the store, a most congenial place with bookshelves all along one sidewall, a good square table with chairs in the center, and a sink on the other wall with many cups that looked as if people often gathered there.

Eventually Rita came in and filled the room with her energy and life. She has short hair and is of medium height, and does not stop moving. I explained why I was there. I mentioned that I had spoken to the town social worker the day before. Rita did not comment on this. Instead she went straight to the situation of the refugees themselves.

She said that many had lived through hard times. What they needed was eye contact and interaction with other people including Germans, not someone else to help them including herself. They were mostly single men alone. That was not easy. "I am a Christian," declared Rita. She reached for the small wooden cross that she wore around her neck. "I tell them that I have Jesus with me. That goes well with them. They are Muslim."

At that point a middle-aged German man walked in and handed Rita three pieces of paper. She went to get him some funds. "Would you like cake?" she asked me. "No thank you," I said. She asked the man to get two pieces, and then to bring them back. After he left she explained that she was his guardian. His parents had died. So she had the funds for him. He was somewhat retarded and needed someone to take care of his finances. It turned out that Rita did many things.

He came back ten minutes later with cake for him and the other piece "saved for Assad." It was a good rich cake. He sat with us and ate it. It was nice that he seemed comfortable at the table. He belonged there too.

Rita continued where she had left off before he had arrived. She had been about to explain to me the regional train tickets she purchases for the refugees. She said that one of the things that we can do to support the refugees is the *Regio Karte*. She showed me one. It is for the trains that go from Elzach to Waldkirch and Freiburg. They are good for a month. Rita buys them and lets the refugees use them, and then bring them back, so other refugees can use the same one.

I could see how that these train tickets would give them much mobility. I later learned that without the tickets, which they borrow for one euro each, the tickets would cost six euros each way or twelve euros for each trip to Freiburg and back. What a difference!

Rita said the refugees help her carry everything in the organic store. She was doing inventory when I came back much later in the afternoon. She also said that the back room was a meeting room for them. She insisted that they needed interaction and dialogue with each other and with Germans.

I asked about German courses. She said they had them in Elzach too, not just in Waldkirch and Freiburg. She said that they had a local couple, they are *Ehrenamtliche*, meaning they work regularly and for no pay. They teach every evening from Monday through Friday from five to seven o'clock.

In the summer, she liked to have parties to make sure there are things for them to do and to bring the refugees and Germans together. She added that she had responsibilities with the store, with her mother, and her other work. Still she does what she can. "We have people from Egypt, Morocco, Syria, Iraq, Afghanistan, and Gambia."

A middle-aged man from Pakistan came in, greeted us, and sat down. His name was Assad and his cake was waiting for him. I recognized him as the man who had been vacuuming at the used-clothing store the day before. He had been in Germany for three years and nine months he told me. He is truly a political asylum case, not just a refugee in the usual sense. He is currently working for a mattress maker in town so he can send school money to his six children and wife back in Pakistan.

Returning to the more usual refugees, I asked Rita what was most difficult for them. She answered that they were not in contact with German people. Sometimes this was because they were in ghettos with other refugees.

Then Rita explained what had almost happened here in Elzach. At first the mayor had wanted to build a house where all the refugees would stay. Rita told him no. If he did that then they would always be in contact only with each other, and not with the community. Who would take them to the doctor? "We need to have others help. We need to spread out the refugees to spread out the needs so more people will get involved in their care. This is better for their learning German too."

What the mayor had first suggested was simpler, but not wiser. However he listened to her. So Rita and a friend Monika placed a request in the newspaper for living spaces. People responded. From this they found different locations, one of which I had visited the day before with the refugee family, and two of which I would visit later that day.

Figure 4.1   Rita Andris in back room of Bioladen in Elzach, Germany.

People were generous, but it was hard when it turned out that the refugees knew no German. Currently there are refugees at nine different locations in and around Elzach.

I mentioned that I had heard people in Elzach had earlier helped refugees in the 1990s. Rita confirmed that and said she remembered it about twenty-five years before. She informed us that there had been refugees from Iraq and from Bosnia. "We even had people staying in a church then." She told me there are people who were active during that time who are still active to this day. "There is a woman who is eighty-five years old and works with us now too. The young people have come forward as well." "All are Christians, they live it. But there is still" – here Rita made a gesture – "still talk. But here we stand. And many women who do the work."

During my next days in Elzach, I would see how central Rita was to efforts with the refugees. She had good sense and just did what needed doing without talk. When people saw what she had done, they figured they could do something too, and some did. Her reasoning with the mayor however had been crucial. It was Rita who had stopped the mayor from putting all the refugees in one building.

Monika's Guests

A friend of Rita's is Monika who agreed to show me her workshop, where she makes Black Forest crafts to sell, above which live ten Syrian refugee men and a family. Monika also has a educated young refugee living in her home with her grown children and family.

As I walked along the main street of Elzach, Monika walked her bicycle beside me. She is a slender woman with delicate features. She has four children ranging in ages from nineteen to thirty-one, three of whom still live at home. She also takes care of her mother in her home as well.

I asked about her workshop which is where we were heading. Rita had told me that Monika had trained in and taught biology. We first entered a small store that sold the locally made goods from the workshop – soaps, wallets, and Black Forest items made out of wood, all carefully displayed. Then we went back to the workshop so I could see how she made the different products. I liked how it smelled.

We climbed the back stairs to where the refugees lived. It led to a communal kitchen where I greeted the men in Arabic. They welcomed me in. It was about lunch time and all the single men were eating together. They were mostly young men in their twenties, but there was also one older man in his fifties. He was the father of eight children whom he misses and hopes to bring from Istanbul with his wife. He too is Syrian. Like so many, the whole family escaped from Syria to Turkey, but only the father took the dangerous journey through the Balkan Migrant Trail.

Monika had written the German name of things on post-it notes and placed them all over the kitchen. She was given a central place at the table.

Someone had gone to Freiburg and come back with good Arabic food – Arabic pita bread, laban, olive oil, zataar. Meanwhile, on the stove, Hussein was making the classic Eygptian dish, *foul madamas*. They encouraged Monika to have some. She wanted to know if people looked at her post-it notes. The older man said it was hard to concentrate on German when he was thinking of his family. I translated this from Arabic for her, and encouraged her again to try some of the delicious food. They had given me the seat at the head of the table.

Then we all began to eat. It was so good. I asked where people were from. It was mostly Aleppo or Damascus. I asked about their learning German. All the talk was in Arabic. They said it did not come easy, and that they had not been here long, seven months at most. It sounded as if it took much initiative to talk with Germans at all. Monika said she needed to leave. The men appreciated her assistance.

I stayed and we talked some more. I liked their company. The older men were good for the younger ones. It gave them some stability and I think they were better cooks. They asked me to stay for dinner too. One said he would make *tabouli* for me. I told them they were tempting me. They knew I had been in Lebanon and that is the national dish. I let them know that they were very good hosts.

I told them this was what they had to give the Germans – social balance in life. Middle Easterners know how to live and make time for family and friends too. Germans, like Americans, work so much. We often forget the importance of stopping to talk and spending with others. When we do engage with others, we often cannot to do this without alcohol.

I thanked them and wished them well. Then I walked down the back staircase and back to *Sünnewirbili* where Monika had agreed to meet me and take me to her home. There she wanted me to meet the refugee Nabil[3] who was living in her home.

Monika's house is back behind the school and the Catholic Church. It is a big house with a garden and three apple trees and a cherry tree in the front. It is so generous to open one's own home to a refugee; I was truly impressed. She had even constructed a separate entrance around the back of the house. Outside of Nabil's rooms, we sat on a makeshift private balcony.

Nabil is a tall slender man of quiet countenance. He asked us what we wanted – tea, coffee, maté. Maté! I told him I had not had it since I was in Syria, many years ago. So he made maté. He even had the silver straws. It is South American but Syrians went to South America and brought it back. Monika and I both had it while he had tea. He is a young, married man. His wife awaits him in Istanbul. He is a trained engineer from a city in southern Syria. I asked him about his studies. He is in the third level of German, a very high level. He wants to go on in German, but he must get very good to do this. He knows English as well.

I asked about his family. They left their hometown several years ago to move to another city in Syria. He has a sister in Latakia, a brother in Geneva, and another brother in the Gulf. This is not unusual for educated Syrian families. I asked him about his coming to Germany. He said he had no option. He had to leave. If not, he would have had to go into Assad's army or into militias of which there were several. From this point on he conversed in Arabic. I call it the point of pain.

Monika listened for a while and then told us she would go work in the garden. I hope she understood that he needed to tell about what he had been through in Arabic because that was the way he experienced it.

He went to Lebanon but was told there was nothing for him there and for that reason he should leave. Where to go? So he flew to Turkey. From Bodrum on the coast he went in a very small boat to Kos. They were at sea for five and a half hours and always bailing out water for the duration of the trip. Thankfully they reached a Greek island and eventually they came to Athens. Then they went by bus to Thessaloniki. They walked some and then they went to the border of Macedonia.

I told him I worked across the border from Idomeni in Gevgelija. He remembered that – where the train was. He was there in the summer of 2015. The train took them across Macedonia to Serbia. Then they walked again to the camp in Serbia and up to Belgrade where they stayed in a hotel and cleaned up, shaved, and showered. From there they walked north for several days to the Hungarian border.

This was the worst part of the whole journey. He said he could have gone with only a few people, but as they went north they found more people along the way who needed help. There were women and children.

People took advantage of them. So eventually they were a large group of about 300. They put the stronger men on the outside with the women in the middle. This way they were safer. He was the leader. He had a map and knew the way at least to the border.

The police at the actual border were brutal. How to get through? They found out it was better to divide up. If they were in smaller groups they could not be taken so easily. The police would come after them and push them against walls. Nabil said the police grabbed him and damaged his upper arm. He showed me where it was still injured. He had just barely gotten away. All they were trying to do was cross through Hungary.

A taxi offered to take them for 100 euros each and then another 100 euros. They got in, but the taxi only took them through the town and then let them out. What was that? They did not know where they were. They had no water.

For three days they wandered. They would sleep at night and got up very early in the morning when the police could not see them so easily. They did not have a map of Hungary and so had to guess the way to Budapest. No one spoke English. No one helped them or even gave them water.

Finally they found another taxi. The driver said 500 euros to Budapest. They agreed. What else could they do? In Budapest they went to a special hotel where they had to wear wristbands showing they were refugees. At least they got something to drink.

It was August and so hot. From there they went to the McDonalds where they made a connection for a car to Germany. It cost 450 euros each. They took it to Passau on the border with Austria.

The police opened the door and Nabil ran out. He was afraid it was the Hungarian police again. He got a distance away and looked back. The policeman was smiling. What? Then he realized. He was a German policeman, not Hungarian. So he walked back and apologized. The man handed him a bottle of water. What a difference.

In Hungary the police treated them like animals. Here in Germany the police treated them like humans. Nabil said if anyone ever tries to say anything against Germany he would stand up for the country in the same way he would for his homeland.

As mentioned, Nabil is tall, slim, has a narrow face and a serious expression. He was in his twenties at the time. Yet in no way would he be someone you would treat with anything but respect. It made sense that he was the leader of 300 people, a gentle leader.

He asked me if I would like to see his rooms in Monika's house. I nodded. We went inside. There was a place for a computer, a small work area. Then was a sitting room. He said the table was from Rita, and the chair was donated from the Treasure Trove. The kitchen was fully furnished. He had a small refrigerator. He could cook and so forth on his own. Then to the front, a bedroom with a view of the garden staring out into all the apple trees.

I walked down to the garden and thanked Monika for introducing me to Nabil. She gave me two apples from her garden. He walked me back to the road toward the pension. He took a bicycle with him. He said a German man had given him the bicycle. The generosity of the Germans in this small town continues to astound me, and him too. I wished him well in his studies and bringing his wife to Germany.

Lutheran Church in a Catholic Region
It rained my first Sunday in Germany, but I still went to the Lutheran Church in Elzach along with a small group of fifteen other hardy souls. The pastor greeted us. I had heard she was a member of the Asylum Circle, which pleased me.

I would attend church throughout my stay in Germany. Americans of my ilk tend to do this. I had been raised Episcopalian, a liturgical Protestant faith, so I was at home in both Catholic and Lutheran services and knew all the main prayers. Only I missed the older hymns, many translated from German, that I had been raised on. In many churches in Germany I found they sang "modern" hymns in new hymnals that no one knew. Thank goodness for the organ.

The Third Village: Whose People Worked Yet Missed the Mark

The third village was one I had chosen because the social worker in Elzach had recommended it as one that provided good services for refugees. However, a problem with villages in general is that they can be difficult to access. Rita was most kind to drive me there or I would have had to take multiple buses. It was also about twice the size of Elzach with some 9,800 inhabitants, but could still be considered as a village or a small town.

We went to the *Rathaus* to see if the social worker could see me. I had emailed her several days in advance. She had new refugees coming in that day and was too busy both that day and the next day. So we went to a café where there were German lessons in progress and introduced ourselves to the teacher.

The volunteer teacher was an older man who had spent many years in Muslim countries including Somalia. The students he was teaching were all Afghans, some of whom were illiterate in their own language of Pashto. I learned from him when there would be other classes at the café and where the main refugee accommodation was.

Then we went to the tourist office. There we learned the name of the organizer of the *Ehrenamtliche* for the town, and even set up a meeting with him after lunch. Rita then drove me to a work project for a while, and later back to where I would meet with the head of the volunteers. I thanked her for her time and all her help. She had to get back to Elzach and her many responsibilities.

Head of Volunteers

The head of volunteers for the small town was a tall man with white hair. He was exactly on time. We went to a café for coffee and I had a big pretzel too. He had only recently retired. Before that he had been the head of the local school and was clearly a community leader.

He asked why I was in Germany and I explained my research. Then I asked about his town. He said proudly that of all the towns, his was the first to construct a new building for its refugees. Others wanted to welcome the refugees, but they did not do anything. The *Bürgermeister*, the mayor, here did something.

Since they had almost 10,000 people, by law they should have 140 refugees. But where other communities did nothing, they had a community meeting of people who wanted to help in the *Rathaus*. A total of 120 people came to the meeting. There was not enough room for all of them. People gave their names, addresses, and emails. They said when the building was built they would help.

People started to contribute clothing and furniture. The need for a coordinator became clear and he was appointed. It was not so much to work with the refugees as to help organizing the people who wanted to help. They found a place where they could store the clothing and furniture. This was all in February 2015. They organized a *Laden*, a store where the refugees could come to buy clothing and other things at a reduced price. They have a store for food and for tools. They also have two stores with clothing, shoes, and toys. I asked who paid for the store. He said the state of Baden-Württemberg.

He said that the mayor of the town is *schlau*, "clever." He had constructed a refugee building and a store. He received help from the people and from the state. "They actually came to us to give us funds." The mayor borrowed the funds on a mortgage, and in twenty years it will belong to the people of the town. Poor people can use it as well.

There are people from Syria, Iraq, and Afghanistan. The people who came from Gambia who have been here will be sent back.

I asked what was hardest for the refugees. He answered:

The language. They must learn German. They must also learn how people behave here. They must learn German well. There is a doctor from Syria. He speaks good English. But Syria needs him. His German is not all that good after a year. He waits. In Germany we have a need for integration, for good workers, but there are men who cannot pass the examinations.

I asked about the women. "There is also a course for the women where they have a room for the children to play in. There is a Syrian woman who has learned German well herself in three months and she serves as a translator." He also said that there was a Turkish family here for a while who knew Kurdish and helped.

We talked about politics for a while. I asked him more about the people of the town. He said that there are three groups:

There are many who wanted to help. There are also many who said they did not want to help. And there are some who said they should all go back. They said we have a standard of living and they will take from our standard. But our Finance Minister said, "No German must give anything. No German will get any worse." It is the Germans who have little who say the refugees should go away. Then there are problems with Muslims, and they are afraid.

Visit to the Refugee Building

After our talk and coffee together, the head of volunteers took me in his car to the refugee buildings. They are outside town in an area that is somewhat industrial. To one side is an old building that is set up on the ground floor so it can hold 400 people if need be. There are divisions of white industrial fabric that could each have ten people in them. If 100 people came on one day, they could be accommodated. He showed me how with the divisions. There was even one man living in one of them. He must have liked being on his own.

Then to the right were the new buildings – two new ones for refugees and across one smaller one for the social workers or staff. There are several stories with kitchens and laundries on each floor. There is a play area for children at the far end of the last one. Over sixty-four men and some families live there. It is isolated from the town.

We were invited into a kitchen area for coffee with a group of Syrians. We went inside and were given chairs immediately. Most had been there for a year or somewhat less. But their German was not good. It turned out that a main difficulty was getting German lessons.

As someone went to look for milk for my coffee, I was given a tour of the facility. All have private rooms. There is a laundry too. The only sign of making the roomsit one's own, however, was an Afghan who was shaking a rug from an upstairs balcony. Still it appeared well constructed. Just big and too far from town. How can people interact with Germans? Or Germans interact with the refugees easily?

I asked this of the head of volunteers and he said the men should play football. I looked at the men around me, most of whom were fathers and wondered.

I talked with the men as we drank our coffee. Several were from Damascus, some from Aleppo and different parts of Syria. I asked them about their German study. It seemed slight. One said he had only had two days of classes. It seemed a problem. They cannot get into courses. Where are the social workers for German classes who have that nice building I wondered? What are they doing? Or are there really not enough German courses?

I asked another what sort of work he wanted to do in Germany. He wanted to be a tailor. I asked the head of volunteers if there were apprentice programs in that. He said that he has a relative in textile design but there are no jobs in that. I told the young man he must be flexible in what he does. And above all he must learn German. He said he does not learn so well in classes. He would like to be with a German family and hear German and have German friends. He could learn better that way. I told the head of volunteers that. He responded that it was good to have a base first. I think people here do not know a lot about language learning and motivation. With friends comes motivation. I passed on the idea of a base to the Syrian man. But he was right. He needs interaction with Germans. I wish I had told him about sports.

Then the Syrian doctor came by. He has been here since the previous September, that is, over a year ago. He said the people were right. He had gotten his first German class in April. He wants to live somewhere else. He said he could not study here; it was too noisy. All he heard was Pashto from the Afghans. I told him to go to the library to study. He said he needs to interact with Germans to learn German. Here it was not good. So, I said, go ask if you can sit in the hospital with patients, not to work, but just to sit and listen to them, or ask how they are. Or you can visit an old people's home. You need to reach out. He did not like that idea. Perhaps it is easier for a woman to reach out to others.

What interests me is that he does not like the building. I imagine that the social worker and the head of volunteers do not hear this, and except for the Syrian doctor who is sure of his status, the other refugees are afraid to say what they actually think about their situation here in the industrial area outside town. I thanked the men for their time and company and went back into town with the head of volunteers. I thanked him for his company too. He is a good man.

Thoughts

I went back to the café where I knew there would be more language classes later in the evening. I met more volunteer teachers. The first teacher was a German woman who had traveled all over Syria and had been to Palmyra and Mari. I told the students they were fortunate to have her as an instructor.

The next instructor was a middle-aged man who was teaching an integration class that was less structured. The Syrians wanted to speak Arabic with me, but I insisted on German. The teacher eventually moved to articulation excercises on the blackboard. He was most patient. A new family came in and the children played quietly in the back as the mother and father both participated in the class.

I went back to where I was staying and wrote up field notes for the long day. At breakfast the next day I called Rita on the telephone. I told her of the problems with the new building, that the refugees did not like it, but in general they could not say so. It was noisy and too far from town. It was in the industrial area and Germans do not go there and were not near. They also had to wait for months for official German lessons.

I told Rita that she was so right to have discouraged the mayor in Elzach from constructing such a building. She asked if I had met with volunteers. I told her I had. The head of volunteers was good, as were the teachers. But all seemed to be under the mayor. Rita reminded me that the social worker had to do what the mayor wanted, and the volunteers did not really have much power.

It did seem a problem if the mayor and social workers do not listen or cannot know what the refugees really feel or think. Rita said they are afraid of getting swamped. I remembered the industrial building with extra places for 400 more people. And yet there seemed to be many people of good will in this town.

This third village had reinforced the value of a clear thinking person like Rita and a thoughtful mayor like the one in Elzach who had listened to her and did not put all the refugees in one building outside town. Spreading out the refugees was a much better policy. Isolation is the last thing refugees need if they are to learn a new language and how to cope in a new culture. The third village had come up with a bureaucratic solution that did not promote integration, but the refugees were not free to explain this to the people in charge.

My landlady for the night could not have been nicer. Her husband even took me to the train station in his car which made my life much easier. He said he was a refugee too, from the Czech Republic. I asked him, "From the Sudetenland? "Yes, in 1946. We had to leave everything." He came to Bavaria, and from there to two other cities. Then he and his wife lived in Nürnberg for fifty-one years and then came to this small town. I continued to meet Germans who themselves had been refugees.

CHAPTER 5

RESPONSES OF TOWNS AND SMALLER CITIES

Bruchsal: A Town with Dedicated Volunteers and Leaders

Bruchsal has 43,200 inhabitants if you include both the city and its metropolitan area. It is the smallest of the medium-sized towns that I visited. I went there because it was the right size for smaller towns. It was also where my German friend Erika had grown up and several of her friends assisted me in making contacts.

The first afternoon in Bruchsal, Roswitha Wallace, a good friend of my friend, met me at the hotel. Roswitha works in medical administration and has German, French, and Polish ancestry. She had lived twenty-four years in Lebanon and Cyprus, knows Middle Eastern culture well, and has a thorough understanding of cultural differences. She had set up two interviews for me with people who had been working with refugees in Baden-Württemberg, the state we were in. They turned out to be among the most important interviews for my understanding of the situation of the reception of refugees in Germany.

The next morning, another friend of Erika's, Maria Frank-Seiferling, an eighty-five-year old lifetime activist, called me and invited me to her home. Maria's mother was from Berlin and her father from Munich. She had recently taken care of her husband who had had Alzheimer's. She had been collecting articles on refugees for me, including important speeches by Cardinal Marx of Munich in which he declared to his priests that they should "stand strong in the debate on refugees that they be treated in a humanitarian way."[1] She also gave me a recent book in German on the

causes, conflicts and consequences of the refugee crisis.[2] Then, with
Maria using her walker, and me happily without suitcases, we both
walked to a nearby ice cream parlor for Venetian ice cream, and then on
to the center of town. It was market day in Bruchsal.

It was the Wednesday market in the market square and the September
weather was warm and sunny. Maria bought fresh tomatoes, vegetables,
and meat, and then she saw a seller who had come over from Alsace.
She knew my father's family had come from Alsace and insisted I buy a
specialty he was selling – donkey salami.

Pastor Dr Jörg Sieger: An Essential Interview

That afternoon Rosewitha's husband picked me up from the hotel and
took me to their apartment for an interview that Rosewitha had set up
for me with Pastor Dr Jörg Sieger. He is a theologian and Catholic priest
who had been head of Caritas, the Catholic Charity for Baden-
Württemberg in Heidelberg, but who was now in Bruchsal. He looked
about forty and had a forthright way of speaking.

I explained to Pastor Dr Sieger the purpose of my research. He said
that all over Germany people were working differently with refugees.
"No one had really been prepared or had the least idea what to do, not
the people or the politicians."

He explained that in the past, officially until the spring of 2015,
there were always the Dublin Regulations. When refugees came they
had to go back to the first country in the EU they had set foot in. That
would be Italy or Greece or Spain. "We knew this. We didn't want
anything to do with them. Italy and Greece did little with them.
We did even less."

He explained to us how it had worked relatively well until after the
Syrian War began. Then the EU spent funds on the Turkish border with
Syria and in Lebanon in 2015. It had paid 15 euros per refugee in camps
and in Lebanon. No one had wanted refugees in Europe.

Then in the summer of 2015, the dam broke when the masses
came and they could not be stopped. In Germany though the
reaction was a new one for our society.

In contrast were the 1990s when there were refugees from the
Balkan Wars, but we said essentially, "We can't, we won't," that is,
not to accept them.

While in 2015 it was a very different situation. They were welcomed! People said, "We can." It was a crisis for children and others, and we collected clothing.

I asked, "Why such a difference in the responses?"

The Reverend Father said, "Emotion played a big role." We all knew the photograph of the child on the beach. I responded, "Aylan Kurdi!" "Yes." He quoted a proverb in German, "Misery you can bear if you do not see it."

"Also people responded to memories they had heard of wartime from their parents and grandparents. We have few people who are volunteers who were men during the war. But many who are volunteers are children or grandchildren of people from the wartime."

I found this most interesting as well. Dr Sieger continued and gave another example. He said that he held a mass for women who had been themselves refugees a long time ago. "None of them then went to a subsequent talk on current refugees. It was enough what they had experienced in their own lives, they needed to move on. But the new younger people can help."

"At the end of 2015, Caritas was founded here. It has helped support the volunteers. There are 10,000 volunteers in Baden-Württemberg. There are 200–300 volunteers in Bruchsal."

I asked, "Who are the volunteers?" Dr Sieger responded.

Figure 5.1   Aylan Kurdi, age three, on beach in southwest Turkey after failed attempt with family to reach Greece.

They come from all generations, all classes. In Heidelberg, there were professors, housewives, students, handworkers. Their willingness to help surprised the social workers and the politicians. Their motivations were different and not always clear.

Some just wanted to help others. Some had religious motivation. For some it was humanitarian, not religious. Others felt that they had so much, they wanted to give to others. Some had been raised to think they needed to help the poor and downtrodden, but it could fall into a colonial attitude with a sort of European hubris that, for example, they would teach them punctuality. Still others felt they had been given something that they needed to pass on.

I told him that when I talked with a group of Syrian refugee men in Elzach, we had lunch together. Lunch included Arabic bread, yogurt, and *zaatar* – Roswitha brought some *zataar*, that is, a spice that includes wild thyme, to show the pastor – I told them that I thought that they had a gift for Germans. "The gift was their ability to drink tea and talk and laugh and make life good together. In the Middle East people know how to balance life and work better." I had had to learn this when I had lived there, I told him. "In America, and in Germany I think too, we work and work. We do not know how to get to know each other." Roswitha nodded. She said that she was in the East for twenty-four years. It took her a very long time to learn this balance as well.

The pastor said volunteers who work with the refugees come away from the shelter and feel they have received a gift. He said, "We in Germany plan everything. And woe if that plan is not followed. It must be followed to the T." I said, "In the East you cannot even talk about the future without saying, *inshallah*, 'if God wills,' for no one knows the future. It shows that we do not control the future."

He said that there is also a very different use of time. Dr Sieger explained how in working with the refugees they had had to work to coordinate the administration of social workers, language instruction, health services, and finances. There were thirty staff members in Freiburg. In Bruchsal there are only three part half-time staff, along with people in the Lutheran Church and the Red Cross.

I asked him what was most difficult for the refugees here. Dr Sieger answered:

What is hardest is waiting. They have nothing to do. Either to stay or go back, for half a year or a year. Most have their family in Syria. It diminishes their strength. They are good here. But their flight is not ended since their family is not here.

Also the feeling toward the refugees here is changing. A part of people here in Germany do not want the refugees. It is about 20 per cent maximum – from those who are afraid of strangers to those who are racists. It continued from World War II. It never went away. It was still there. These problems with refugees have allowed this to come up again, to resurface.

Dr Sieger gave an example from a class with parents. "A woman was talking about questions. At one point she said, 'This is our land, it is just for us. Let them work in their land for themselves.' It is a very narrow view."

I thought that as Americans, as a land of immigrants, we did not have such a strong sense that the land was ours. I was reminded of Native Americans who understood even better than European-background Americans that the land did not belong to anyone.

Returning to Dr Sieger, he explained how, "In the 1960s and 1970s, we were quite old-fashioned ourselves. Women had to have permission of their husbands for passports and work. Homosexuals would get criminal records. When the guest-workers came, we became more open and had different cultures here. But still we refused to contemplate about migration. We only thought of Germany for Germans. We thought of people who had been here for three generations as 'of migrant background.'"

Frankly, I think that is what people in Germany still think today.

Dr Sieger continued: "For example, at a meeting recently a woman wanted to speak for Bruchsal. She had only been here for three years. A man told her not to speak. He said she needed to be here for twenty-five years before she could speak!"

"So what happens now, no one knows. It is all changing. It used to be when one bought a house it was for eternity, but not anymore. However still it is so in our thoughts. This land has become other. Yet still in our thoughts, we think, 'We must go back.' There is 'this wanting to go back' in Poland, in France, in the Netherlands, among the Swiss.

So, if we can keep the refugees in Turkey, it is not orderly, but it keeps them there."

"As for the cost, realize that if we spend 6,000 euros/refugee in a year, that money is recycled through the economy. Many people have been hired in Karlsruhe who were unemployed. Now they are working in part-time work at least for the refugees. Through this German society gains."

"Why do people not know this?" I asked. Dr Sieger responded that there are many lies. But in fact it is investment that helps the general economy. He continued. "We had stopped constructing buildings for the poor, council homes. But now with the refugees, we have started anew discussions of poverty, and of relations of men and women. We had believed there was equality already."

I asked where the refugees here came from. "Afghanistan, Iraq, Eritrea, Syria, and Pakistan." I said that the Afghans probably would not be allowed to stay. He said that if we allowed them to stay, we say we have not done so well in their country.

As our conversation wound down, Dr Sieger said he wanted to learn Arabic, but people were not up to teaching him. I think he is shy. But he knows Hebrew. That will help.

I thanked him for his time and his insights. He had given such a full picture of the people who worked with refugees in Germany, of how refugees were thought of in Germany over time, how this had changed and was continuing to change. His thoughts would frame much of my thinking throughout my journey through Germany, and I would ask people questions based on what I had learned from him. He was also the only one who acknowledged that equality had not been reached between men and women in Germany, as is true in my country of America as well.

Refugee Accommodation

The next day a relative of my friend Erika in America asked me to meet her on the market square. We went to her favorite bakery where we had cappuccino together and *Nusshörnchen*, a nut and cinnamon croissant. She wanted me to visit the tourist attractions in town, including a famous baroque palace. I was looking forward to visiting two *Unterkünfte*, that is, refugee accommodations, that morning. I could tell we did not share this interest, so I thanked her and we went different ways.

I found a taxi with a Pakistani driver. He got me to the two refugee buildings. I walked into the courtyard of the first and met a woman who looked German. It turned out she was the social worker, Gudrun Pretorius. I explained why I was in Germany and in Bruchsal. She explained that there were many refugees living outside the refugee buildings which was a positive sign. That was what we all hoped would happen. She invited me into her office which had a good feel to it.

Frau Pretorius explained the process by which refugees qualified for asylum. This directly affected where they lived since they had to stay in the refugee buildings or "camp," if there was one, until they received a positive *Bescheid*, "notification" or "decision." Once they received a positive decision on asylum, there were workers who would help them find a place to live in town.

I asked how they qualified for it. She said it was not easy. There were only a few places refugees could go for the three required interviews in the official BAMF offices. For example, those in Bruchsal had to go to Heidelberg or Karlsruhe. Sometimes they had to wait for half a year or even a year for the first interview since the offices were overworked. This was the waiting that the Reverend Dr Sieger had referred to.

I asked her how many refugees there were in the refugee accommodation now. She said that there were 120 in one building and eighty in the other building. It was mixed consisting of families and single men. In the beginning, though, there had been many more. There had been 500 in one building and 140 in another.

She added, "Actually we had 770 at first. It was so different. They included single men, some hurt from the war. And they were from fifty nationalities. This was from September 2, 2015, through October and November. It included many from the Balkans too. It was good. It was the first place they felt at home, at peace. We greeted them with friendliness. We did not treat them differently."

"And we gave the weak and the children the best places. The others understood. There was one room with 30 young men. This made room for the young children to be with families."

Frau Pretorius continued. "German volunteers come to work with the children three times a week here. And there is a volunteer who comes to hold a music school for the children once a week here as well."

Initially she had thought they should pair a foreign family with a German family. But now she knows that is not how it works. Rather, individuals must first negotiate the relationship casually. Then maybe later a family can build such rapport.

We went on a tour of the refugee building. When we arrived at the middle of the building, I asked what the building had been used for before. Frau Pretorius said it had belonged to a firm. It had had smaller divisions, but the whole building had been massively renovated and painted for the refugees.

On every door were the names of the occupants. I did not find this the case in refugee buildings in other cities.

We came to one unit where there was a Syrian family. The mother came out and we spoke in Arabic. I asked her how she was. She said she wanted to leave the "camp" because it was not good for the children. But the problem, she allowed, was that she did not know German. "Why not?" I asked. She said she had given birth and then she said it had been too much work. It must not have been easy in those early months.

"But you can learn," I said. "First you need to listen. Do you know how I learned Arabic? Arabic is hard." I told her about going to southern Lebanon where no one spoke English and living and working in a small village for a year. "How old are you?" She said she was twenty-eight. "You are young. You will learn fast. The women learn faster than the men." Her daughter came along. Already she was speaking German. "You can listen to your children too. In America mothers learn English from their children."

Then we went to the playground and up the stairs outside where there were West Africans drinking dark tea. From there we went inside on the second story where there were rooms with six men in each. As Frau Pretorius had said, it was not easy. There were special rooms, including a playroom for children for when it rains. There was a kitchen for families separate from the kitchen for single men. All were very clean. She said the young men had had to learn how to keep things clean. They had.

In the front of the second story were other offices. In one a woman took care of making sure there were enough funds and next door was a room full of files. Then we went downstairs. I thanked the fine civil servants. I had to get back to the hotel for another interview later that afternoon.

Volunteer Coordinator

I was at Roswitha Wallace's home again and the doorbell rang. It was Maria Frank-Seiferling. And then it rang again. Rolf-Dieter Gerken came in. He is the coordinator of volunteers for Bruchsal. He sat down and only wanted water. The others of us had tea with honey.

I asked him about the refugees in Bruchsal and where they stayed. Herr Gerken said that they had two small buildings for the many people who arrived. The number of refugees coming to Bruchsal was unprecedented. The response had been spontaneous. Fifty people had volunteered to help. This was in September of 2015 on Eisenbaum Strasse where I had visited. He added, "Eventually we had 120 refugees there. People came who had time and the knowledge of how to help. Some just in the evenings, some just part of the day. They helped in teaching German, and with the children in the afternoon, that is children from two to fifteen years of age."

He explained that by 2016 there were fewer refugees staying in the camp. They help them move when they go out to other living arrangements. "Those who helped them in the camp can stay connected when they have private living quarters in Bruchsal as a sort of partnership." This is an especially good sign that relationships have been built with local people and refugees.

I asked Herr Gerken how frequently the volunteers in Bruchsal met. He said they did not meet as a whole group. Rather they met in their sub-groups. The teachers met with fellow teachers, those who work with children with like workers, and so forth. "They meet every two months for dinner in a good restaurant that has pizza." He smiled as he said this. He added there are between 100 and 120 active volunteers now.

I asked him about motivation. Unlike Dr Sieger, Herr Gerken was not interested in this. He said for some it is related to the church or religion. There are volunteers who have an immigrant background and knew they could help. Some are immigrants who a long time ago came to Germany from Turkey, Iran, or Syria.

I asked about the question of coordination among the different organizations of Caritas, the local city hall, the district center, and so forth. He said they worked well because they had different projects.

I asked about changing political climate in Germany and especially here in Bruchsal. Herr Gerken noted, "There is AfD [Alternative für Deutschland]. It is at best 20 per cent. But it gives no direct interference. It is not yet visible. He explained that those on the right have 'light contact with foreigners.'"

Then he discussed a current area of dispute in Bruchsal itself, namely the question of the building of a community center in a residential area of the city that would be for the refugees. "People fear it would affect property values in the area." Roswitha added that her boss, an esteemed eye surgeon from the Middle East, had just bought a big house near there. He is a Baha'i and said as he was once a refugee, he does not care if his property goes down in value. There would be a demonstration against this community center on Saturday. I said that I would attend.

I asked Herr Gerken what work he did before he took the unpaid position of Refugee Volunteer Coordinator. He told me he worked in informatics and had a background in organization. He is originally from Bremen in the north. His wife is an active Catholic and they both know Dr Sieger. Now he has been coordinating volunteers for three and a half years in Bruchsal. Herr Gerken stayed to talk with us further. He said it had been hard at the beginning since so little had been communicated between people and institutions.

I shared with everyone the table of contents of my proposed book. Herr Gerken's response was, "I am most interested in integration." This told me that I needed to include a focused section on integration. I was glad Herr Gerken had called this to my attention.

A Chance Meeting and a Demonstration against Refugees

For my final days in Bruchsal, Maria Frank-Seiferling was kind enough to allow me to stay in her upstairs. On the way to moving from the hotel to her home, the taxi driver I happened to meet turned out to be a neighbor of hers. He was Syrian and had been in Germany for 40 years. So I introduced him to Maria when she came out to greet me. He invited us to his nearby home for coffee later in the day.

But first it was market day again and we walked to the market square. The weather was still beautiful. "A gift," said Maria. There was also the demonstration that day against the community center for refugees that was proposed to be built in a residential area.

The people against the proposed community center had a display of posters spread out. They included doctored drawings of the community center, making it seem a whole story larger than actually proposed. Below there were photographs of animals that might be lost due to the community center, as if that were a major concern. They had their arguments written out to the effect they were not against all refugees. They were only against those who come for economic purposes. Specifically they did not want them in residential areas like northern Bruchsal.

Maria and I engaged a middle-aged man who was a major organizer of the demonstration against the center. I asked him if he had ever met a refugee. No, he had not. I told him that was the main difference I had seen — those who saw refugees as a category and those who met them as persons. I suggested he try meeting one so he could see them as persons. I told him there were many volunteers in Bruchsal. He seemed like a good man, why not come and help? I asked to take a photo of him and Maria together. She told him she was a member of the Green Party. He said he was too. They laughed and I got a good photo. It turns out Maria says ironically that she has been a member of the Green Party since 1979 since she was involved early on in environmental affairs. The Green Party was officially founded in 1980. She is member number 99 — one of the earliest.

Roswitha went to the demonstration later in the day and encountered more acid responses. Perhaps it was Maria's walker and my grey hair that made people behave better.

A Syrian Dinner and Hospitality in Bruchsal

Back at Maria's home, I helped her take down laundry from the lines in the small garden and then we had naps. It had been a good day so far. Later in the afternoon I reminded her that Sayed Hallak, the Syrian taxi driver, had invited us to his home for coffee. He had given me the address.

We found the apartment, only five minutes from Maria's. It was up narrow stairs but Maria managed. Herr Hallak greeted us and introduced us to his wife and one of their sons.

Thus began an evening of many hours of talk and Syrian food the likes of which I had not had in many years. It began with Arabic coffee. Maria said she would have tea, but I asked if she had ever had Arabic coffee. "No." "Then you should try," I said. "It is very good and more a ritual than a drink." The daughter made it for us.

We talked about so many things I cannot remember them all. I told them why I was there. They asked Maria where she was from and about her parents. She told them she had worked for seventeen years as a hospital nurse in Hamburg.

Herr Hallak had come to Germany in 1974 to study. He had worked different jobs there. His children were born in Germany but they went back to Aleppo, Syria, his hometown. That worked for a while. Then for the sake of his children's studies they returned. His wife came back in 2010 when she studied German for the first time. He insisted and she learned well. She has been working in Germany for several years now.

The oldest son works in programming in another town. The oldest daughter is married to a doctor in Paris. The second daughter is finishing a degree in pharmacy at the university in Heidelberg. The other son is studying biology. He also plays soccer.

Herr Hallak said he had wanted to go back to Syria to make sure his children grew up with appropriate behavior. In particular, he wanted to make sure they respected their parents and would care for them. He had seen too often in Germany that children left their parents at eighteen and never returned. Now as a taxi driver he helps older people. He said that he often asks, "Do you have children?" "Yes, but they do not come." In the Middle East this would be inexcusable.

Maria said that she was one of eight children and yet her mother had died alone in Munich. It was sad to her. I said in America it varies. I have a son and two stepsons. My son calls me every day. I took care of both my mother and my father. But there are many older people in America who are alone.

Then dinner came. Frau Hallak had made *tabouli* for us. It was delicious. And *kibbi nayi*, and other *kibbi*, and another *kibbi* dish without meat. All delicious. We ate and ate. I do not know when she and her daughter made all this good food. For dessert, we had a milk pudding with rose water and nuts on top. And peppermint tea. So good.

I asked if I could take photographs of them for a souvenir. So the women put on scarves. I took photos with Maria sitting in the middle as befitted the oldest person. It was a lovely evening.

"Herzlichen Dank, es war ein wunderbarer Abend," said Frau Maria Frank-Seiferling. "Heartfelt thanks, it was a wonderful evening."

Roswitha's Experience

The next day Roswitha called. She told about her experience at the demonstration the day before. There a man had asked her if she had signed the petition against the community center for the refugees. She had told him she was not going to sign it. Why? She did not believe in it. He asked was she not afraid to sleep at night? She told him not at all. Was she not afraid of being attacked? Why not?

Figure 5.2   Maria Frank-Seiferling with Syrian family in Syrian family home, Bruchsal, Baden-Württemburg, Germany, 2016.

She said that she had lived in the Middle East and there was no reason to fear. Why were they trying to make people afraid? There were more problems from the Russian Germans than from any people from the Middle East.

The man had some knowledge of the Middle East. He told her to remember what happened in Homs. That was in Syria she had told him. It had nothing to do with the people here, she had said. Finally she had told him, "Why are you trying to make people afraid, and yet you offer no solution? You are like people from the AfD." He had not liked that. "You are a good man, why waste your time standing here doing this?"

Sunday Evening International Café
We agreed to meet to go to the Sunday International Café at St Paul's Church where they had weekly cake and coffee for refugees and local people to meet and talk. We got there and we were almost the first. There were three German women who had put out the cakes from the

local baker who donates them every week. They also put out teas, coffee, and games for the children. I spoke with the German woman who was in charge.

Some refugee children came in. Then some men came in, first an Afghan man. We all sat at one table where Maria and another German woman were seated as well as a boy who playing a board game with dice. Then a group of men came from the camp where I had visited. They filled up another table. I went over and greeted them in Arabic and shook their hands. They got cake and tea too.

We sat down and proceeded to talk. One of the Syrians was from al-Sweida where I had stayed in Syria. The Iraqis were from Baghdad. They do not have official language courses yet and have been here a year. I think that means they will not get asylum. We talked. Someone asked me about Trump in America. I had been trying to forget about him. But as long as we spoke in German, it was valuable. I was pleased the refugee men had come to the gathering.

Then it was time to go. I had watched the few middle-aged German men. In general they do not know how to interact with Middle-Eastern men except perhaps as experts in telling about German culture. I think it would be better if they had something to do with them, like make something or fixing something together.

At the end an Iraqi man showed us a photo of his wife and children from his phone. "What a lovely family," I said, adding, "*Mashallah*," "what God has willed," which is what you always say in Arabic to show thankfulness and to keep vulnerable people safe. He hopes to bring them to join him. I hope so too. It was a lovely gesture to share their picture. He misses them, and they him. That is what seeing refugees as people entails.

The next morning it was difficult to say goodbye to Maria. I thanked her for letting me stay in her home and for all her help. I hoped she would continue to see Herr Hallak and his family. I would miss being with caring people like her and Roswitha.

Refugees were fortunate to be in Bruchsal where both volunteers and civic workers like the social worker were so dedicated and capable. I especially liked that the volunteers continued to keep contact with the refugees after they left the refugee accommodations. It is this sort of network of contact that bodes well for their future in the town.

Bamberg: A University Town Where Research Did Not Work

Bamberg is in Franconia in upper Bavaria. It has a population of 70,000 inhabitants and is thus the largest city I had been in so far for any extended stay. It has medieval buildings and is the home of the University of Bamberg, which includes the Institute for Migration Studies.

Professor Heckmann Schedules a Late Meeting

I had written ahead to a Professor Friedrich Heckmann of the Migration Institute, telling him what I was researching, and asking to meet with him. He was retired but had published much in the field, appeared still be active in research, and was the senior member. He had set an appointment for five o'clock in the evening.

I arrived on time across the river at the Institute for Migration Studies. Professor Dr Heckmann is tall, older, and had studied in Lawrence, Kansas. After briefly talking about Germans in America I got down to business. I knew his most recent book was focused on integration. So I asked, "What do Germans mean by integration?" Professor Heckman answered. "Integration means participation in all spheres of society. Especially it means language today because today we are a knowledge-based society. So migrants must have language."

I said that Americans encourage people to learn language through work, while here in Germany they want people to learn language before they can work. Professor Heckmann acknowledged that the United States was a work-based society. He added, "We do not want them to retreat into their own areas. If there is continuous migration, there will always be such areas. Where there is a welfare-based society as here, if we want people to earn the minimum, which is 8.5 euros/hr., and have health care, and so forth, they have to learn the language."

I said there were places where refugees had to wait months for language classes. He said they were supposed to get them after three months. I remembered the third village I had been in where the Syrian doctor had waited eight months.

We discussed where they stayed. I told him about the mayor who had constructed a new building for the refugees outside his village. The professor did not recognize the name of the village. He said at the height of the incoming, they put refugees anywhere.

I asked Professor Heckmann why there was such a difference in the German response to the refugees from Bosnia and the new refugees now. I wanted to confirm Pastor Dr Sieger's thesis, and allow him to elaborate on recent German history. His first response was he did not know.

I said they were both Muslims and the Bosnians were European Muslims. But now the response has been one of welcoming, whereas in the early 1990s it was not so. Then he said that there have been changes since the law of 2005 and in integration policy.

Professor Heckmann continued. "After the migration pressures of the 1990s disappeared, in 1998 there was a new government of Gerhard Schroeder [SPD] and Joschka Fischer [Green]. They officially adopted Germany as an 'immigration country.'"

Professor Heckmann reported that in his 1981 thesis, he had predicted this. But that was very early. In the new century a new approach developed. The new elite became proponents of integration and immigration. The elites put pressure on the populists. (There was demographic need for this.)

He asked if I knew of the Migration Institute in Washington DC. I was taken aback that he asked me this. But then I had not been playing the academic game of impress the other with your erudition. Instead I had been continuing as a field anthropologist and asking basic questions, and trying to confirm his knowledge. Heckmann recommended that I read the recently published report he had written for the Migration Institute regarding the development of a new consensus on integration and immigration.[3]

I mentioned how impressed I was with the volunteers in Germany. Professor Heckmann said he saw them as part of this process as well. He said he had predicted that if immigration increased, then there will be an increase in violence against immigrants. It has doubled. As for the volunteers, he saw helping as a form of helping oneself – a sort of exchange. For retired people, it gives a sense to life, makes it meaningful.

He suggested I look at a study by the Bertelsmann Foundation on these "helpers." He also suggested I talk with Ulrich Glaser in the *Rathaus* in Nürnberg who coordinates volunteers there. Heckmann himself lives in Nürnberg which is not far from Bamberg. He told me that they had closed many former refugee buildings there because they had spread out 8,000 refugees in 172 locations across the city. Clearly this was from Ulrich Glaser so I thought that I might visit him to learn more about the larger city of Nürnberg.

Professor Heckmann stood up to signal the end of our meeting. He had purposefully set up a late meeting. He suggested I visit Caritas. Bamberg also had a former US military barracks where they put people who will not be given asylum before they would be deported.

I asked about his latest book on integration. He offered to loan it to me. I thanked him but said I would buy it and he gave me a flier.[4] I asked him when he would have more time. He said he was writing a report so after the end of September. I would be long gone by then. He did not know how I would get back to my hotel. Luckily I had kept the card of the taxi driver and so was able to deal with this myself.

Member of the Migration and Integration Council

The next day, while in a bookstore, I found myself talking with a young clerk. She said people were afraid of the refugees. I asked why. She said it was "fear of strangers." I was surprised. Bamberg is a university town with many international students and many tourists. Here of all places, among young people like the clerk, I had trouble understanding this "fear of strangers."

I continued on toward the main square. As I got closer, I began to hear music, good classical violin music. There were two musicians, a violinist and an accordian player playing. I went closer to them. There was also a woman there listening. We began to talk. It turned out she was British, had lived in Bamberg for years, and taught English there. I told her that I used to do that too.[5] I mentioned I was in Germany to learn about how people were working with refugees. She said she was on a council that worked with refugees. "Do you have time for coffee?" I asked. "I would like to learn how the council works."

We found a cafe and she told me about the International Council and about the city of Bamberg. People of different nationalities, depending on their numbers in town, served on the council for six-year terms. She told me that, in total, 20 per cent of the population of Bamberg had a migratory background. They come from 130 different countries. It is a university town. But this percentage was common across Germany. That meant that about 5.5 million of the population of Germany have this background and most of them cannot vote.

She said her own children, born here and with a German father and a British mother, are considered of migratory background, although they are German citizens.

She talked about the school system in Bavaria and a meeting the next day on countering racism in the schools. I asked if the fear of strangers was a fear of Islam. She said that there are a lot of lies on the internet about Islam wanting to take over the world. People do not know any Muslims. There is not enough dialogue. I was glad we had met and thanked her. I would go to the meeting the next day on countering racism in the schools. Unfortunately it reminded me of similar meetings back home where the speakers' status was higher than their ability to communicate.

On the way back to the hotel, I went into a telephone store where I talked to a young black man. I asked if he was from Bamberg. "Yes." "A Bamberger?" "Yes." But he said he would rather live in a larger city. "Like where?" I asked. "Like Nürnberg. It has 500,000 people," he said. "Ahh. Bamberg has only 70,000, too small," I said. He agreed. He said his parents were from Togo.

The Beer Capital of Germany

I had searched for Caritas for two days, including that afternoon and found one office, but no one was there. On my way back to the hotel I had noticed a beer garden.

So that evening I went back to the beer garden for dinner. There I learned that Bamberg was the beer capital of Germany. A German man explained that many farmers made their own beer and shared it at an annual festival. "Bamberg is known for its dark beer or its smoky beer. It is more concentrated." Some Americans at my table said a brewer from St Louis had come there and bought a defunct brewery. The German man knew him. "Copeland," he said.

After the Americans left, I talked with the German about refugees. He suggested that I visit his hometown of Erlangen, a town of only 25,000 near Nürnberg. They had a program for refugees. At a town hall meeting, 100 people had come to discuss issues and work together. I thanked him.

Syrians on Lovers Bridge

Bamberg sits on the confluence of two rivers so there are numerous bridges. As I walked back to one of the bridges, the *Loewe Brücke*,

I noticed that there were hand-combination locks hanging on railings on both sides of it. It did indeed look strange. Later a Syrian woman told me it was the "bridge of lovers." They put their names on the lock and then throw the key into the river.

When I was over half way across the bridge, I saw three women sitting on a bench on the bridge. They had headscarves, but they looked Syrian to me, not Turkish. So I asked them if they spoke Arabic. "Yes," they were surprised and pleased. I sat down on a bench next to the oldest one. We all talked. They were from Aleppo and had come here three years before. The woman's son had come "forty" years ago, which in Arabic meant not the actual number of years but a long time, to study here. He was an engineer. He had married a German woman and had children who were also professionals. The rest of the family had come three years ago when things got bad, probably in 2013, before the surge in the summer of 2015. But they were not refugees, the older woman made that very clear. They were "family joiners." They have their own houses. They were wise to come when they did.

The older woman has four sons and three daughters. But it sounds as if she is lonely. She says hello to the Germans, but they do not talk back and she does not know German. I think she needs to learn, but it will take time. As she said, "We Arabs love hospitality and friends and talk and being together. The Germans keep to themselves." As they said this, they made faces of closed-mouths. I said, "I think they are more reserved." It will be a growing experience for both.

In the end I asked to have a photo taken with them. The mother reminded me to say, "These are Syrians who came as part of a family, not refugees." "Yes, I will remember."

It matters to people not to be considered as refugees when their identities are so fragile.

Hotel Staff with Refugee Aunt

The woman at the desk in the hotel in Bamberg had always been particularly kind. We got to talking. It turned out her aunt's family were refugees too from land that had been part of Germany but was taken by Poland at the end of World War II. Before, they had substantial land holding. But when they had to leave, they could only take what they could carry. They took the papers for their land, but they were told by the Poles, "You are not coming back." They went on what her aunt, who was fourteen at the time, called "the trek." It was hard. Their culture was different than that of Franconia where they were sent. Years later when some went back to see their land, the aunt could never go back. She did not want to.

I told her how people I had studied earlier, who had been forced from their homes in Macedonia, remembered the last time they closed the door. They never forgot their homes. They always dreamed of their homes and the backyard gardens. She shook her head. Then she said, "How can people not think of what these people have left when they had to lose their homes?" "I do not know," I said. "I am an anthropologist and I study immigrants and refugees. I learn much from them. They see life more clearly."

I told her I had read a book on the millions of Germans who came to Germany after World War II from the east[6] and how they were mostly older people, women, and children, since the men were in camps or were dead. It was so hard then, and there was virtually no outside aid for them.

She said they were Germans and the Germans had started the war. I said, "They were refugees and refugees always deserve assistance." I think a lot of Germans know about the experience of refugees from their relatives.

But I was not making headway in Bamberg. Rather than hit my head against a wall, I decided to go to Nürnberg, the nearby city of half a million. Perhaps the bigger story of refugees in northern Bavaria was clearer in Nürnberg.

Nürnberg: A Central City of Immigrants and Refugees

I took the train to Nürnberg, less than an hour to the east of Bamberg.

That first day I walked across what had been the old city to the *Rathaus*. It was mostly stores and new buildings, although there were a few old churches and a clock tower. Nearly 90 per cent of Nürnberg was destroyed in World War II. The old city, which had been beautiful, was gone.

Professional Coordinator of Volunteers

In the *Rathaus* I went up to the office of Dr Ulrich Glaser whom Dr Heckmann had recommended and I had emailed. I knocked on his door, but no one answered. I waited. When Dr Ulrich Glaser arrived,

I learned I was most fortunate to have found him, because as he hastened to tell me, he was busy the next day and Monday was a holiday.

We sat down at the table by the door and talked. I asked him if he was the coordinator of volunteers. Dr Uli Glaser explained that he was a "professional" coordinator. That is, he is paid for his work. He has worked for volunteer affairs all his life. Then he quoted to me in German:

Bürgerzeit	Citizen's time
Bürger Wissen	Citizen's knowledge
Bürger Geld	Citizen's money

Truly these were the constraints that all civil servants worked within. He elaborated that he coordinates not only the volunteer offices, but also works with foundations and coordinates fund-raising with companies and corporate responsibility. I could see why he should be paid. This is much greater responsibility than any other volunteer coordinators.

He knew from our correspondence that my interest was refugees. He explained that earlier refugees had not been in his purview. Other agencies in Nürnberg had worked with them. In the early 1990s, there had been hundreds of thousands of refugees from former Yugoslavia. Near the end of the next decade there were asylum-seekers, but they were fewer in number. Then they had increased.

He reminded me that the Central German Agency working with migrants, BAMF, is in Nürnberg. Also the main agency that works with the unemployed, and now with employment, BA, is also in Nürnberg. I asked why these were here. Dr Glaser explained that it was from the 1950s when there were so many migrants and refugees who were already here. Nürnberg is centrally located. Then he reminded me of the major changes that had occurred in Germany in recent times regarding immigrants.

Up to 1998, with Conservative governments in Germany, they all said, "Germany is not an immigration country." And yet it was taking in more immigrants than any other country at the time.

In 1998, the Green Party came to power. And it became possible to become a citizen between 1998 and 2005, when the law changed.

I asked about the difference of response to the Bosnian refugees in the early 1990s and the new refugees now in 2015, both of whom were Muslims. Dr Glaser said that in the early 1990s, there was still the hostility of the East Germans against the Bosnians. They had only lived under totalitarian regimes – first the Nazis, then the Communists. They did not know migrants.

He wanted to know if I knew the definition of *Migrantionshintergrund*, that is, "one with migrant background." He explained that it meant a person had at least one parent who did not initially have a German passport. He said that 20 per cent of the population of Germany had this type of migrant background. In Nürnberg, 40 per cent had such migrant backgrounds, while for people under the age of eighteen years old nearly, fully 60 per cent had such migrant backgrounds.

I was impressed. Truly his city was an immigrant city. But since the most recent group of immigrants in Germany was the *Russlanddeutsche*, I asked about them and their politics. Did they have more right-wing views as a German sociologist had just told me at breakfast in Bamberg? He concurred. Dr Glaser said they had kept their Russian-speaking contacts. Some of their comments on social media were quite awful, he allowed. He wondered if I had heard of the story of the rape of the young girl that the Russian media spread? Yes, I had heard of it. That story was the one in Berlin that had turned out to be false. It should have alerted us to the Russians' ability to set up false stories and pass on false news.

Dr Ulrich Glaser then told me about the housing of the refugees. This is a special responsibility of the city and required much effort on the part of city officials.

With a population of 520,000 inhabitants, there are 180 housing units with refugees in them, spread out across the city. Many refugees are in smaller units, although there are still a few with 200–250 refugees in one building.

He said they had 8,500 refugees. The refugees started coming in 2014. The numbers increased until there was a tremendous influx by September 2015. They continued coming in February and March of 2016. They are fewer in number now. They used to come at a rate of over 300 a week. He said they rented all the space they could. Some were industrial places for 800 people. Now those places are all closed. It was 67 per cent men. The highest successful asylum rates were people from Syria, Iraq, and Iran.

I asked Dr Glaser about volunteers. He said that it varied with time. Still, the number from the end of June 2016, from quarters that had refugees and along with churches, could be conservatively estimated to be 4,000. He explained further that the figure represented about 1 per cent of the adult population of Nürnberg. As to who these volunteers were, he said that they tended to be better educated and 70 per cent were women. He added, "We also try to have one full-time paid counselor for every 100 refugees. Applying for asylum is a complicated process. These counselors can help individual refugees."

I asked about neighborhoods and what they did when they were going to put refugees in a housing unit in a particular residential area. Dr Uli Glaser said that when they found a unit to rent, the locals there did not have a choice. They tried to inform them. They would organize a social gathering to tell them about the situation and try to calm them. They hoped for a positive attitude. He said he had been a moderator at several of these. The atmosphere was tense. I mentioned I had been at an anti-refugee demonstration in Bruchsal. I said they had used animals as an excuse not to build the community center. "It is housing values," he said, among other things. "What do you say to this?" I asked. He said, "I tell them housing values have only been increasing in Nürnberg."

He added that they also have a small unit for homosexuals. They have another unit for women who have been traumatized while fleeing so they do not have to be with men.

I asked what was most difficult for refugees. Uli first said, "Maybe the language. No, expectations. They had very high expectations. They did not know they would have to accept German rules, things like the equality of women."

Back to volunteering, he mentioned that for people over the age of fourteen, a total of 40 per cent are volunteering. But with Germans, it is the sporting clubs that are the object of major volunteering. This is very different from volunteering to help with refugees.

He gave me handouts with general information and statistics, newsletters, information on volunteers, activities, and a volunteer survey. I thanked Dr Glaser for his time, information, and articles. He was clearly busy and had been most generous with me. Nürnberg is most fortunate to have such a person dedicated to municipal work. And I was fortunate to have found him in the limited time available.

Visit to Refugee Dormitory

The next morning I went by taxi to the refugee accommodation that Dr Uli Glaser had suggested I visit. I arrived in mid-morning and started to talk in the hallway with several of the men who were waiting outside the main office, including a Syrian man from Aleppo who had been in Nürnberg for about ten months. He wanted to get his German class started. He had his wife, who was pregnant, and young son with him.

When there was a break, I went inside the main office to talk with one of the officials in charge, a Frau Suzanne Gauermann. She had understood from Dr Glaser that I just wanted to talk with the people there. I told her I hoped to talk with her too when she had time. She was clearly busy. I told her I would come back.

I went outside the main office to another room where I met one of the official translators. He translated from Arabic, Kurdish, Persian, and Turkish. He had been in Germany since 1979, mostly in Ulm.

When I asked what he thought the Germans thought of the new refugees, he said they were very nice with them. Of course there were people against them, but in general he felt that 70 per cent of the Germans supported the refugees. Then he named associations that helped: AWO (Workers' Welfare Organization), Caritas, the Red Cross, and the city of Nürnberg.

I asked how much the refugees received. He said, for people without food and who lived in refugee accommodation, they received 320 euros a month. People who received their food there got 184 euros a month. They also have their health, education, integration course, and language course paid for. This was much better than in other countries like France or Britain. I added that this was more generous than in the United States too.

Then the translator had to go back to work himself. The first Syrian man I had spoken to then asked me up to his unit with his family. So I went up.

It was a good-sized space with four beds. The windows were open and it was airy. His wife, who is eight months pregnant, was resting. Their young son, about four years old, was there. The father made Arabic coffee for me on a burner. I was honored to be in their unit. We talked. He said he had waited for the *Bescheid*, the decision for asylum. He still did not have it. I asked how long it took. He said some got it quickly, but those who had been there for eleven months had to wait a long time. I think a lot of people came at that time.

I told him they were fortunate they had come. So many people were stuck in Greece. He knew some people there. They could go nowhere. Still it was not easy just to wait. He wanted to visit his parents in Turkey. They were in Mardin and Diyarbakır. They have diabetes and are older. That is hard. "Do you want to bring them here I asked?" "Yes. They need calm." But he must have asylum first. He wants his children to know his parents. I can understand that.

I thanked him and his wife for their hospitality. I went back to the office. What a fine family. I wish I could do something for them, but it is in the hands of the German authorities.

Talk with an Asylsozialberaterin, "Social Consultant for Asylum"

I went back to the main office where Frau Gauermann had finished working for the morning. There was a social worker there with her too. I told Frau Gauermann that the people there thought highly of her. They had told me that when we had been talking in the hallways. They said she knew what they needed even before they asked. She was pleased to hear that.

She said this was the second time she had worked with refugees. The first time was from 2009 to 2012. Then there were refugees from Afghanistan, but also from Russia and from the Balkans. There was more diversity, but they were fewer in number.

I asked her when she came back to work again with refugees. She said she came back in December 2015. Then she gave me a printed article with photos of the original camp in Nürnberg. It had big tents where the walls of the rooms did not reach the ceiling, and the only furniture was beds, nothing else. I read it later when I got back to the hotel. It was a booklet, "*Ein Leben im Transit,*" or "A Life in Transit,"[7] with photographs that showed how difficult it had been with so many people living in one room. It was never really quiet and there was no real privacy. It was mostly single men, with eight to a room, and they had lived like that for four months.

Then on 12 July 2016 they came to the building we were in, across from the Siemens building. It was an office building that had been totally renovated into living quarters. It has three stories with kitchens on each floor. It also has a children's room and a prayer room. Currently 238 people were living there, but it can hold 305. What an improvement over the original accommodation with tents!

I asked Susanne what was the hardest thing for the refugees. She said to wait for so long when the situation was not clear. At the *Bundesrat* or Federal Council so many refugees have requested asylum. They must go through three different interviews. But all people are different. The final decision makers only have papers; they have not met the person they decide about. Before, Syrians could bring family members. Now it is much more difficult to bring family.

Frau Gauermann continued. "It is also difficult to get work permissions. While they wait for the decision on asylum, they can qualify for secondary work permission if they meet the following four qualifications." She then listed these as: finding a work place, going to the *Auslander Amt*, going to the job center, and proving that no European could do the job. "If they ever get through this process, what boss would wait for all this time? So it is ridiculous."

I asked her what other people I should visit or contact. She gave me good suggestions. I thanked her. She knows the refugees well and the difficulties they face better than most.

I went back to the hotel and tried to contact the organizations she had suggested. But perhaps because it was Friday, no one responded. Then I thought, it is Friday; I took a taxi to the mosque.

The Oldest Mosque in Nürnberg
It turned out that there are multiple mosques in Nürnberg. So when I asked the Kurdish taxi driver to take me to the mosque, and said I was interested in Syrian refugees, he took me to a mosque known as "the Arab mosque." It is also known as "the Mixed Mosque" since people from all different backgrounds go there.

As I got out of the taxi, there were men coming out of the mosque from Friday prayer. We spoke German and a little English at first. Then I spoke Arabic and the smiles came out. They were Syrian. Why had I not spoken Arabic at first? They could not have been kinder.

One man had been in Nürnberg for many years. He always came to this mosque. He said it was the oldest mosque. "People from all over come here," he said. "From Tunis, and Africa, from Syria, and all over. The sermon is in Arabic." I told him I wanted to talk to the imam.

I wanted to understand how the German people were with the new *lajeen*, the new refugees.

He said he would ask, and he went into the mosque. Much later he came out with a large prayer scarf for me. It was white with little grey and silver sparkles on it. How thoughtful. I had a scarf but should have brought a bigger one. He told me to follow him inside. I went upstairs and took off my boots. He put them on a shelf.

The Young Syrian Imam of the Mosque in Nürnberg

Then he introduced me to a tall young imam, Imam Abdulrahman Alhout. He, too, is Syrian. What a pleasure. There was a man there who spoke English and Arabic. Should he stay? I spoke my village Arabic and the imam said we would understand each other. He invited me into his office.

I liked him right away. I gave him my card. He said he was doing his doctorate in theology in Erlangen Centre for Islam and Law in Europe, here in Germany. I said that was very fine since Germany was strong in theology. I asked him how long he had been here. The young imam said he had been here four years. He had come at the beginning of the war. He had family. Ahh, I said, family connections. How fortunate and how wise to come then. He nodded. He too was from Aleppo.

He asked if I would like coffee and which kind, German or Arabic? I asked if he would drink too? Yes. Arabic then if it is not too hard. No. It is good. He told me where to sit and he would go ask for it. He motioned to the table. "Dates from Mecca." He had just come back from *hajj*, the pilgrimage, two days ago. "*Hajji!*" I smiled. "Was it your first time?" I asked. "No," he said. "My third." Third time! I was impressed. He was happy. I mentioned how in the Balkans where I had lived they did so many rituals with the birth of the Prophet. "Mawlids," he said. "Yes. They are so beautiful," I said. "Even more so in Syria," he said.

I asked the imam how many mosques there were in Nürnberg. He said there were eight. There are three Turkish mosques, one Bosnian one, one Albanian one, two Pakistani ones, and this one, the Arabic one. That makes eight. "But there should be no division in Islam," I said. "Yes. This is the central one. The oldest one." "How old is it?" I asked. He said it was thirty years old. "We have 2,500 people for Friday prayers!" That is impressive. "And for the children?" I asked.

"On Sundays we have classes for children from ages five to twelve. On Qur'an, on Arabic, on *terbiye*, how to behave."

I asked what people thought about Islam here. The imam responded.

> The German people are good people. They are better than other European people. They do not sit around and talk and talk. They like to work.
>
> In politics there are those who make problems to try to make people afraid of Muslims. So it will be hard for people to rent to Muslims. The other day my wife was walking with our children and a woman screamed for no clear reason. We are peaceful. But some people make problems.
>
> As for the new Muslims here, it is hard now. They should not just take. They must learn the language and work hard. Germany is *"Bilad amal,"* "the country of work." There are services, but it is not enough just to take. The good person does work. How can we thank Germany – with work.

I would like to hear his sermons. I think he is probably a good preacher. He understands about Germany and about the difficulties of new migrants and refugees too.

I asked him who was the imam before him. It was an Egyptian. Better a Syrian like him now, young and dynamic.

I thanked him and left. The Syrians I had met at the outside doorway were there again. I tried to give back the scarf but they told me to keep it. They were so kind.

They went inside to pray and I went to find food. I was famished. I had yet again missed lunch. I found a Turkish place and sat down with a German woman. We talked. She mentioned an organization, Die Brücke, for Christian–Muslim understanding. Then I went to a street and tried to get a cab during rush hour. Not easy but finally I got one. The driver was from Fürth. That is the city next to Nürnberg where Henry Kissinger was from.

Sunday and Good News from Hungary

I attended a Lutheran service on Sunday at St Jakob's Church, an old church that had been destroyed in 1945 and rebuilt in 1965. Its spire had a rooster on it. It was not a traditional Lutheran service, but a more modern form. They even projected the hymns on a screen in the front like the Baptists back home. It was friendly and there were different generations present. I spoke with the pastor and others.

Later that day good news came out of Hungary. Orbán's referendum, against following EU quotas of refugees, had just failed to get the requisite 50 per cent of vote to be considered valid. But there had been other news that week, not so positive, of a bomb attack on a mosque in Dresden. The hate crimes on refugee shelters had also continued there.

I had followed through to contact the dialogue group for Christians and Muslims. The person in charge turned out to be a Lutheran pastor. He had mentioned at the end of his email that he was visiting a Turkish mosque on Monday, the Holiday of Unification of Germany, to affirm his group's commitment after the bombing in Dresden.

Holiday of National Unification at a Turkish Mosque in Nürnberg

Holidays are difficult times for foreign researchers. Regular offices are closed, and people are not available. This Holiday of Unification was the twenty-sixth anniversary since 1990 to commemorate West and East Germany coming together to become one country again.

When I received the email from the director of Die Brücke, telling me he was going to a Turkish mosque, I decided to join him. He was surprised when I showed up. I had not realized that he was being taped for a media interview that day.

I went into the gate of the mosque complex and upstairs with the pastor. There I met a representative of the mosque, a man in a handsome suit who spoke good German and Turkish. He would give the Turkish interview so the imam would not have to do so. I liked him. He had his young son with him for the holiday too. He asked how I knew Turkish. We stood by the door upstairs and I explained in Turkish briefly about Baba Rexheb, my teacher in America with whom I had spoken Turkish. The German pastor announced that he had understood most of what I had said. He said he knew Arabic too since he had studied in Damascus. He received his advanced degree in Islamic Studies.

Then we went to the table and they brought tea. At that time two German media people arrived. I just moved back. Their target was the pastor and the imam.

The media people went away for a while. The pastor asked me about my background. Then he said he had asked for this meeting at the mosque to reassure the Muslims that "We are together after what had happened in the East last week."

But he wanted me to know that people at this mosque were under pressure. The mosque was AKP, that is, the Party of Erdoğan. There was much tension. The pastor said they were cutting many of the connections that they had worked so hard to make with the German community. This was not good.

Then the pastor put on his long black cloak and white tie so he looked his role. He went downstairs to meet the imam who was waiting there and who stood tall, dressed in an all white robe with gold trim and white headgear. White and black.

I went downstairs too and we all headed toward the mosque. I put on a headscarf. We took off our shoes and went inside.

It is one of the largest mosques in Bavaria, and the walls have exquisite blue tiles from Iznik, the center of tiles from Turkey. The two religious leaders stood in the middle of the mosque and talked. Then they did the photo shoot with the pastor giving his practiced greeting in Turkish.

The media people needed to talk with the mosque representative so I went back upstairs for more tea where I ended up talking with older Turkish men who were also up there drinking tea. Then they called me to come back across the upstairs balcony and over to the mosque side. The mosque representative had time to talk with me too.

Volunteer Mosque Representative and Integration

The mosque representative led me upstairs in the mosque to a meeting room where he, his young son, and I sat down. I asked him first about the mosque. "When was this founded?" "In 1989," he replied. "Before there was a factory here. We changed it." I said I had heard there were three Turkish mosques in Nürnberg. He said there were five and listed them.

He said he came from a typical immigrant family. They were originally from a city in the north. His father had been invited to work in Nürnberg. Of the children, he came first as a four-year-old, and then his brothers. It was hardest for his older brother who had school in both countries. His younger brother was born here in Germany.

Figure 5.3   Imam and Lutheran pastor in mosque in Nürnberg.

I asked him about "in-te-gra-tion" using the German pronunciation. He responded that he thought integration was an "empty word," (*boş bir lafttr.*) He continued, "My German is quite good." Indeed from all I could see and hear with the Germans that was true. What worried me here was that I had heard similar talk over the weekend in Nürnberg from other researchers whom I had questioned.

The mosque representative continued. "I have been working for over twenty years. I have three children. I am integrated." But then he asked himself, "Am I integrated?" I once asked that of a minister of integration. She said, 'You speak German.' 'Why do I not feel this then?' I asked. 'That I am not integrated so?' She did not say anything. "If integration means to speak German, I speak it well. What else do they want? I do this job at the mosque as voluntary work. What is this integration? Certainly I have the language. I see 'integration' as an empty word."

"I do not see it as coming from outside. If I want to feel part of this – it is a feeling. If I had this feeling, I am here, together. If you do not have this feeling – You can have programs however many you want."

I said that I thought of integration as a two-way street. That means that not just the migrants and refugees must change, but also the Germans too. "Oh no," he said. "Here it is only the new people who MUST change." I said, "Some refugees said no one here talks to them. The neighbors do not talk to them. They do not say hello." I was thinking of the Syrian woman on the bridge in Bamberg.

The mosque representative said that is not just a problem for outsiders. If a village is Catholic and a Lutheran comes, they will not talk to him. "Will this change over time do you think?" "Maybe with the young, but I do not think so."

"Still the Germans have good qualities," continued the mosque representative. "When I was young, I would eat at their houses. I had German friends. There is 40 per cent racism, but not always."

"The East Germans are more problematic," he said. I asked if it was because they had fewer migrants. He did not respond. The representative for the mosque wanted to continue to talk about refugees. He added, "If I were offered a job in East Germany, say in Dresden, I would not go for the sake of my children."

Then I asked him what the Turkish community had done for the new refugees in Nürnberg. He said that when they first came, in August 2015, "We made *helal* soup for them. As Muslims, we did this the first weeks. The person in charge of food for the camp did not know this. We had a five-mosque committee. The nearest camp had 280 people of the first people who came to this city. They only had four square meters for two families."

Then he elaborated. They would go and ask what they needed – a suitcase, clothing for women or girls, scarves for Muslims, or men's clothing. Many people gave. They gave thirty bicycles for example. They repaired some. They were all working, but they did what they could. Some gave money. "We worked together with the Arabic Mosque." I asked, "With Imam Abdulrahman Alhout?" "Yes."

I mentioned the difference between the reception of the new refugees and when the Turks had come fifty years ago. He acknowledged this, but said that the Turks had come as workers. "And now there are seven to eight Turks in Parliament."

Then we talked about sports – basketball, hockey, even baseball for a short time. I could see his son was interested in this too. I thanked him again and left. He called a taxi for me.

On the way back it turned out the taxi driver – Pehlivan – was a Turk from West Trakya in Greece. How rare. He said no Germans knew there were Turks in Greece any more. I told him I taught about Muslims in Europe, that was why I knew, and that his people were brave to stay. He said that Greece's joining the EU gave them more rights in Greece. Only Greece is so much poorer now. I came back to my room and wrote up the notes.

I was honored that the mosque representative had felt that he could speak to me about his feelings on integration. That is a personal topic and most important. It deserves respectful consideration.

Unification Day in Dresden in 2016

Meanwhile in Dresden in the East on that day, there were demonstrations and Pegida marches against Merkel. There were cries of "Traitor," and "Merkel must go!" with 2,600 police in attendance.

Merkel herself had come to town. She must have known it would be problematic. There were even posters of her in Nazi uniform. It was embarrassing to me as a foreigner to watch this shameful behavior and I think to Germans too, apart from those demonstrating against her.

This is twenty-six years after German unification and this is how some in the East have become after so much has been expended for them. There was a speech the next day on television by a young Muslim in Germany in which he suggested that the Saxons of the East needed integration courses.

As mentioned the week before, some people had placed a small bomb in the entrance of a mosque in Dresden. No one was hurt but the imam and his family were in the mosque. It seems Dresden is a place of growing xenophobia and right-wing extremism. In 2015, there were 106 attacks on asylum shelters there, and fifty more in the first half of 2016.

The German National Museum

It rained later on the afternoon of the holiday so I walked to the closest museum, the German National Museum. I began in the Middle Ages section where there was remarkable artwork and statuary. Upstairs there were astrolabes from Syria from 1000–1200, remarkable instruments.

But the globes took my breath away. There was the Beheim Globe, the oldest in the world from 1492. The man who made it had lived in Portugal before he returned to Nürnberg. The west coast of Africa was well done, but there was no New World. Noah's Ark was between the Black and Caspian Seas. The next globe was from 1520 and had some of the New World.

Then on to Albrecht Dürer (1471–1528) who was born, and lived, and worked in Nürnberg. They did not have many paintings or engravings by him. But I especially like the paintings of his master and his mother.

On to the museum store where I was hoping for books on German history, something beyond the shallow tourist ones I kept finding. No such luck. But among the postcards there was a classic Woody Allen quote: "The more I listen to Wagner, the more I feel like invading Poland." That kept me chortling through the rain as I walked back to the hotel.

For dinner at the hotel there was good potato soup. A single young German woman was eating alone in the hotel restaurant. Could I engage her in conversation? I asked if she were there on business. Yes. Nothing further. I tried again. Where was she from? That worked better. She was from the North and was in Nürnberg to do a week of studies for her work. She had two children.

I told her why I was there. Then she started to talk in German. She was from a small town. They had 127 refugees, mostly from Syria. There are two in her young children's classes. She said it was hard for them. I asked if there were an interpreter. "Only for problems, and not all the time," she responded. "Do the children learn fast?" I inquired." "Yes," she said. Her son hugs Muhammad and has him listen to videos with him. "That is good," I said. "That really helps."

Such small examples always interested me. With the number of refugees she had described, the town must have about 8,500 inhabitants. It would fit among the villages I had studied. I liked to hear about German children helping refugee children. I thanked her for telling me about her town and family.

International Women's Café

The next day I took a taxi to the International Women's Café. It was not what I expected at all. The women who work there are not volunteers, but all professionals who have worked on asylum issues for at least ten years They work for the EU from which they get most of their salary, with 25 per cent from other sources and 20 per cent from the city of Nürnberg.

Their main purpose was to help women get asylum. The woman in charge wanted me to make an appointment to talk with her. But this was my last full day in Nürnberg. I had called the previous week and no one had responded, perhaps thanks to the holiday. I could see she was impatient so I asked her immediately what she saw as most difficult for the refugees. She answered, "the restrictive laws."

As follow-up, I asked her what she thought about integration. She said, "There is the possibility for integration, but in the situation of living in an asylum house with 200 others, how can they find integration? As for the mainstream, integration means learning the German language. It is very important. Also the allowance for work and respect. Hate and fear are counter-productive."

She went back to the problem of restrictive laws. "For example in Bavaria, there is a law that refugees could not be put in private dwellings." "That is ridiculous," I said. "The idea," she said, "was to send them back. But then some mayors did not have big buildings for them. So some went into private buildings. They stay in the big buildings during the asylum process. But this can last two to three, or four years. When those from Syria and Iraq got preference, others had to wait."

Then she abruptly left and went to her back office. Meanwhile, however, I had a good conversation with one of the other workers. She had arrived on a bicycle and had very short hair. I had thought she was German, but it turned out she was from Turkey and had been in Germany for thirty years. We talked about volunteers. Then she told me about herself and how she said she did not speak Turkish on the street or in the metro. She was very careful where she spoke it. That made me sad. Langauge is a delicate issue here.

Lunch with the Pastor of Die Brücke

The pastor's "bridge" group that he planned was to be solely men. He told me they were thinking of having a program that instead of discussing *Leitkultur*,[8] that is "the dominant or core culture," they would discuss *Leidkultur*, "the culture of suffering." A nice play on words. He explained that it was the idea of the mosque representative who had been the spokesman for the imam at the mosque the day before. Clearly he knew German and German culture well.

I mentioned how I had stayed at the mosque the day before, after the pastor had left, and that I had talked further with the mosque representative. We had had a good discussion of integration. The pastor was all ears now and wanted to know what he had said.

First I asked him what he thought of the man's German? "It is very good," he said. "Do you think he is integrated?" I asked. "Yes, I do." "Well, he has another view." He was surprised. "Integration is not just from outside. It must be from inside too," I said. I wondered that the pastor did not know this. Could he not see the racism involved in integration when people know they were not truly accepted no matter how well they speak German?

I steered the conversation to the issue of apartments in Nürnberg. The pastor said that the costs had almost doubled in the last two years. Demand had gone up. I asked if there was no rent control. He said there was none that worked. So people were forced to go live outside town in suburbs like Langwasser where the Russians live.

The pastor wanted to work with Muslims as a single group, say "The Islamic Forum of Nürnberg," just for men. But he thought they need to meet in a different place. Not the upstairs of his office where it is too closed in. It needs to be open so men can drop in and see there is an imam there. Maybe in the Turkish restaurant we were in, only upstairs. He wanted my opinion so he thought we should go to his office.

On the way to the office we had begun talking about how hard it was for refugee men to concentrate when their families were still in Syria. In his former parish there was such a man. Eventually, with his help, they had gotten the family to Lebanon, then to Turkey, and then to Germany. He was a different man when the family came to join him in Germany.

He said it was bad that it had gotten so much harder to bring family members now. I asked when that law had come into effect. He said he thought it was the previous spring. "What was the reason for the change?" I asked. "Numbers," he said. "With the families it is just too many people now." "Ahh," I said. "But that is so hard on the families."

We talked about volunteers. He said he had been extremely proud. He talked about "the welcoming culture." He said that there was a long history of "social courage." In West Germany they had had this. As for East Germany, they had never worked on "the dark spots" in their history.

I told him the theory of Dr Sieger, that it was the children of people who had been refugees who were able and willing to help refugees, but not the people who had been refugees themselves. That squared with those in his parish, which was in northern Franconia near the border with the East, where many of the volunteers had what he termed "broken biographies" in their background. That is, they had parents who were from the Sudetenland or East Prussia. Of the fifty people who were the most active in his parish, "the pillars of his parish," two-thirds had parents who has been refugees. As the political landscape got more rightist and more green, even those not affiliated with a church came to help. I thanked the Pastor for his time and insights and wished him well in his endeavors.

I was glad I had come to Nürnberg. It is an important city with its high number of refugees and migrants. I had met with most knowledgeable people there from Dr Uli Glaser and the Social Consultant for Asylum, to the young Syrian imam and the Turkish mosque representative. Finding places for refugees to rent was an ongoing problem and working with neighbors to reassure them about their own home values before the refugees moved in was most wise. But the discussion with the mosque representative had also made me reflect on questions of integration of Muslims in German society.

Schwäbisch Gmünd: A Town of Integrated Civic Engagement

I took a train to my last medium-sized town of Schwäbisch Gmünd. With about 61,000 inhabitants it was not large enough to be named on the list of stops on the sign above the train station platform in

Nürnberg. Like Bruchsal, and unlike Nürnberg, Schwäbisch Gmünd is in the German state of Baden-Württemberg.

The reason I had chosen to come to Schwäbisch Gmünd was I had been there on my pilot study the previous spring. My friend Siglind had seen an article in a German paper on the mayor and his work with refugees and had passed it on to me. I had written to the Oberbürgermeister and we had met the previous spring. His comments and actions on how citizens form community, and how refugees integrate were the most thoughtful I had encountered across Germany. As with Elzach, I had vowed to return.

Schwäbisch Gmünd was also the hometown of artist Emanuel Leutze, who had immigrated to America as a child in 1825.[9] He had early shown artistic talent and had returned to Europe to the famous Düsseldorf School of Art in 1840.

In 1849 Leutze had begun painting the work that most Americans know although few know the artist's name. The painting is of George Washington standing tall with an American flag behind him in an open boat in the middle of an ice-filled river, as his men row valiantly on a cold and windy night. It is *Washington Crossing the Delaware*.

What is most fascinating is the reason Leutze painted it at this time in Europe. Leutze was trying to give courage to those who had fought for democracy in the failed revolutions of 1848, and to remind them that democracy was still possible. Leutze sent this painting to America where it was immediately recognized as a masterpiece. He later returned to America.

When people know about its immigrant artist and the time of its painting, *Washington Crossing the Delaware* takes on new significance. But inspiration can move in both directions. I hope this book allows Americans to be inspired by Germans and their leader now too.

First Morning: The Gmünder Way

It is always wise to begin with the *Rathaus*. I had written to the assistant of the mayor to ask for an appointment. Still I wanted to let them know I was actually in town and ask for suggestions of other people to talk with. So the first morning I walked to the *Rathaus*. The mayor's assistant suggested I make an appointment by telephone with the head of refugees at her office by the train station, which I did.

Then I walked across the handsome city square to the other end where there was another municipal building and the office of Herr Hermann Gaugele, the Head of Integration. It turned out he had relatives in Minnesota.

When I explained my interests, Herr Gaugele immediately started talking about the *Gmünder Weg*, that is, "the way to integration in Schwäbisch Gmünd." The mayor had coined the phrase so that even the process was part of the community. Herr Gaugele said it begins when a refugee comes to Schwäbisch Gmünd. "We have someone to meet them at the bus or train station, someone who knows their culture to help them." I asked if this person were a volunteer. Yes.

He noted that they had their main office for refugees just to the right of the *Bahnhof*, the train station. "We call it PFIFF." (This stands for Projektstelle für Integration und für Flüchtlinge, that is, "Project Site for Integration and for Refugees.") Further, *ein Pfiff* is "a whistle," whose metaphorical use implies something that has zing or pizazz and a device for getting attention – an attractive name for an office to deal with refugees.

Briefly Herr Gaugele explained that there were five steps to the *Gmünder Weg*:

(1) welcome;
(2) possibility of language learning, from beginning up to advanced, including for those who are illiterate. And this was without regard to the regulations that say people have to wait until they are guaranteed asylum before they get the integration course. "Our mayor says all should have language courses;"
(3) participation in voluntary activities;
(4) education, training, employment; and
(5) providing individual accommodation.

Herr Gaugele then said he thought he had the explanation of the *Gmünder Weg* in English. As I skimmed this I saw that the mayor had begun this project in June of 2013. It was so early I gasped. "Yes," said Herr Gaugele. "He was a visionary. And notice how many institutions he assembled at the outset – churches, other institutions, clubs, associations, so it was a united front."

He asked if I had seen the camp in Schwäbisch Gmünd. I told him that I had been there last spring. He said there was a new one that opened a few weeks ago and was much nicer.

On the subject of *Ehrenamtliche*, the volunteers, he said some had been active in this work even twenty years ago. But sometimes they think they know what the refugees need more than the refugees do. Some thought the refugees preferred to be in town rather than on the edges. But this is not always true. Some refugees said they wanted to stay further away on the edges. The mayor is good. He hears what the refugees say.

I recalled from my discussion with the mayor the previous spring that he preferred to have the refugees in smaller groups, preferably three to four living with the owner of a house. This was more likely in smaller villages outside the city. He said the city paid the bus tickets, or organized bicycles for travel into town.

I asked Herr Gaugele what he saw as the greatest difficulty for the refugees. He said it was that that we have a culture, and they have a culture. When we come together, we must move some, and they must move some. However many steps we have between us – we must find some common scene from our differences. Then he gave an example. He said:

> We have women from Iraq, Yezidis whose men were killed. They cannot swim. But here in southern Germany swimming is important. We wanted the children to learn to swim. The pools were full all the time, except on Wednesdays we had a little open time that could be just for them. But they said, "We cannot get wet on Wednesdays. It is forbidden. There is no compromise." Then they thought, if no one sees us, maybe it is OK. So they did it. They compromised.

Herr Gaugele had phone calls. I thanked him for his time and asked if I could meet with him further. He had given me handouts I wanted to read and then come back and discuss. How many towns had heads of integration like him?

Summer Community Events

That afternoon I went back to the coffee shop where I had been kindly provided with dinner my first evening. The young man of Turkish ethnicity whom I had met there was working again. He had been born in

Germany and so, with the new laws, had the possibility of getting German citizenship. He needs this, as he wants to become a teacher. He had invited me to meet his mother since I was the first American he had ever met who speaks Turkish.

He showed me a handsome color program from the Staufer Festival, a thirteenth century city saga that had been performed in Schwäbisch Gmünd in early July 2016. It was a grand spectacle that had included 1,300 performers, all from the town, and some refugees even had bit parts.

But before the Staufer Festival, the young man told me how they had had an *iftar* dinner, that is, a dinner for the breaking of the Ramadan fast at sundown, for the whole community in the smaller square by the large church. One thousand people had come! The Turkish cook whom the main mosque had brought from Turkey for Ramadan had done the cooking. It was free for everyone – citizens, resident Muslims, refugees, everyone. He even had photos on his iPhone. The mayor spoke from a stage they put up by the church, and the imam recited the *ezan*, that is the call to prayer. "It was so beautiful," he said.

When his shift at the coffee shop was over, we walked to his family home so I could meet his parents.

A Turkish Family

We walked about twenty minutes and went upstairs where I took off my boots at their doorway. I met his father, a kind man who was going to the mosque for the regular Thursday meeting later that evening. His mother came in from work. She was in her fifties and had four children, three boys and a girl. The others were all married and lived in the region. Only the youngest son who had brought me there lived at home and was still going to college.

We sat at the dining room table and talked. His father asked me what I thought about Gülen, the Turkish Muslim leader who has lived in exile in Pennsylvania since 1998. And then we talked again about the *iftar* for the whole city. They told me it had been on 18 June, and 1,000 people had come. They had built a stage and everyone was invited. Germans and Turks and all people had come. There was food for everyone: salad, soup, meat, pilav, and baklava.

"It was so connective, it was truly a community event. It was the first time all the foreigners came," they said, meaning the Germans.

Apparently in the past, the mayor had come to the mosque for Ramadan, but this was the first time it was celebrated outside in the church square. Remembering it, there were tears in their eyes. I think they felt respect in the attendance of others at the *iftar* dinner. This was most wise and gracious of the community.

We talked about this and that. The mother works and so does her husband. They have a nice apartment. She pickles many of the vegetables from the garden and makes all her own food, including all the bread and noodles. She took me up to the attic where she had the *yufka*, a special Turkish bread. It was made on a *saj*, a special oven. It lasts a year all covered with towels. So much work. "You just add a little water and you can make different foods with it too." I told her that this was *san'at*, "a form of art" to know all this.

The difference of being in a home and in a hotel is so great. Throughout my time with them, the son had brought out food for us to eat – stuffed grape leaves, noodles, white cheese, homemade bread, and Turkish tea that he had made and that was so good. It was truly an evening to remember with a warm and loving family. This hospitality is a feature of Turkish and Middle Eastern culture that I hope Germans appreciate as well.

Office of Refugee Accommodation

My plan for the next morning was to visit the head of volunteers in Schwäbisch Gmünd. Unfortunately there had been a miscommunication and the woman in charge of volunteers was on vacation until the end of October. I had a noon appointment set up. I just needed something worthwhile for the morning.

I decided to pay a call on the *Gemeinschaftsunterkunft*, the district refugee accommodation office. I had talked to them on the telephone the day before and gathered a visit would be challenging. Still I decided to go. It was very different from the municipal offices.

As I had expected, the administrator in charge was far too busy to see me. So I asked if she had an assistant, who could talk briefly with me, all the while looking for a likely face. I motioned to another office across the hall so we would not disturb anyone, just as an assistant readily looked up at me.

The assistant reiterated what the mayor's assistant had suggested. To understand the *Gmünder Weg*, it was best to go to PFIFF since they did such good service for refugees. Her office did technical services like trying to get refugees quickly into work, language courses, mini-jobs, or half-time work.

She explained that when a refugee says, "I have a job," they had to check and see. The same went with a place to live. If it cost over a certain amount, they had to check it out. These were regulations to protect both refugee and community adherence to laws.

I asked if she had seen changes in attitudes toward refugees here. She said not so much. She explained that they had had a lot of refugees. But they had been straightforward with their *Ehrenamtliche*. They had seminars for them. "We emphasize self-help, not looking down on them. We work to be objective. When people give two hours a week, we think that is plenty. Not more, it is enough. Sometimes two hours a month is also good. Whatever works well for the *Ehrenamtliche*. We do not want to make work for us," implying that if the volunteers are overworked then they will stop helping and there will be more work for the regular staff.

I asked what she thought was most difficult for the refugees here in Schwäbisch Gmünd. She said that what refugees here found most difficult was when somebody comes for some time, say two years in our buildings, and works for the city with the understanding that if you do this, then you will receive what someone else has been given due to their work. When the time comes, though, the city no longer has similar benefits to give out, such as a flat. When people have nothing, they try to get what others have gotten. Jealousy then sets in.

As for changes in Germany in general, she acknowledged that there had been evidence of this in the news. "But we see the positive here. For example last year there were floods here, last spring. The refugees helped people. They pulled a car out of the flood waters." I remembered the floods. I was in Germany then and had just missed the flooding in southern Germany.

She continued. "We have a community here. Refugees participated in the Staufer Saga. The refugees are helping. We work together. With the *Ehrenamtliche*, we tell people the truth, that it is hard work. We are honest, above board."

I mentioned how it seemed that the Turkish people felt they were not so integrated and the refugees have brought this out in them. She said they had something called *Dost Ladies Club*. It meets twice a week.

It is space for talk and drinking tea or coffee. It is for Turkish women to drink coffee or tea, and Arabs too.

By this time the main administrator, the one who had not had enough time to speak with me, had come in to see what we were talking about (I had thought she would come). She sat down and joined the conversation. She mentioned *Duldung*, which has the general sense of "forbearance" or "patience," but here it is used bureaucratically to refer to "when there is a negative decision on asylum." The administrator then explained that these people stay in an apartment that would generally be used for homeless people for the waiting period until they are deported. In contrast, those with a positive decision can move into a regular apartment. The job center pays their rent, a low price to be sure, if they do not yet have a job.

I explained that in America, refugees were only supported for six months. We put them to work as soon as possible. Churches help with all the extras and getting them settled in. They also receive food stamps which provide food purchasing assistance. However, beyond six months, the US government did not give much more financial support. I said that Canada was more like Germany with more institutionalized plans for immigrants that it extended to refugees.

She said that they even have a project for people who must return to their country. "We help them get set up back home, with say a tractor." I was impressed with that. But most do not want to go home. They wait for the police to tell them they have to leave, which is not good for the children. At this point the administrator returned to her office.

The assistant then mentioned that there was even a place for traumatized people in Stuttgart. She had sent a young Afghan there whose father was killed. People there share their stories. I said it was wise to have a place for people who have been traumatized. "And it is good you can recognize this in refugees." I told her about the Iraqis who came to Dearborn, Michigan, who had experienced multiple trauma from the first Gulf War. "They could not work at all. We supported them." She said, "We have different training here. But we can recognize trauma." I thanked her for her time and expertise. I was most fortunate in the assistant and her knowledge and caring.

Eventually I got back into town for my interview in the refugee headquarters where refugees go when they first come to Schwäbisch Gmünd.

Refugee Officer

This was the famous PFIFF office next to the train station that I had been hearing about since I had come to town. Daniela Dinser, the Refugee Officer, was in charge.

The office itself was on the second floor. As I climbed up the stairs, there was light streaming in through the windows. There was a woman speaking extra clearly in German to two young refugee women in one room, while a couple waited outside the door of another room. There were toys for children to play with in the end room. I sat down next to the couple to wait.

Daniela Dinser opened her door and invited me in. She looked active and together. She had the infamous three monkeys on her desk: "See no evil, hear no evil, speak no evil." I accepted her offer for tea. I briefly told Daniela Dinser why I was there and then said I wanted to hear about PFIFF. I told her where I had been that morning. Her office and that of the district administrator were quite different.

The phone rang. It was the mayor. She mentioned that I was there. The mayor agreed to meet with me on Monday late afternoon at 5:15 pm. That was good.

Daniela said she was the *Flüchtlingsbeauftragte*, the Refugee Officer. It was her responsibility to deal with all problems related to the refugees – school, work – whatever comes up. "We seek out the appropriate contact to solve the problems. Then we bring them together – the people, the churches, whatever."

She took a direction I had not anticipated. "You know how it is with children when they go in the church when they are young with water?" "You mean baptism?" I said. "Yes. The people who are there. When they go to school, we have someone to go with them. Sometimes the refugees are older than school age."

Then it hit me. "The godparents you mean? You have volunteers who act like godparents to the refugees when they take their children to school the first time. But they are Muslim, so that would not be a term they would know," I said. I must think what there is in Islam. But yes, people from outside the family who have responsibility for them. I liked her analogy.

She added, "Volunteer work is so important." She continued. "We have what we call 'platforms.' These are things we do together, citizens and refugees. It is very important. With language, it is so important too.

I bring my three children to these too. We live it also. Not only *über*, but also *mit den Flüchtlingen wir sprechen*. That is, "We do not just speak about the refugees, but we also speak with them."

But then she continued in a totally different vein.

> Many problems that the refugees have, they are problems with us.
> We have our traditions and rules. I need to see my roots to be able to be open to new things. Then we are not afraid of the new. It is a societal problem that we as Germans have with our background.

I had never had someone speak this openly about being German. Clearly Daniela Dinser, in her work with refugees, had thought deeply about what it meant to be German. She continued.

> It was only with football {soccer} that we were able to say we were proud to be German. Twenty years ago we could not say this. I am a German. Now I can say that. I am happy that I live here. The refugees are welcome.

I think this is most important. To welcome people, it is most important to know who you are and be at peace with this. I was honored she had been this open with me.

We got into a discussion of changes in responses to refugees. I mentioned the change from response to Bosnians and the new refugees now. Daniela said that when they had voting recently in Baden they found that more rural people had voted right-wing. They were "late settlers." I said, "Yes, the *Russlanddeutsche*. I had thought of them as refugees." But Daniela said, "We had not considered them so. We considered them Germans. But culturally they were not German. They had problems and were more Russian."

I mentioned that I had heard that they had problems with alcohol and crime too. Also in America recent immigrants are negative about the newer immigrants. However, I saw the *Russlanddeutsche* as refugees too, even if they did get citizenship immediately.

Daniela Dinser said she was trained in the law. She had practiced law for three and a half years and then wanted work that gave her more time. I asked what sort of law? She said family law. Then we both laughed.

I said "Community work does not give you more time, does it?" She shook her head. I knew this from my own experience working in the Arab-American community in Dearborn, Michigan. Community work is never done; it does not have a nine to five daily schedule.

She showed me a page from a German law book on asylum law. People get asylum for political reasons. The constraints include:

- Only those who come by air or by the North Sea can qualify for asylum. (None of the refugees here have come this way. Thus Germany is protected from offering asylum.)
- Those who can be defined as "refugees" can stay two to three years. In addition, they must keep proving it. That is, that they cannot return.
- More recently most Syrians were only granted permission to stay one year. This prohibits them from bringing their families.

Daniela Dinser said they also have about forty-five Yezidis, all women and children, no men since they were killed. Most of the children saw their fathers being killed.

I asked her what was the greatest difficulty of the refugees here? She showed me some very fine contrastive cultural visuals that compared differences in Germany and some problems that might occur with treatment of children and women, attitudes to homosexuality, and so forth. One of these had to do with punctuality. She said Gisela Erler made the handouts with input from refugees. Still I could tell she was not particularly interested in punctuality.

Looking at her I said, "What you wanted me to ask was what is the greatest difficulty of the German people with the refugees." Indeed, that is what I had hoped to learn from people indirectly.

She nodded as she said what she had said before, only more clearly.

Our problem is with our roots. This is my tradition. Many people are afraid of refugees. They do not know them. They are afraid of foreigners.

If they knew their own identity, it would be easier. We need a way to get together. These are our traditions, our roots, our laws.

I said, "In America, we do not have so much history. But I do not have fear. I know my family's journey. I talk to people on the train. I talk to people with beards. I am at peace with myself."

She gave me some handbooks that they give the *Ehrenamtliche*. I thanked her again. Then I high-fived her. We do this in Detroit, blacks and whites and all people, when we feel we understand each other. Schwäbisch Gmünd is most fortunate to have Daniela Dinser as Refugee Officer.

Then I took the bus back to the hotel. I was learning the ropes in Schwäbisch Gmünd.

Church with the Russlanddeutsche

On Sunday as usual I tried to go to church. I sought out a Protestant church but the hotel staff had no idea where one was. I found one on the internet and took a taxi there, only to find a locked door. Other people with a car had come there too looking for the Protestant church. They let me ride with them as we sought out the open Lutheran church. It turned out to be across from the big Catholic one, very near my hotel. The people I was with turned out to be *Russlanddeutsche*.

As we headed into the church, the woman who had driven the car explained to me that they had come to the church for a baptism. So we all sat up front on the left side of the church in what used to be choir stalls. Two babies were being baptized that day. I sat with the *Russlanddeutsche* since I had come with them. The baby whose baptism party I was with was named Anastasia. She was dressed all in white and was very active.

Down in the main part of the pews of the church there was a peppering of older people. There were a lot of empty seats. The pulpit was raised high with an impressive canopy above. I understood very little of the sermon, perhaps because I was counting names of men who had died in World War I, listed high on the wall across from me. There were 183 names. I had no idea there were so many Protestants from Gmünd.

Later I went across the city square where there is a monument to the war dead of the city. The total war dead in Schwäbisch Gmünd in World War I was 670. The total war dead from World War II was over 1,000. It was a terrible loss for a town of this size.

After the service there was no coffee hour, which tended to be the general practice in German churches. That was their way. I went back in the church and saw a woman whom I assumed to be German. I asked her about the *Russlanddeutsche*, if they were mostly Protestant. "Some are," she said. "They all come here for baptism. But they do not come back to church."

Then she explained she was a *Spätaussietler*, a late resettler. She had come from Rumania forty years earlier. She then explained that she was very different from the *Russlanddeutsche*. Her people all spoke German, although an archaic form of it. And the children spoke German and had gone to German schools. She said that they had wanted to put her children back, but she said no, let them stay in their grade. By the end of the year they were fine. She said she had even worked as a *Putzfrau*, a cleaning lady. Later she did other work.

"And how has it worked out for your children?" I asked. "They went to university. One is an engineer." I smiled. "And the other has a good job. Now of my grandchildren, one is working for Bosch." I said, "See the difference from if you had stayed in Rumania!" "Yes," she said. "People back in Rumania, the young ones have all left for western Europe. There is no work there." I thanked her and said goodbye.

Return to the Office of Integration

Herr Hermann Gaugele had given me much to read and think about in my first visit to the Office of Integration. I had gone over the materials and had questions for him. He also had more materials for me about the Integration Roundtable.

The Integration Roundtable of Schwäbisch Gmünd is made up of seventy people who meet about four times a year to go over their commitments to integration activities. It includes important people from institutions, churches, international organizations, clubs, industry, and bureaucracy. A woman, Frau Martina Häusler, whose major responsibility was this Roundtable, explained this to me.

While we were talking, another young professional woman came into the office. She worked at the local university 50 per cent of her time, and for the community and city the other 50 per cent of her time. She also worked for the Integration Roundtable and its different groups.

I asked about the German courses because I knew there was a problem in other cities with not having enough of them. The results in the last three years in seven classes had been 85 per cent successful at the A-2 level, the second level of study. Herr Gaugele was rightly proud of this. He showed me the whole report for 2016 as far as it was completed, with all the statistics for the city and its minorities.

It showed that 36.5 per cent of the city inhabitants of Schwäbisch Gmünd had a migration background, and that there were more from Russia than from Turkey. In 2015 there were 724 foreign refugees who had remained in Schwäbisch Gmünd. He even gave me a copy of a book on integration in Schwäbisch Gmünd that had been published in 2009.[10] Clearly Schwäbisch Gmünd had been working on integration for many years, well before the new refugees came. I later talked about this with the Mayor. Herr Gaugele explained the two types of integration: those who are new, and those who have lived here a long time. "We were all together at first. But now we see that there are problems."

I mentioned how touched the Turkish family I had visited was with the *iftar* last Ramadan. It was truly a community-sharing event. Then they told me about another event on 1 October for "the Breaking of the Bread" for Christians. Both Muslims and Christians came, about 400. It was at the Cultural Center. The idea is to get all involved, with a different way of thinking.

Herr Gaugele said that what is important is to have partners. "It says we need your support, and we will support you. For example with the fair, it is not enough to just walk around. You need to get people involved, working in groups. And you need to do this in small steps."

I asked what they would do if they saw that a refugee had problems and could not cope. One said, "We would try to do something with the living arrangement usually. Often other refugees are most helpful." Herr Gaugele said his experience in the *Jugendarbeit*, youth work, helped him think differently about things like this.

I asked about sending some of the refugees back. "Yes, last year about 145 returned. We think that what they learned here helped them. There is a special program too."

The second woman who had come in asked if I knew about *HuT, Handwerk und Technik*? I had read that it was most popular with the refugees, but I was not sure what it entailed. Herr Gaugele said it was led by a wise older retired man who is an *Ehrenamtlicher*, and "truly honorable." He was known to go into apartments where refugees lived and bring them to his small factory that has many tools for wood-working and metal-working. He teaches them how to use the tools by talking and showing them. They learn by doing. This is most valuable. They learn skills and ways of German security with tools. They have overalls of different colors to indicate knowledge. Early on it is blue. Later it is red. What they learn is valuable for obtaining work later.

There is something also for girls, but it is handwork and talk. It is better to have men and women separate. A woman leads this. I asked if it were *Dost*? They thought maybe so. I explained that *dost* was a fine word in Turkish that meant "friend." The second woman who had come in asked if I knew Turkish. I began to speak Turkish. She was surprised. I had not realized she was Turkish, she was from Afyon in Turkey, and her name is Sema Toykan. What a pleasure. She asked me to join the other women for lunch that day upstairs in the same building.

From the book that Herr Gaugele had given me, published in 2009, I could tell that they had been working on integration much earlier. There was even a group photo in the book including Prof. Heckmann. So there were outside consultants from Bamberg and the European Forum on Migration. But the main assistance I learned had come from the Schader Stiftung, a well-regarded private foundation that specialized in practical solutions to social issues that had worked with Schwäbisch Gmünd later. Herr Gaugele said that they showed Schader what they were doing; Schader evaluated it, and helped them make integration even better. "We have had foreign people for forty years, twenty years, we wanted to make it better."

In the welcome map, he showed that they had a club for late settlers, and two groups for *Russlanddeutsche*. I asked when the *Russlanddeutsche* came. He said they first started coming in the 1970s and then ever since. The Turks first came in the 1960s.

I thanked Herr Gaugele for his help and time. He took me up to Sema Toykan's office where there was another Turkish woman. Martina Häusler also joined us so we had a total of three women and together we had a good lunch.

Lunch with Three Women Who Work

The Turkish woman from the community had brought pizza from the Kebaphaus that her family owned. I told her I had gone there for lunch the day before yesterday and that I remembered it from the previous spring. She remembered me. She is on the Integration Advisory Council for Schwäbisch Gmünd, which is important.

We had pizza, coffee, and Sema Toykan had made a dessert that Martina brought whipped cream for. Three of us knew Turkish, but not Martina, so we mostly conversed in German.

The office had a beautiful view with much light. It was good to be with women. Martina asked about my project and I explained it.

We all enjoyed the lunch and the company. Then, before Martina had to leave, I asked the question. What, in your opinion, is most difficult for the refugees. The Turkish woman on the Integration Council answered, "Family. The hardest thing for the ones who are here as single men is being without their families." Then Martina said in her mind it was insecurity. "They come to Germany for the security, but then they find that they are waiting, waiting, waiting. There is insecurity in that they do not know what will happen next. Can I stay in this secure country or will I be deported? And then there are negative voices from the AfD." Sema said that there are negative tendencies too.

> Always there are some prejudices. There are people who are open, and others – why they are just that way – they do not try to understand. It is the small things that would help people be aware of how to handle foreigners. The prejudices are hard.

For example Sema talked about what is written in a newsletter on "language courses." Now if a Turkish woman in Turkey wants to marry a Turkish man who is already in Germany, she must pass a test in German. But if a woman from Thailand wants to come to Germany, she does not need to pass a test in German. The requirements are not the same.

After Martina left, we talked more in Turkish. I told them about what the refugee issue revealed about the host culture. Partly Germans could use this to rethink how Turks have fared in their country. It brings up issues of integration of Turks who have worked hard in Germany and not been granted acceptance.[11] I told of the young woman in Nürnberg who had been in Germany for thirty years and was ashamed to speak Turkish in the street or metro. That is not good. She was amazed that I loved the Turkish language and had spent so many years studying it.

The Turkish woman on the Integration Council mentioned what some of the refugees said about integration materials. Some of these materials included things like: "Wash everyday. Don't beat women." The refugees were confused. "Do Germans have trouble with these issues? Do they not wash? Do they beat their wives? Why are they telling us these things?" She said at first they did not realize that these were against stereotypes of Muslim men. Then they were insulted. They were right.

I asked them, "What is integration?" The Turkish woman on the Integration Council said that she is here. She seemed sure of herself. But she said as she left, that with another mayor, he might not be so interested in her contribution to the Council.

I said people should never be left out. People like her know what others think. They hear and see. It is a wise mayor who put her on the Integration Council. They need her voice. I thanked Sema too. As the Turkish woman and I walked down the stairs, she said it is good that Sema is here. It shows they have not forgotten the Turks. I saw what she meant. To have hired a Turkish professional here matters a lot.

I walked back to the hotel and checked on what people thought of the second Hillary and Trump debate. In the back of my mind I was worried about my own homeland. Then I wrote out questions for the interview with the mayor. I left early to the *Rathaus* so I could be there by five o'clock in the evening.

The "Lord Mayor" Richard Arnold of Schwäbisch Gmünd

As I had already had a generous interview with the Oberbürgermeister Richard Arnold the previous spring, he was kind to give me time again. The mayor invited me into his office and announced that he had half an hour. I handed him *stollen*, a small loaf of dried fruit bread, the man in Daniela's PFIFF had told me to give him. It was marzipan, which he loves. He tried to give me some but I told him it was all for him. He obviously needed it. I wondered if he had eaten all day.

We talked. He is tall and good looking. He is high-powered mayor like diplomat Richard Holbrooke of the Dayton Peace Accords. He was of course in a suit.

I told him I appreciated his five-step *Gmünder Weg* more now that I had seen many other cities in Germany and understood it much better. My first question was if the consulting in earlier days in 2009 and 2013, with the European Forum on Migration and the Schader Foundation, had helped?

The mayor answered that at that time they had had two groups in Schwäbisch Gmünd: the *Russlanddeutsche* and the *Spätaussiedler*. "We consulted with the outside groups to put in a strategy."

I asked, "What made Schwäbisch Gmünd reach out for outside help then?" He responded.

It was not refugees. We saw that we had many who had come from Russia. We also had many who had come from Turkey too, second and third generation. They had problems with integration.

So we were well prepared when early refugees started coming too. They were not treated like immigrants. They were treated like objects. Some thought if they were treated that way they would go away. In 2010, we had refugees from Gambia, Nigeria, and Afghanistan.

The way these refugees were treated was unacceptable. We changed the way before the large wave of refugees came to Europe. We organized 'A Treaty for Humanity.' This was with the churches, the organizations, the clubs, societies, and companies. We had it in mind but it needed to grow. This became the *Gmünder Weg*.

I mentioned that I had not seen a similar program in other cities. The mayor said that was because it had grown from within, from involvement of the citizens, teachers, schools. "It is a strategy of the community."

In the interview with the Mayor the previous spring he had told me how he had put refugees in the home of his own elderly parents. Imagine this as a model for the town! This was a powerful way to emphasize the humanity of the refugees. The mayor had explained that his father was born in 1931 and his mother in 1936. Before the refugees came into their lives, they were talking more of illnesses and they were closing up into their own world. Since the two refugees had been living with them, they had opened up. His mother was learning again about things beyond the borders. His father enjoyed hearing stories of what was going on at high school from the sixteen-year-old from Afghanistan. The town doctor had even suggested prescribing, instead of seven pills, one refugee!

In the current interview, the mayor continued with more passion,

The most important outcome is not integration but confidence. We work on confidence building. To invest in integration you need confidence.

That is why we had the October 1 event, "the Breaking of the Bread" with Christians and Muslims. We were celebrating *Gemeinschaft*, "community." It is a feeling. We Germans like to argue and reason. But it is not through reasoning that this comes. It is a feeling.

I did not hear this expressed anywhere else in Germany this way. The Oberbürgermeister of Schwäbisch Gmünd had thought long and hard about integration and how to achieve it. It made me think again of the representative of the mosque in Nürnberg and his thoughts of integration.

I recalled four projects with refugees he had told me about the previous spring. These included two that related to gardens. Schwäbisch Gmünd had had a *Landesgartenschau* (a state exhibition on gardening) for citizens from all over Germany in 2014 that was most successful. It got its citizens, including 100 refugees to help. All who worked over fifty hours were given a bright green jacket, cap, and bag. The mayor said he got this idea from the London Olympics, so that the refugees looked like everyone else who had helped. The other garden project, including citizens and refugees, was planting bulbs in and around the town. This spring they had 17,000 tulips from this.

Another project was the Staufer Festival that is held every four years. The mayor explained that the Staufer were an imperial family celebrated on stage there. That year the event was held from 24 June to 10 July, with 1,000 citizens and refugees as participants.

The last example of integration of citizens and refugees was the Fire Brigade Volunteers. Refugees were allowed to join in the training. In Schwäbisch Gmünd the Fire Brigade is volunteer and part of a citizens' unit. The training is intensive – four full weekends from October to March. There were thirty-two refugees who stayed throughout the training. Of these six passed the exams. They are not easy. Finally three more passed with all the other locals. As for those who did not pass, they can try again.

I asked the mayor, "What have been the major changes over time with your program?" He said:

We learned that we needed to let them show their talents. They need confirmation. Also pace. They are not used to the pace here. Partly it is the language barrier, detailed advice in German, and the physical feeling that comes from fear of deportation. It is important that they give an effort for professional training. This cannot be underestimated.

Then my last question. "What are you most proud of? The mayor answered immediately:

That we have over 1000 refugees living in town and that we still feel responsible for each other. We still have strong social cohesion in town. But this relates to confidence building.

Again he returned to the importance of confidence building:

If I want investment, I need capital. If we want integration, we need confidence.

I thanked the Oberbürgermeister for his time and expertise at a most busy time of year. I went out to his front office where Daniela Dinser was waiting. We went to the waiting room where I wanted to talk with her.

Another Talk with the Refugee Officer

As we sat in the mayor's waiting room, I asked her what I should have asked her when I met with her the previous Friday in her office. "How long has PFIFF been in existence?"

"Since last February," she said. She added that it had not been easy. "No," I said. "Community work is the most difficult there is." Again I remembered my work in the Arab American community in Dearborn, Michigan, when I had been much younger.

I asked if she would go to Berlin soon with her PowerPoint presentation. She smiled. She had told me the previous Friday that she did not like PowerPoint but she had to use the application. She was giving a presentation in Berlin on the *Gmünder Weg*. She was going to take her mother who had not been to Berlin in forty years and who was looking forward to it.

Figure 5.4 Refugee Officer Daniela Dinser and Lord Mayor Richard Arnold of Schwäbisch Gmünd Baden-Württemburg, Germany.

Then I said I wanted to share with her how the mayor had responded to my last questions. I said I had asked him what had been the biggest surprise or change over time. He had said that he had not realized that the refugees needed to let their talents show themselves, and to receive acclaim. He had also spoken of pace.

"The mayor spoke of pace?" she said with surprise. "We cannot keep up with him." "Yes," I said, "he said that the refugees had trouble with the pace here. I think he must be a multi-tasker." "Oh yes, he is. All the time." "I imagine working for him is challenging," I said with a smile. She nodded.

I asked to take her photograph with the mayor. He had just come out of his office. I took it by the outside door to his office that has a sign on it, *Die Stadt der glückliker Politiker*, "the city of happy politicians."

I thanked Daniela Dinser and the mayor again. I went back to the hotel, ate my cold chicken wraps, and typed out many pages of notes. Then I wrote thank you notes to Hermann Gaugele, to Sema Toykan, and to the mayor. It was after midnight when I turned out the lights in this remarkable town.

Of all the communities in Germany, I continue to think back to Schwäbisch Gmünd for its well-thought-out programs related to refugees at all levels. It had evolved the *Gmünder Weg*, a local way of working toward integration of refugees over the experience of working with three cycles of migrants and refugees. Volunteers were free to develop programs like the one that taught refugees about German machines and technical handwork in the volunteer's small workshop. It involved seventy local institutions in the Integration Roundtable that meets four times a year. The committment of Lord Mayor Arnold was known throughout the region. Refugee Official Dinser was especially competent as was Herr Gaugele in the municipal office where annual evaluations were completed and made public. Civic events, like the Iftar dinner, made the local Turkish people I met so proud. The way the city encouraged refugees to become involved in city gardening, in the city Summer Festival, and in the volunteer fire department was especially creative. If any community was a model for what could be done with refugees it is Schwäbisch Gmünd.

CHAPTER 6

RESPONSES OF LARGE CITIES

The large cities I researched all had over a million inhabitants. They differ significantly from the medium-sized towns or cities in that community is harder to define. In the large cities a sense of community may be expressed more as sports affiliation or even dialect. Here I was especially looking for programs for the refugees.

In the pilot study I had visited both Munich in the south and Hamburg in the north. I planned to return to both cities. Due to the New Year's Eve incident in Cologne in 2015 in which men of Middle Eastern background assaulted many women in the square by the cathedral, I added Cologne to my large city list.

Munich: The Rule-Tight City

Church Service and Making Connections

Attending early Sunday church services is wise because while the priest may be trying out his sermon, he is likely to have some time after the service to talk. Therefore I got up early Sunday morning in Munich, had breakfast, and got to the Lutheran church before half past eight in the morning.

The church, St Matthäus, was a large one. I entered and followed people who were going into the chapel. Eventually there were eighteen parishioners, a piano player, a sacristan, and the pastor. The service was a formal one with communion. The sermon related to the Gospel of Matthew and the pastor's recent trip to Sicily.

As we walked out afterwards I thanked the pastor. He suggested it was the first time he had seen me. I explained how I had just come to Munich the day before. I asked if he had time to talk. We went back into the chapel.

The pastor had been in America at New York University. I explained what I was doing in German. Then he told me about his work. "I am of the Order of St John. We have three houses, about 1,500 refugees." He explained how St Matthäus coordinates all the different oriental churches in Munich. They have invited the oriental churches to meet here – the Syrian, Iraqi, Eritrean, Coptic – they have liturgy in Arabic. They have language courses too. "They have people who came to Munich fifteen to twenty years ago. They can help better than we can."

He said that as a Christian man he wanted to help Christians – the Copts, the Chaldeans, and so forth. He gave the example of a Coptic priest who collects funds to help the Egyptian Copts in Germany and in Egypt too. He mentioned that Christians had trouble in refugee houses. There was fear of mobbing, of Muslims surrounding them, so they did not tell that they were Christians. His group tried to get them to other houses so there would not be these problems.

After he spoke positively about the Assyrian Church of the East from Iraq, I requested contacts and he said he would call me later in the day and send me the names of several of the leaders of these groups and their contact information. I thanked him.

The pastor did send me the name, address, and contact phone information of the Assyrian priest whom I called. We spoke in Arabic and agreed to meet the next day at noon.

The Assyrian Church is a very old Christian denomination, originally from northern Iraq. Back home in Detroit we have several Assyrian churches whose people as an ethnic group are known as Chaldeans. They have been leaving Iraq for decades.

Planning and Research in "Rule-Tight" Munich

On Sunday afternoon I took in a city tour of Munich. I had been there before and had seen the tourist sights, but I had forgotten what a wealthy city it was. It was rebuilt rapidly after the war and is the headquarters of major corporations like Siemens and BMW. It has important scientific universities and is the publishing center for Germany. Munich has 1.5 million inhabitants.

I had put off visiting Munich until after Oktoberfest, the famous beer festival that goes from the end of September to the first week in October. Oktoberfest is not a good time for research and everything is more expensive then.

Munich, like the rest of Bavaria, is largely Roman Catholic. On my visit the previous spring I had inadvertently come at a time of the Catholic holiday of Corpus Christi which falls on a Thursday and was an excuse for people to take off that Friday too, so it was a wash for meeting people at Caritas, the Catholic charity.

That spring as I came into Munich, I had a Syrian taxi driver who told me many of the Syrian refugees had left Munich for the north. He had been in Munich for twenty-five years and knew the region and situation well. When I questioned him, he explained that Syrian refugees had come through Munich – it was a major transit route for refugees. But then they had moved on up north to Bremen and so forth. When I asked why, he had said, "It is tighter here." I had asked if he meant the government and he nodded. I assumed he referred to regulations and behavior in general. I would soon learn the extent of this to the detriment of my research.

My first day in Munich that previous spring I had sought to visit a program for refugee women that I had contacted several times by email in advance. I telephoned and was told to call back at different times since the person in charge would be in at noon. She did not arrive at noon. Then I was told she was at meetings all day. After six hours of such waiting and calling, I was finally told I needed to give 14 days' notice before I could visit. Since I had written ahead, I began to wonder about the program itself. So as not to be caught in this predicament in the fall, I had carefully written to the same program on refugee women, well in advance. The response I received was a refusal to be allowed to visit.

Returning to my spring visit, I had discovered on my own, a young refugee center on Marsstrasse near the train station in Munich. As I had looked in the window I could see a young man at a table. I tried the door and it was locked. He motioned me to another door, which was also locked. He came over and showed me how to push a small button. Then a doorman came who let me in.

The Young Refugee Center had only been founded the previous month, in April 2016. It was the first of its kind in Germany for unaccompanied minors. I knew unaccompanied minors were a special concern. In my mind they were the most problematic of the refugees. With no close family to help them mature, and with a background of war experience, violence, and often exploitation, they were the most likely refugees to get into trouble and cause problems. Indeed, in July and again in October 2016 Afghan unaccompanied minors had been responsible for two incidents of violence against Germans.[1] It appears the incident in Kandel in December 2017 was also by an Afghan unaccompanied minor (see endnote 5).

The people downstairs explained to me that when the unaccompanied minors came from the train station, from other parts of Germany, or even Austria, they would come to this center. Doctors make sure they are under eighteen years of age and also check their medical condition. This includes both males and females. Sometimes people have to guess their own ages. They stay at the center for three to five days. Then they are sent to other places in Germany. There may be two other centers like this in Germany, but this was the first. It looked very fine to me, like a new building or at least one that had been newly renovated.

They gave me the names of two directors. So before I came in the fall, I contacted both directors, asking if I could visit and talk to them about the center and how it was progressing. My request was refused. I asked if I could talk with them without visiting. This was also refused. When I discussed this with Germans, they said they were probably afraid of negative publicity. But to refuse to talk with an academic who was writing on positive programs is just the opposite. I was not met with this kind of reception anywhere else in Germany.

Caritas for Refugees

The next day, a Monday, I walked to the address I had from the hotel staff and the website of the Caritas group that works with refugees. Only there was no Caritas there. Instead I found a café out back. But where was Caritas? I asked the café owners. Caritas had moved two years ago and not updated their website. But where did they go? No one knew.

Thank goodness I had phone numbers from my research the previous spring. I called and talked with a woman on the phone. At last she gave me the address of the place for Caritas for refugees – a long distance from the *Bahnhof*. This was not as convenient for refugees as the former location. I would need to take a taxi.

On the second floor was the Caritas office for refugees. When I explained my interest I was directed to a young man who could talk with me. He turned out to be of Persian background, but born in Germany. I asked the young man about the Caritas program that he was a part of. He explained that Caritas Alveni, "alveni" is Latin for "just arrived," is social work for refugees. The program was about fifteen years old, and had started with one camp or accommodation. Now it serves fifteen to twenty camps around Munich.

He told me that in Munich there are good camps with their own kitchens and doors that close. But in the surrounding territory, there are also *Traglufthalle* with as many as 300 people in them. In these the walls do not go to the ceiling. There are six people to a room. There is no privacy. It includes families and single men from all countries.

Traglufthalle, "air halls," are like small airplane hangars. They can be constructed rapidly and are not meant to be permanent. He explained that they had worked to close these sorts of accommodations. It was not good for people to live there. After one year, they would close all fifteen of these. What happened was that, at first, they had housed refugees in sports gymnasiums of schools. But then the schools wanted their sports gymnasiums back. So they went to the *Traglufthalle*.

Caritas Alveni supports most of the refugees in Munich. There are 10,000 to 15,000 refugees here. When I asked why so many, I was told that refugees had come to Munich first. It is near the border, near Austria and Italy.

Caritas Alveni has 150 workers supporting this work. They are paid for by the city of Munich and by Caritas. I asked about the background of the 150 Caritas workers. The young man said they had mixed backgrounds. Most had studied orientalism, and had backgrounds in cultural or ethnological studies. Some had pedagogical and social work backgrounds, a mixture of everything.

He said that for every 100 refugees, there must be one social worker. At each accommodation, there were three assistants from Caritas Alveni to help the social worker and the refugees.

Also they had former migrants who know Arabic and Urdu to help so they do not need translators. This troubled me, for translators are very important for working with documents and for cultural issues. I wondered how many of the 150 workers really knew Arabic. To speak it is different from working with documents.

He said they had people with backgrounds in early childhood education to work with the children – one for every thirty children.

I asked about getting a positive *Bescheid* for asylum. He explained how some get it in two months, and some in two years. He said the Syrians got it the fastest, Yezidis, Christians, and Kurds as well. But the Afghans did not fare as well. Still, he explained that it was not always so good to get the positive *Bescheid* fast. Because then you had to move out of the camp and find other housing. That was not easy. If you cannot find alternative housing, then you go to another camp, or to where Germans put their homeless. These accommodations were not so good because some of the others living there are drug addicts or alcoholics. He said they could ask for a six-month extension, or ask for a social appointment due to the shortage of apartments.

I asked him what was hardest for the refugees. He said, "Their illusions. They have heard that they will be given an apartment, money, and a car. They come here and find out it is not true." I ask them, "Where is my car?" Then they see the truth. "Where is my apartment?" I was getting to like this young man. He said that the first week is the hardest. They realize they have nothing here.

I thanked the young man. We went out of his office to the main room. There was a young Syrian standing there awkwardly. But no one in their whole office knew Arabic – remember, no translators. Then they realized that I knew Arabic, so they asked for my help.

The young Syrian man had gotten a negative reply to his request for asylum. There were no reasons given. He had contacted a lawyer, but wondered if he needed to contact another one. He was deeply upset. He was only twenty years old and had no family with him. As he stood there I could see he was quaking with worry and fear. I tried to reassure him. "Have patience. You have done what is right in seeking an attorney." My words were not reaching him. So without thinking I just reached out and hugged him. It calmed him. The others were surprised.

I asked in German, "Why was he turned down? He is from Syria." The main people in the office said, "They are just playing with him." "Playing?" I said, horrified. Another Caritas person then went over to try to work with him with more seriousness. I hope he gets real help. He looked over at me with a smile. Maybe the hug had helped.

Then I asked for brochures on Caritas Alveni. I also asked the young man I had been talking with if I could visit a refugee accommodation, any one that they suggested. He said he would ask the higher-ups. He came back and said unfortunately no. What were they afraid of? I had visited refugee accommodations in all other cities and towns in Germany, but apparently this was not to be allowed in Munich. I then asked if I could speak with a volunteer at one of the camps. He would call me back on this. I never received this call.

It was getting near noon, and I had an appointment with the Assyrian priest. I needed to call him to get the address where he worked. I got through and the people where he worked said they would call me back. Good. I asked if they could call a taxi. This they did and I thanked them.

I went downstairs and waited for the taxi driver. He turned out to be an Uzbek who had been here for eighteen years. We talked about Munich and its people in Turkish. I asked him where it was better for foreigners in Germany. He said, "Not in Munich. Here people are isolated and nationalistic. It is better in the west and north." "How about Köln [Cologne]?" I asked. "Yes, that is better, more integrated to the rest of Europe. Hamburg is good too."

Victory over Bavarian Bureaucracy in Visit to the Oldest Refugee Camp

While I was still in the taxi, my phone rang and I got the address of where the priest worked, but it was a strange street address. I gave it to the taxi driver. What I did not understand was that the address was not a house but a major city refugee camp with gated security.

The Turkish-speaking Uzbek taxi driver got me to the security gate. This in itself was not easy. He called the phone number I had and the people inside the camp answered. So the man at the security gate let us through, and the taxi entered the road into the camp grounds.

A woman came out and we talked some. Then an older man came. I said I wanted to talk with *Abouna*, the Arabic polite form of address for a priest meaning "our father." They would look for him. When I started to speak in Arabic, things got better.

Suddenly a handsome man in a white shirt came up. It was Abouna Markus Zaia. He said he had just come from the doctor. Together we went into the large five-story building. Immediately to the right I saw a large poster with the words *"Die Johanniter"* written on it. I figured that must be the St John Society that the pastor had referred to in church the day before. I signed in with my name and time of arrival, and was given a red ID lanyard.

Several men came up to Abouna. Clearly he had many roles in the camp. To the left was the cafeteria. He explained to me that the building we were in was for single men only. It was five stories high. The adjoining building was two stories high, and was for families and had some single men too.

I asked how many refugees there were in the complex. He said 800. Later, on the way out, he explained that the complex could hold 1,200 people, but they had 800 there now. I asked where they came from. He said from all over: Syria, Iraq, Afghanistan, Pakistan, Eritrea, Ethiopia, Nigeria, Morocco, Iran, and Azerbaijan.

We walked down the long corridor. Reaching one door he opened it. It was a German class with all male students. I looked in and wished them "good learning" in German. The teacher thanked me.

We went further down the corridor into a main office. There we had the misfortune to meet a tall older German man. He was a manager of sorts. He said I had to have permission from the city to come there. He said people from all over wanted to visit. I said that I was not a journalist; I was a professor and academics did research in different ways. This was the eighth German town I had visited for this research. He was not impressed. I said I did not want a tour. I just wanted to talk with Abouna, that was all.

We melted away from him and into a room where there was no one. We quickly closed the door. I said I thought Bavaria had more rules than other German states, and people seemed inordinately bound by them. What was the stereotype – "Austrians trying to be Prussians?"

I asked if I could call him "Abouna." He nodded. I said I had worked in a village in Lebanon with a Maronite priest, Abouna Boulos. He said, "They, the Maronites, are connected to Rome. We are not." He is of the Assyrian Church that is affiliated with the Assyrian Church in Chicago.

I asked him how long he had been there. "One year," he answered. But by this he meant he had worked at the *Unterkunft*, the refugee lodging, for one year. Earlier he spent six years in Rome where he had completed his MA. Then he was asked to come to Munich. He had come as a refugee from Mosul in 2006. He has his whole family here except two sisters who are married and moved north of Mosul in Iraq.

He emphasized, "All that we had has been destroyed – our whole neighborhood by DAISH, that is ISIS. All the people were forced to leave, they have nothing, all 5,000 left." They went to Kurdistan and some went to Turkey where they have stayed. Others went to Lebanon and remained there. Some went to Jordan where some have stayed. And some have gone on to America or Australia or Canada. For there is no work, no houses, no church, and no security where they used to live.

There are some refugees who traveled from Turkey to Greece and then further up north to Europe. He thinks 50,000 passed that way, Christians and Yezidis. I told him I had worked in the camps on the Balkan Trail and did not see many Christians. He said that they did not want to call attention to themselves as Christians. He said the Christians of north Iraq and the Yezidis in Mount Sinjar left everything to DAISH. But many were still waiting to come to Germany in camps in Greece or along the Balkan Way in Bulgaria, Serbia, Macedonia, and Croatia.

I asked about who got the positive *Bescheid* to stay in Germany. He said the Yezidis did, but not 100 per cent. If they had asked in EU countries earlier, they could be returned to those countries according to the Dublin Accords. All the Christians were granted permission to stay.

They needed to get housing. But people do not want to rent to those who do not have work. Then they get permission to stay in the camp for about six more months. He explained that it was hard to get work. You need the language and it takes two to three years to learn German. So people stay in the camp. Sometimes you end up in a pension, like a hotel with two rooms.

Abouna then said that this was the first camp in Munich. It is also the biggest camp in Munich. People were able to take language classes here from the first day. There are language classes for men, classes for women, and classes for children. They even have classes every day to help children with their homework when they come back from school. I said this was a good idea since the parents mostly could not help them.

Then I asked my general question. What do you think is the hardest thing for the refugees here? Abouna said, "First the language. Then it is integration into German culture." I asked for an example of what he meant by the second point. He said, "For example the Afghans come from a culture where alcohol is forbidden. Then they come here and alcohol is all over. Or," and he pointed to his watch, "there is punctuality. That does not matter so much in Afghanistan. Here it does."

I asked what integration meant. "It is to learn the culture of the new country," he answered. Then he noted that there was *unsuri*, that is, racist nationalism, in the north and especially in the east of Germany. "Not so much in Bavaria," he said.

I asked him about members of the Assyrian Christian Church whom he serves. He told me he serves families in four cities in Germany and four cities in Austria, some of whom have been here for thirty to fifty years.

I asked about the role of Die Johanniter, the Society of St John, in the *Unterkunft*, the refugee barracks or lodging. He said it was for security. He felt that it made a difference, especially for Christians, and all knew of it including the Muslims. But it should be added that Middle Easterners have respect for clerics of all religions, which is why Abouna was respected by Christians and Muslims alike.

Abouna said that to talk about religion was forbidden in the *Unterkunft*. "You would be expelled from the lodging if you talk about religion. There was one who was talking about fundamentalism (Muslim). He was expelled from the camp."

I asked if the refugees were part of the executive board. He said that two of them helped the administration.

I asked about the volunteers. Abouna said they help with security, with language training, and with connections or networking. I understood they also take people for doctor's appointments. "How do you get *Ehrenamtliche* here?" He said they come from Christian Life, from the nearby Catholic Church and from the Lutheran Church. He added that when he first came, he taught German for eight months.

I thanked him for his knowledge. As we walked out, an older refugee man came too. He must have been waiting for us. As we walked down the steps, Abouna pointed out how the refugees had improved the appearance of the front of the building by planting flowers in big pots. They sit out here for peace. As we walked to the security, I asked him where other Assyrian priests in Europe were. He explained that there are three others in Germany, one in Denmark, two in England, and an archbishop in Sweden. Again I thanked him.

As I went into the hotel, I could tell it was getting colder. Later in the day I should go buy a coat. Somehow I had lost my leather jacket on a recent train trip.

From Coat Buying to Police Barriers and Pegida

Later in the afternoon I set out to a well-known department store to buy a warm coat. When I came to a square known as Karlsplatz, I saw police setting up barriers. Why should they be doing this on a late Monday afternoon? Then I saw the Pegida flags – the anti-Islam organization founded in Dresden. I heard the demonstration would begin at seven o'clock that evening. I needed to find and buy a coat, and come back in time to see how the demonstration would pan out.

I found a store and bought the coat. By the time I came back to the square again, the crowd had grown somewhat bigger around the barriers and the Pegida flags. I found a restaurant across from the demonstration site for dinner so I would not miss anything.

But before I went into the restaurant, I talked to a young policeman and asked him about the demonstration. He said it was a lot of money for not much. I asked if it were every Monday. He said it was, but it was not always in the same place. He added that it cost the city a lot in police pay. I asked if he got overtime pay for this duty. "Only if it is on the weekends," he said with a smile. By this time, inside the barriers I could see some chairs. There were about seven people, mostly older men, sitting there. Not an impressive demonstration as of yet.

I watched the demonstration site from upstairs in the restaurant. By the time I finished dinner there was a big crowd all around the barriers. First there was classical music and scenes projected on a screen above. Then a man read a speech about what they believed about Islam in Europe. He spoke into a microphone. By now those inside the metal barriers – you could see through the barriers – were about thirty seated and ten standing with flags and posters. Those seated were mostly older while those standing were mostly younger, both men and women, although many more men. They clapped when the man finished. Then an older woman from Munich spoke. Her speech was rigid, racist, and ethnocentric. I left part way through it. I do not know how long it went on after I left.

There were easily eight times as many people outside as inside the barriers. I do not know if they were all against Pegida but they did not clap for the speakers. There was a man in clown costume who blew bubbles. There were some with posters against the Pegida positions. There was a man with a poster – "Welcome Refugees." There was a young man who yelled at the Pegida people periodically.

The City Center

The next day was a rainy day as I headed to the city center. I talked with the taxi driver, a Dari speaker from Afghanistan, about the Pegida demonstration of the previous evening. Yes, every Monday there is a Pegida rally in Munich against Islam. He said it was unfortunate but there was nothing they could do. I said that I did not think it was about religion. He agreed. "It is all about politics," he said. I asked if it was due to people from East Germany. "No," he said. "It is people from here too."

Then I asked him about other parts of Germany. "The north is better – Hamburg, Cologne, Frankfurt," he said. I thought again, I need to go and see this for myself.

He dropped me off by the city center. I could easily walk to the new *Rathaus*. Just walk ahead and then turn left, I was told. When I went out to the square, there was a fifteenth century building. It turned out to be the new *Rathaus*, neo-Gothic and baroque. It was truly an impressive building with huge stairways. It turned out the office on refugees was in another building and their meetings were in the morning of that day, which I had missed. Although I am not sure they would have let me attend.

As I walked down the staircase I noticed a memorial to the 1,000 Jews of Munich who were deported in 1941, including ninety-four children. After five days they were all killed. It was on the wall of the *Rathaus* when you come inside the first steps, but I had not noticed it until I was leaving.

I mention this especially because Munich is the only city that refused the *Stolpersteine*, "stumbling stones" – the bronze plaques with names and dates of birth, arrest, particular concentration camp, and death – that are found on the sidewalk in front of places where Jews had lived in towns and cities all over Germany. I find these most moving. The Jews of Munich reportedly said they did not want people stepping on their names.

Then I went back out of the square to the bookstore I had seen when I first walked by. I asked for books on refugees. The young woman working in the store brought over twelve books for me to look through. On a rainy day I found this better than visiting a museum.

I returned to the hotel. Nothing in Munich held me. I would follow the advice of the many taxi drivers and go north.

I took the train to Stuttgart and from there through central Germany north to Cologne.

Cologne: Toleration and Organization Spread across the Rhine

Arriving in Cologne from Munich I could not help but compare the cities. Munich is the third largest city in Germany after Berlin and Hamburg, whereas Cologne is the fourth largest city with 1.24 million people. However the television stations in Cologne were significantly more cosmopolitan than those in Munich, and this was from comparable hotels. The television programs in Munich were almost exclusively in German, with foreign programs dubbed in German. In contrast in Cologne there were several channels in English, several in Russian, and in other languages including Spanish, as well as many in German.

On the web in Cologne I found many addresses of help groups for refugees, many more than I had found in Munich. In fact I barely found anything like this in Munich and I had looked. It was significantly more organized for refugees. As for Caritas, the number of agencies within the Caritas office in Cologne was impressive.

However, much of that first night in Cologne, I kept getting up to hear how the final debate was going with US presidential contenders Hillary and Trump. I was worried.

The "Refugee Coordinator"

It was still raining on my first full day in Cologne as I walked to the *Rathaus*. I went in and people were helpful. A woman came over. Yes, there is a man who works on refugees here. She called him. Then she took me to see him in another building.

On the way in the rain, she said she was a refugee herself. She said her family was from a region taken by Poland – it must have been East Prussia. She explained that they had come to the West. "Was it hard?" I asked. She nodded but was not sentimental about it. I told her about my friend Erika who is from the Sudetenland. "Yes," she said, "My husband is from there too." So she understood about refugees herself. I think this is true for so many in Germany. People are quiet about it, but many have personal experience.

She took me up to the third floor of a building that she used to work in. We went to a room in the far back. I would not have found the room myself. There the coordinator for refugees worked. I thanked her.

The coordinator sat at a desk with a large map of Cologne to his back. He said he was new in the job. He began by saying that in the past, they had not done enough. They had relatively smaller groups of people, like Turks and then Russians, and they were not seen as a problem.

Bells were already going off in my head. The location of this man's office was most inconvenient. He was new at his job. I knew that Cologne had large numbers of Turks and Russians.

The coordinator continued that now in Cologne alone, they had 13,500 refugees who came basically all at once. These were new refugees. They did not want to have ghettos forming. They knew that not all would qualify for asylum. However they would give them help and treat all with humanity. "We must integrate them into our society. We have only begun to think about that in the last 15 to 20 years," he said. "Those focusing on this are in the Office of the Oberbürgermeister and the Sozialamt that coordinate activities and government policies to epitomize integration."

We got into a discussion of integration. He said this was a major concern in Germany. I said the Turks were concerned as well. He said, "A problem here is the difference with men and women. German men and women are equal while in Turkish culture this is not so." This statement of gender inequality regarding the Turks always signaled "end of discussion." I knew he would not want me to talk about private and public culture among Turks or whether German men and women were equal.

So I said, "Let us go back to Germany and integration." He said, "We are only beginning to integrate 13,500 refugees. And we have the *Ehrenamtliche* to help in this with welcome groups." Then he explained how they were sent to help them, especially with language teaching. These included language courses, and conversation groups to try to make the large groups smaller and also to help integrate them to work. He added that there were problems when the refugees stayed a long time in the camps all together. They could get aggressive, and there were different nationalities.

I asked if he thought the society was still mostly positive toward the refugees. He said that he thought it was mostly positive. But there were some attitudes, such as that they were criminal, that did not help. They were not necessarily true – here it was more the North Africans – but it was spread out to all the refugees and it did not help.

I thanked him, but I did not ask him my usual question as he was very new to his job and I felt some distance. I went downstairs. Then I called Caritas and got the name and address of the person who works with refugees.

A Journalist Who Tutors and the New Year's Problems

I walked quickly in the rain back to the *Hohe Strasse*, the main shopping street and to the café where I had stopped the previous afternoon. I got a sandwich, tea, and a piece of apple pie, and sat down near the window. I ate and thought.

Near me, next to the window was a young middle aged-woman reading a pamphlet with *Gott* in the title. Most of the people in the café were older.

I ate my food. I looked over again at the youngish woman and asked her if she was from Cologne? She answered that she used to be, but now she lived in Krefeld between Düsseldorf and Cologne. I told her I asked because I was here to learn about how refugees are doing in Cologne. She explained that she worked with refugees in her children's high school. Immediately I was interested. I asked her what she did. She said that she helped refugee students with German. The school put out a request for help. She worked professionally as a journalist, the weekend through Wednesday. Her name is Sandra Schuffelen. She could only help at the high school on Thursday and Friday, she said.

She explained that the refugees are thirteen to sixteen years old. "What an important age," I noted. "It helps the teacher to have someone else working with the refugees even for a few days," she said. I asked if the teacher were good. "Very good," she said. She explained that the teacher did not have special training for this, but she was very good. "She cares, and she has authority. She knows how to teach." I said that was very important. Later she said the young people could tell if the teacher cared or not. One boy in another class said he would not do the homework because the teacher did not care about them. "No," she said. "The teacher is a tool whom you have to work with to get where you need to go."

I said with a new language, the teacher is even more important. The teacher becomes the language and the culture. She mentioned that there was a boy from Syria, an unaccompanied minor. His mother and sisters are in Turkey. She wished she could have them come to be with him now.

I explained what I was doing in Germany, how a publisher in London wanted me to write a book on the new refugees. But I had said I would write on the response of Europeans to the refugees, and mostly on the response of Germans because they are doing the most for them. And so I was going from small towns to middle-sized towns to big cities, learning what people were doing with refugees in Germany. I was just in Munich where I had even gone to a Pegida rally. She said that she would be afraid to do that. "No," I said, "you wouldn't. There were not that many people supporting Pegida. They have gatherings every Monday. There were maybe only forty people inside the police barrier."

She asked about our election in the United States. "How can people support Trump? How can so many people vote for him?" I said the primaries were different. But she said the polls say it is close. I said my brother who works for NPR (National Public Radio) does not trust the polls. But Hillary was highly favored then. This was before Comey, head of the FBI, came out with the emails against Hillary just before the election.

I asked her about the New Years' events in Cologne.[2] "Did they ever find out who caused the problems?" I asked. "Was it by the *Bahnhof*, the train station?" "No, by the *Dom*," and she pointed toward the cathedral. "It is the main landmark in Cologne." She explained further:

The problem was there were hardly any police there that night. No one expected any problems. So when there were problems of sexual assault, the only news that came – I was working that night – were a few reports of sexual problems, but nothing systematic. People could only help each other. It did not come out until a few days later. That was really the problem, the time lag and the lack of police that night. If there had been enough police, there would not have been the problem. We are a tolerant town.

So they do not know who the men were. They were probably a mixture of people. Some North Africans, but some Germans too. There was some talk on Facebook of telling men to come here to do this. But no one knows for sure. In any case, it was convenient to blame it on the refugees. And the attitude has changed so much here from before with regard to the refugees.

I asked her what she saw as hardest for the refugees she worked with here. She answered, "To be far from their families. So they try to make up for this with relationships with other refugee students. It is not always good for language. They need family."

"The program is a two-year program. It is funded by Evonik, a major chemical company." It impressed me that a company was supporting a special educational program to help educate refugees. "We have eighteen students, many from different countries. The program lasts for two years. The teacher is from Cologne. The students are mostly from Syria, Iraq, and Afghanistan, but also Nigeria, Poland, and Romania. They know each other from the camp. At first this was a problem and they even fought at first."

I thanked her. I said she was doing the most important work. I also told her about the mentoring program I had researched in Hamburg the previous spring. I think close teaching and mentoring of refugee students is crucial for their success in Germany. But I know even more the importance of such close teaching and mentoring from my work in bilingual programs in America during the Lebanese Civil War. Students came from similar situations of war, trauma, and family disarray. When one teacher or one teaching aide or mentor spent time with students, it often made the difference whether students would stay in high school or drop out. As the mayor in Schwäbisch Gmünd had said, confidence was crucial. So was timing of this intervention.

Caritas

As I crossed the Rhine River for the first time, I felt strangely at home. True, I like rivers and had grown up on an island in one, but this felt especially right. My mother's father's family had been Rhinelanders.

When I arrived at the Caritas Center, I asked the taxi driver for his card just in case. On the second floor I was fortunate to find Tim Westerholt, the Management Head for Technical Service for Integration and Migration. I asked him to tell me about his work.

Herr Westerholt explained that he only worked with refugees after they received a positive *Bescheid*. But each year, the positive "decision or notification" had different ramifications. In previous years it had meant a three-year residency permission. This year however it granted only a one-year residency permission. That is, the refugees must keep proving they are still in danger in their home country.

He explained that there are fewer refugees coming. Now they must wait at least one year to have permission to bring their family. Last year they were allowed to move anywhere in Germany after they got a positive *Bescheid*. Now they must stay in the city where they have been. And now all need to go to a lawyer. So the situation has changed in Germany since the summer of 2015 when there was what was known as "the welcome summer."

I asked if it was the New Year's incident here in Cologne that changed it. "No," he said, "there were always people who doubted and did not want them. But their voices did not come out until then. Only after that, people could say, 'You see.' From those reports, their voices came out. Still though we have the *Ehrenamtliche*, the volunteers."

Then he referred to a brochure on "Service for Integration and Migration." He explained that they sent people to integration courses. These are mostly language courses at the different levels. He noted that at Caritas they even went with people to the courses to make sure they were right for them. These also included how to get oriented to German ways. He said this was like shaking hands, when to do so with women, and cultural orientation. He said they also helped with transfer of school degrees. They called lawyers for them and helped them work with the lawyers on residency in Germany.

Finally, the young Caritas manager noted that they worked with refugees on how to "become German." For migrants as precedent, say from Italy, it takes three years, then they need a certificate of fluency in German, and they have to be working. They all have difficulties, and they are all somewhat different.

Then I asked him my basic question. What do you think is most difficult for the refugees now? He said, "The times of waiting and waiting and waiting. They say, 'I'm here for one year and four months. Why do I not have the right to go and work?' And now there are two to three classes of refugees. Those from the Balkans at the bottom, those from Syria are at the top."

I asked about housing. He said, "We are trying to give back the sports halls where the refugees have been living to the schools. Where will they stay?"

"What are the most you have in one complex?" He said, "In Hercule Sense Caserne, with containers in the front, 500–600."

I asked if there were people whom I should meet. He suggested I meet with Cardinal Woelki who had given funds for refugee projects. Then he gave me three other suggestions. He mentioned that he lived nearby in Kalk where there were many Moroccans. He was surprised that they were not supportive of the new refugees. I said we knew this from America. The most recent immigrants do not support newcomers. They are too fragile and insecure themselves. It is sad but true.

I thanked him for his time and went downstairs where I asked the older receptionist to call the previous taxi service. The driver who came was different. He was a tall and solid Turk. We started speaking Turkish very soon. He had been in Germany for many years.

I told him I was studying the relation of Germans with the new refugees. Our talk moved to the relation of Germans and Turks. He said, "They do not like us."

I asked if there was an area in Cologne where Turks lived. He said he had bought a home where just Germans lived for himself and his family. He would say hello. People did not greet him back. He made a garden and gave his German neighbors food from his garden. He also gave them some *börek*, a thin yufka-dough pastry with cheese and sometimes vegetables in the middle. "Why do you give us this?" they asked. "We Turks are this way," he had answered.

The neighbors were a man and a woman and when they got older, one had to go to the hospital. When the other went to the hospital, they gave the key to their flat to the Turkish family. "Why do you give it to us? There are German neighbors." But they trusted the Turkish family more.

"What a wonderful result," I said. "You were so patient and so kind!" He said, "There are good Germans too. It takes time." I told him that my husband says it takes Germans three days to decide if a stranger is worth speaking to. He said, "more like three years." We laughed. But it was a good result. If only more Turks and Germans could come in contact in good ways. I worry about separation. Then the stereotypes can continue.

He asked for my card. He said he wanted to see my books. I thanked him. He opened the door for me. I shook his hand. Such a fine man. Germany is fortunate to have him.

Caritas Torture Victims Center

The next day I got up, dressed, had breakfast, and headed by taxi to the Torture Victims Center in Cologne. I had an interesting taxi drive. The taxi driver was a Turkmen who, when I asked him if he was from Cologne, said he had been here for twenty-seven years. And before that? "Berlin," he said, "for two years. And you will ask before that," he said –

"where am I from? Iran. But before that my family was from Turkmenistan." He spoke Persian, Turkish, German, and other languages I am sure. "My children were born here. But when people ask where they are from, they do not know what to say. I told him in America it would be easier. "Yes, but not here."

I told him that I was from the northern part of North America, from Michigan.

We talked comfortably in Turkish. He explained how world religions come from hot regions. That is why they have hell, *cehennem* – the Muslim word for "hell." But if they had started in Siberia, there would be no *cehennem*. In Siberia, people would like that. I agreed. We know what it is to be very cold. "And to be very warm is very fine," he added. "It is not hell. Hell would be good in Siberia where the cold is so horrible. Imagine it being warm, ahhh." We got along so well.

He found the short street where the Victims of Torture Office was located. He said he enjoyed talking with me, and I with him.

I had come early. I greeted the receptionist who was a middle-aged man and told him that I was the professor who had called the day before and who hoped to see brochures. Waiting on chairs were a Kurdish mother and daughter. It looked as if the mother was the one with problems.

The male receptionist took me out to where he had brochures in the hallway. He started to hand them to me. They included such titles in German as: "Overcoming the Problematic Obstacles: Interpreters as Language and Cultural Investigators in Psychotherapy and Counseling," and "Survival of Victims, Giving a Future after War and Torture." There were also brochures in English such as: "Resilience: Developing Ways Out of Adverse circumstances; "Refugee Children in Europe: Good Practice Guidelines; Psycho-social Context, Assessment and Interventions for Traumatized Children and Adolescents;" "Reaching out for a New Future," and "Wounded Soul Brochure for Those Touched by War and Human Rights Violations, Therapy Centre for Victims of Torture." I was impressed with the quantity and quality of the brochures. Clearly this was not a new office.

I had questions, but I wanted to wait until we were back in his front office. We returned there. Then I asked, "How long has this Center for Victims of Torture been operating?" He answered that it had been operating for thirty years. That is, it has been there at that address that long, he seemed to imply.

"Who were the first people who came here as victims of torture?" I asked? "Turks," he said, "from political problems, they were tortured before they came here." That would have been in the 1980s after the coup and perhaps Kurds as well.

He said, "We give psychotherapy for refugees who have suffered torture. We have 100 clients, and we work in sixty languages of the whole world and their contexts. A man cannot be healthy when he still has this. For true social security, he needs this therapy. People must first be stabilized."

I asked about funding. He said, "We are part of Caritas, for fifty years we are linked. But for funding we have mixed sources. We get funding from *der Bund, das Land, und die Stadt* – that is, the country, the state, and the city; and from Caritas, and the EU."

That impressed me. Then I asked how many people worked there. He answered, "About twenty, but not all are full-time. We have therapists." I asked if *Ehrenamtliche* worked there too. "Oh yes," he said. "They help in different ways. Sometimes they take care of the child of a victim of torture during the appointment, or help bring the person here. There are many ways to help. '*Wir schaffen das*.' ("We manage it," echoing Merkel's words.) It is a big *engagement*, that is, involvement."

"As for the population of Cologne itself, about 30–40 per cent of them have migrant backgrounds. But we have engagement." I asked about the mayor. "Henrietta – ?" He could not recall her surname either and he checked on the computer. "Reker" he said. "She was elected in 2015. You know she is *parteilos*, that is, she is independent." I said was not aware of that and asked if it were unusual. "Yes," he said. "It means she is more Green." I asked if she were pro-refugee. "Yes," he said. Then he asked if I knew that she had been attacked. No, I hadn't. I asked who had attacked her, if it was a German. "Yes," he said, "someone against her refugee policy. We also have tendencies against them here too."

It was 10:00 am and there was a young woman waiting for an appointment at that time, I think to do work, not to be counseled. I thanked the receptionist. He had given me much information.

It Would Not Happen Again

On Saturday I bought my train ticket to Hamburg and took a tour of the city of Cologne. It began at the cathedral. I had time to go inside the Cathedral before the tour. I lit a candle. I like this city and its people. Imagine a large city with a woman mayor. The "stumbling stones" to remind people where Jews had lived came first from Cologne too.

Alas, not much survived the war. Much of Cologne is new buildings. Even the layout was redone after the war to accommodate automobiles. I did see a police school on the far side of the Rhine with big posters, encouraging young people to apply. At least one of the young people had Middle Eastern features. The sign at the bottom was *Wir leben Integration*, "We live integration."

I later learned that Cologne was the most politically liberal city in Germany after Berlin. Apparently Cologne has one of the largest gay communities in Germany too, about one million LGBT. Since the Middle Ages, it had the slogan: *Leben und leben lassen*, "Live and let live."

After the tour I went to a large bookstore across from the cathedral that had been recommended to me. I found more good books in German on the refugee question and ended up buying several. When I came out toward the front of the cathedral I could see that there were many police at the train station.

Still when I had walked across to the bookstore, it had felt good and the crowd was ethnically mixed. A taxi driver explained the police presence as common weekend fare. They had learned from the New Years' ordeal. It would not happen again.

Sunday in Cologne

The earliest service at the Antoniterkirche was at ten o'clock in the morning. The church was a former Benedictine monastery that became Protestant in 1820. When I arrived, there were about thirty people spread out in the church. According to the announcement there would be a concert there the coming week with the Gregorian Chorale of Cologne. No doubt the audience would be larger for that. It occurred to me that the religion of Germany was music.

The service was good, and the sermon was based on the lessons. We even passed the peace. I had not seen this at other German churches, although it is quite common in American churches, where you greet people seated around you partway through the service.

But it was the sculptures in the church that gave me pause. There was a low-hanging angel over a war memorial that was powerful. There was a Christ on the far wall. And on the way back from communion I was met by a tall authoritative seated Jesus, face forward, with his palms upturned on his knees. He took my breath away.

Later I found the church had a small store area. They had postcards of the sculptures I had seen in the church. I found out they were by Ernst Barlach, a famous German sculptor who was born in 1870 and who had died in 1938. He had fought in World War I and become anti-war as a result. The Nazis called his work "degenerate art." It is remarkable that the church has three sculptures by Barlach: the hanging angel over memorials for World War I and now World War II, the Christ on the wall as on a cross, and my favorite, *Lehrender Christus* – "Teaching Christ" (1931) – the one of Jesus seated with his hands on his knees palms upward.

AWO: Workers Welfare Federation

I had been hearing about the important work of the AWO throughout Germany. I had made the appointment with the AWO office in Cologne the previous week.

When I arrived in the AWO offices, Frau Blickhäuser, the Head of the Office of Citizenship, was on the telephone, working with a volunteer. She motioned me to sit down. She had some booklets and an article out so she was prepared for me. I sat down at the round table. The office had a good feel to it, with her rounded desk that was welcoming and large enough for many papers, and a sizeable window behind her.

Frau Blickhäuser explained to me that AWO stands for Arbeiterwohlfahrt or Workers Welfare Federation. There were several organizations that supported their work with *Ehrenamtliche*, both city and private. She had been doing this work for eighteen years. She called my attention to a recent article she had published in a journal on "engagement in the time of flight."[3] I was especially pleased that people in the actual field of refugee work were writing and publishing.

Frau Blickhäuser said there were several forms of *Ehrenamtliche*. There are the traditional kind found in churches, political parties like SPD, CDU, in sports and so forth. They include both positive and negative aspects. Then there are those with whom she mostly works. These are the people who are more interested in working for hospice, for AIDS work, or other societal work. It is her job to consult with them and advise them in this.

I asked her, "Who supports your work here?" She explained, "The city and the community. There are fifteen centers for this in Cologne. So people work with children, in hospice, in schools, in kindergartens. I find what they need and match them."

I asked her, "Where does the term, *Ehrenamt* come from?" I had been wondering about this for a long time. For some reason I was sure she would know. She did not disappoint. She told me that it was a traditional term. "It is almost 100 years old. It comes from Marie Juchacz, the founder of AWO Arbeitwolhfahrt. The etymology includes the word *Ehre* or "honor" or "honorary," implying "unsalaried,"and *Amt* or "office or charge," implying regular work to which one commits.

We talked about other organizations in the city that do similar work. There are also ethnic ones. All can get some funding from the city if they follow the rules, have worthy purposes, and do some good. They were listed in an AWO pamphlet that she showed me. Some were Russian – you could tell by the contact names. They were seeking *Ehrenamtliche* to teach German and to help in different ways. I asked Frau Blickhäuser about the *Russlanddeutsche*. Yes, they still speak Russian. It is a problem. The young ones learn German, but Russian is still their main language.

I asked about refugee accommodation. She said they were various in size, from only ten people to up to 1,000 in Diakonie, a particular Protestant-supported accommodation which I visited. They were spread out across the city. They are not centralized which is good. There was a map that showed that all the districts except two had refugees, while two districts had more than the rest.

I asked if finding rental units was a problem in Cologne. Yes, for everyone it was. There is a shortage. She added, "Not just rental units, also schools, and kindergarten places. Try to find 3,500 to 4,000 kindergarten places all at once!"

There were welcome initiatives in all areas of the city. She explained that there were forty-five to fifty people working in these, all *Ehrenamtliche*!

I asked what the welcome initiatives did. She said they would greet refugees when they first came, teach them German, help them find a school, and help them when they had problems. That struck me as extensive. Then there were structures for special advice for refugees. These included an anti-discrimination bureau, therapy for victims of torture like the one I had visited, a disability center, a place for unaccompanied minors, and one for LGBT.

Without me even asking, Frau Blickhäuser spontaneously said to me:

The biggest problem for the refugees are their false hopes of what life will be like here, impossible dreams that they bring with them. However we have unemployment here. And we have no work for men without education or training. It can lead to trauma when men sit on a bed, with 100 other men, and they have nothing to do. It can lead to depression, and aggression in young men or even hooliganism.

Islam is also a problem for us. In the last five years it has gotten worse in the Turkish community, the Salafism. Those with Erdoğan. It did not used to be this way. There is DiTiP (DiTiP stands for Diyanet İşleri Türk-İslam Birliği which funds Sunni Turkish mosques in Germany and is controlled by the Turkish government in Ankara.) In a sense we have a movement to the right among migrants. But it is a politicization of religion.

We discussed integration here; I said I had heard from Turks that they felt they were not integrated, even when they spoke German well.

Frau Blickhäuser had a strong position on this. She said, "Why do they think they do not have to struggle? Germans with minority spouses have to struggle too." She gave the example of an Iranian man married to a German woman. Reportedly, he does not feel respected by Germans, that integration is something within. But Frau Blickhäuser said that they need to understand German culture, its structures and ways. "For us integration is not inner. And many of us have to struggle. Why shouldn't they too?" She added, "It is patriarchy that keeps us down. And they are part of it too. They too have work to do."

I thought this was a valid point. It took a woman to make it. Women struggled in every culture I knew including my own. Men often did not realize this.

Then she stood back. "In the 1960s and 1970s, we made mistakes. We did not think the Turks would stay. Neither did they. We did not give them German classes. Their children were supposed to go to school. I know, my father was a teacher or principal then. But it did not go so well. Only now it is a different story. Now they are in society and need to participate more."

Continuing on work with *Ehrenamtliche*, Frau Blickhäuser spoke on the *Integrationszentrum*. This is the six-month course that refugees all take after they get their positive *Bescheid*. People ask why only then? Because there is a shortage of teachers. A major part of the *Ehrenamtliche* program is education and mentoring. In Cologne they have 600 people working in this aspect. It often involves visiting a child in a school to help him or her. It is one-on-one. They also have this for adult education. Here there are thirty volunteers working in this.

There is a newspaper in Arabic that includes events and announcements online, including concerts. Some volunteers help here. Yet another area for volunteer help is conversational German and speaking courses. These are after the regular integration language courses. There are courses at the university, courses for women, on the hotline, and for those who have been traumatized. In the area of recreation, there is of course football, and other sports in the refugee accommodation too. To help integrate into the labor force, there are volunteers who help with apprentice programs and others who help going over opportunities to see what is available for work.

I asked again about the funding of her work in matching volunteers to the many needs. She said that 50 per cent of it was funded by the city of Cologne. She also got funding from the foundation of the Cologne City Guide – we are helping.

But that is for the work of the *Ehrenamtliche* in general. For the work for the refugees, 90 per cent of cost comes from the federal government.

She mentioned that she had applied and been approved for a grant of $ 6,000 from Ford International for intercultural classes for reading mentors for twenty classes. I congratualated her on this.

I thanked her for her time and all she had told me. But what made me happiest was hearing about and seeing the *Ehrenamtliche* wherever I went in Germany. She was pleased. Before I left I asked for some handouts, including one she had co-authored on engaging *Ehrenamtliche*.[4] Truly working well with volunteers is a major skill and something all of us need to cultivate. Cologne was fortunate to have someone of her organizational skills and experience.

In Cologne, the number of organizations and quality of people working in them for the new refugees impressed me. The city itself was positive despite the New Year's incident. I could see why refugees and migrants would want to live in this most cosmopolitan city on the Rhine. It had a mayor who was pro-refugee and, for a city this size, it offered much more in institutional strength and had a great ability to build on the toleration of its people, which also expressed itself in volunteer work at multiple levels in many practical ways.

Hamburg: The Northern City of Visionary Programs

Like Cologne, Hamburg is a river city, but on the Elbe River. Due to its closeness to the North Sea, it is also a major sea-going port. Ships from all over the world come to its massive harbor for transfer of cargo and for dry-dock maintenance. It is the second largest port in all Europe. It is also the second largest city in Germany with 1.8 million inhabitants. Hamburg is its own city-state. With its financial, media, and commercial wealth, it has the ability to chart its own way.

The Weichenstellung *Program for Refugees Students*
I had gone to Hamburg the previous spring because of a specific mentoring program I had first heard about through the German Marshall Program in Washington, DC. I had been on an expert panel on refugees on Capitol Hill with Dr Ivan Vejvoda, vice president of the German Marshall Fund. He had mentioned this mentoring program to me that was being implemented in the Hamburg schools by the Zeit Foundation, a major German foundation.

The mentoring program was called *"Weichenstellung."* On German railroads, the *"Weichenstellung"* is what directs the trains to the correct tracks, a sort of "strategic course setting" – a good image for mentoring. When I had asked, Dr Vejvoda even gave me a flier on the program. I was immediately intrigued. Education for refugee children is crucial and anything that can help educational transition is doubly important. I read all I could about the program. Before I went to Germany that spring, I explicitly requested an appointment at the Zeit Foundation in Hamburg to learn more about the program.

When I first visited Hamburg in May 2016, I arrived early for my appointment at the Zeit Foundation, located in a handsome neighborhood in what must have been a wealthy home. Dr Tatiana Matthiesen was most gracious and kind in explaining the program and answering my questions. She even explained that her father was Spanish and her mother German. She had truly succeeded in the German system herself.

The *Weichenstellung* program had originally been designed for students in German schools who showed promise but whose families for whatever reason could not support them strongly. It was a program to help students reach their potential. The idea was to provide mentors for these students for a period of three years around the critical period just before students are divided into academic or non-academic trajectories around age ten. A third of the students turned out to be migrant students. Dr Matthiesen said the program was deemed successful. It has since been applied in the south in Baden Württemberg and in another state in Germany.

The program began in 2013, before the main refugee surge. Someone then realized that the program could be adapted for refugee children who were spending their first year in a preparatory class to learn the language. For refugee children, it was changed to a two-year program. The mentors were university students who themselves wanted to be high school teachers. They were paid 15 euros an hour and would mentor groups of three to four refugee students for four hours a week. Once a month there would be a cultural event to help the refugee students learn about the city. This is the program that Dr Ivan Vejvoda had told me about.

I asked if the mentors got together to talk about their experiences. Yes, each month they did this to discuss problems with each other under supervision. Each mentor had a supervisor.

They had conducted a pilot program at a local school in Hamburg with new refugees. They had 135 mentors and 450 students. The teachers asked that instead of just taking students with promise, they take both strong students and those with difficulty in learning. Their goal was to get them into the ordinary system.

Dr Matthiesen then showed me a short video on the program. It featured a mentor and his mentees and was most impressive. You could see how much the refugee teenage students looked up to the mentor. I asked if I could talk with several mentors. Dr Matthiesen said she would contact them and see if they were willing. I was very pleased with this. I thanked Dr Matthiesen for her time and commended the creativity of the Zeit Foundation.

Figure 6.1 Sanim and Maryam, *Weichenstellung* mentors of refugee students, with refugee backgrounds themselves, Hamburg, Germany, 2016.

Mentors of Weichenstellung: *Two Future Teachers of Caliber*
The next day I was most fortunate to meet with two university students who also worked as mentors in the *Weichenstellung* program. Both were from migrant backgrounds, had been born outside Germany, and had come to Germany as refugees themselves.

We met in a coffee house in downtown Hamburg. I thanked them for meeting with me and asked them to tell me about themselves.

Samim, a dark-haired young man with an infectious smile, said he had come to Germany from Kabul with his family when he was eight years old. His father was a doctor, and his mother a teacher, but neither could practice in Germany. They had lived in a camp when they first came to Germany. There had been no special programs in 1998 when Samim came. He just went to a German school and did not understand the teacher or the school. He said it had been hard. And yet he had succeeded. He already has his BA in biology and Spanish and is working on his Masters degree. He plans to be high school teacher, which in Germany has much status. He said he already has requests to have him teach. Schools need teachers who can work with refugee children and now he has worked in this program.

Maryam, who is also dark-haired and very attractive, came when she was one year old from Afghanistan. Her father was a petroleum engineer and had been an ambassador to Beijing but this did not transfer to work in Germany. At first they were sent to Rostock in the East. Her mother worked in a home for the elderly, and her father had difficulty learning German. Only recently has her father begun helping refugees. He knows German now. She is working on her BA at the university.

I asked about their experience with the program.

Samim said he had been working for seven months. He works with two groups – Syrians, and Afghans; and an Iranian, a Kosovar, and a Russian. All except the Russian live in camps. All are fourteen to sixteen years old and in the preparatory year for learning the German language.

Maryam has one group – three Syrians and an Afghan. Her group includes an unaccompanied minor whose family is in Turkey. That is very hard because he is so alone. He misses his family. The border is closed now so they cannot come. She has been working in the program for three months. She has four hours a week with the students in classes, and then the cultural events.

I asked about examples of the cultural trips. The last one was to a bowling alley. It made me smile. I knew there were not many bowling alleys in the Middle East. They had wanted to throw the ball over their heads at first. Truly bowling was a novel experience. Another trip is to the university to see it and learn about it. I liked the sound of trips as a group.

Maryam said, "My boys, they are so good with each other." Samim said, "We need to build emotional relations too." I asked how they did that. Samim said, " I told them, I was in a camp too. And there was no program. They listen. 'You are an idol,' they told me," Samim continued. "In a camp there are fifty other families. Some young people do nothing, some take drugs. But with our families, education is king. I have my BA. I am working on my MA. They know that they are in a good place. It is worse elsewhere. Many have been out of school, either back home in Afghanistan, or in Turkey, or wherever, two to three years out of school. The hope is to go to a regular classroom."

I asked if they would work with them again next year. "No, I will have new mentees. But I will keep contact."

When there was a bomb attack in Kabul this spring, one boy stopped paying attention in class. The main teacher asked Maryam's help. His best friend had died. She was able to talk with him – in his language. Samim said one of his mentees had a similar problem. "His best friend in Aleppo died. I called him on the telephone. He said that his marks had gone bad. He said I was the only one he could trust. We went to the park. That was so important."

I thanked both Samim and Maryam. Both were interested in spending a year in the United States to improve their English. We talked about different places that would be good for their different interests. I thanked them again.

Clearly this mentoring program should be replicated in schools where there are refugee students. A major feature is using university students as mentors. So often people want to use same-age mentors. It is culturally wiser to use older students, especially people of backgrounds who themselves can be models. The refugee students look up to these mentors. It gives them a special and personal relationship. It is also valuable for the mentor to learn to teach in small groups. The small groups are beneficial to the refugee outside the mentoring time as well. The monthly cultural experience is also wise.

Return Visit to the Zeit Foundation and Dr Matthiesen
When I returned in the fall, I was so pleased to see Dr Tatiana Matthiesen again. She had arranged a luncheon together. We walked to the restaurant from the Zeit Foundation. At the restaurant she told me about a recent event in Berlin on 13 October 2016 with President Gauck of Germany. He had asked 100 young people:

  — How will Germany be in twenty years?
  — How should it be in 2036?

The young people were from all over Germany, from different classes, different regions, different disciplines. They were from thirteen to twenty-five years of age. The planning for this was done by two foundations: the Zeit foundation and Telekom. They had young people, including Samim, the mentor whom I had met, as a delegates. There were even ten delegates from young people in their *Weichenstellung* program in Hamburg, in Baden-Württemberg, and in North Rhine Westphalia. The interacting of the young people in groups around the questions posed by the president of Germany and actually meeting the president was remarkable. What an amazing experience for the young people!

We moved on to discussing what she called teachers having cultural sensitivity. The ZEIT foundation has done workshops on this for ten years in ten countries. They see cultural sensitivity as a form of positive action. This is certainly even more important with the new refugees. I noted how multicultural Germany was. I asked to what extent of Germany had *Migrationshintergrund?* She said 30–35 per cent had migration background at least.

I also asked about the *Weichenstellung* program. It is still most developed in Hamburg, but it has been expaned to North Rhineland-Westfalia where there are ninety students, and Baden-Württemberg where there are seventy to eighty students. Next year they will add a program in Schleswig-Holstein, a third state.

I thanked Dr Tatiana Matthiesen. The research and publications of the Zeit Foundation are worth following. We have much we can learn from them.

Initial Visit to the W.I.R. Program and Fear Among Refugees
The next morning in Hamburg I decided to try to learn more about the W.I.R. project – the initials stand for "Work for Integration for Refugees." I had heard good things about it, despite the website not responding to inquiries. It appeared as if there was a technical problem. The website was designed for inquiries. I took a taxi to the nearest office to arrive during project hours.

I went into the building and up to the fifth floor. The W.I.R. office was mostly full of men sitting and waiting. There were two women up front answering questions. I picked up brochures and got in line. Could I make an appointment? No, there was no one there who could possibly talk with me. I was told to go to the website. Clearly the woman did not know the website was not functioning.

I ended up being sent to another W.I.R office in St Pauli. A young Afghan who was standing off to the side showed me the way. He was deeply afraid of being sent back to Afghanistan. The presidents of Germany and Afghanistan had worked to send Afghans back and to accept them in Afghanistan. He had been in Germany for a year but did not have the residency permit yet.

When we got through security in St Pauli we were shown upstairs to the office of the W.I.R. coordinator who was not there that day. Still, there was a nice young man, who had only been there a week, but he would help us as much as he could. I asked about how many refugees there were in Hamburg. He had no idea. I asked where the funds for the W.I.R. come from. He did not know that either. What he did know was that the W.I.R. program was the first in Germany and was unique to Hamburg. He said it was designed for those who do not have their *Bescheid*. They can qualify to register for it after being here for three months. It gives the possibility for work. This filled an important gap until an asylum-applicant can qualify for the job center. That is, until they get their residency, or the papers that say they cannot be sent back. "How many people are in the program?" I asked. "Since last April, 1,000, so now about 2,000."

I asked if other cities were interested in the W.I.R program. The young man said that Berlin had expressed interest, but it was a question of money. The first year they had so many refugees, but now the numbers were not so great, they could have more coordination.

I thanked him for his time and information. We went downstairs and I said I would buy the young Afghan lunch. No, he had classes to go to. I wished him well. "Do not worry. You will not be sent back. You are intelligent and good. Keep working in this program and get work here. You will make it." I pray he does.

A Syrian Pharmacist in the Main Library and Crossing Divisions
I took the subway to the *Hauptbahnhof* and got out. I thought I would try
an address on Steinstrasse that I had gotten from the *Rathaus*.
So I walked along behind the *Bahnhof*.

I must have been tired. I went into what I thought was the right
building, despite it saying *Hauptbibliotek* on it. Yes, it was the main
library of Hamburg, and what a lovely library! As I walked along behind
the stairs what I noticed was a café with people studying and helping
each other. What a good atmosphere. There must be *Ehrenamtliche* here,
I thought. I saw a woman sitting alone studying. She had a scarf on.
I went over and asked if she was studying German? "Yes," she said with a
smile. I asked if she spoke Arabic. She nodded. We started talking and
I sat down.

She told me she was from Damascus. She had been in Hamburg for
two years. Her husband was an engineer and had worked for Bechtal in
Saudi Arabia. She was a pharmacist. She had three children, two girls and
a boy. They were all here. Her oldest daughter was twenty-eight and
worked in graphic design. Her second daughter was studying logistics at
the university, and her son, the youngest, was still in school. They have
their own home and did not have to live in a camp.

She said they were very fortunate, and yet it was still hard. Her
husband cannot find work, nor can she. To practice as a pharmacist, she
would have to pass many tests. She also needs references. How to get
references from Syria after she had left? Of course she is persona non-
grata for leaving. But the Germans do not seem to understand that.
We laughed at that but it is hard. Imagine, references.

We talked about the parental generation of migrants. I told her in
America it is always that way. The parents sacrifice for the children,
especially professional ones. It seems like such a waste, though. She said
that they did not qualify for programs here because they had a home.

But before the personal things, she talked about the positive things
that had occurred in coming to Germany. She said that in Syria there are
many groups – Alevi, Christian, Kurdish, and so forth. She said, "We
did not talk about certain things so we did not know how they felt. But
we are all here together now. Our neighbors are from Iran. At first my
husband was worried. How will we do? Her family is Sunni Muslim. But
we get along so well with our Iranian Shi'a neighbors," she said. "And in
class, we are all different. We were nervous at first. One day a Nigerian

Christian and a Sindhi Muslim from Pakistan fought over a chair. The next day we all laughed about it. A chair! We saw here it does not matter." She said that the divisions were made by politicians. "We are all people. We learned that here."

We ended up eating cake together. I wished her well with learning German.

The Friday Soup Kitchen at St Georg's and Mehmet

On Friday I walked to the church on the street behind the hotel. It was St Georg's Evangelical Lutheran Church and had been a beautiful baroque church. It was destroyed in July 1943 in the major bombing of Hamburg, the worst bombing of any major German city during the war. It was raining when I visited the rebuilt church, but I went there that day because the hotel staff had told me there was a soup kitchen on Fridays. Indeed, I found a line of people there so I went in.

Those in line looked to be mostly Europeans. The parishioners who were working the soup kitchen were rightly proud of their work. A tall woman began to talk with me. She suggested I also talk with Pastor Gunter Marwege. When I found him, he was modest and proud of the work of his church. He told me that while there were not many refugees who came to the soup kitchen on Fridays – I do not think they live in this area of hotels – the church had done much when the refugees came the previous fall of 2015.

He described the "welcome month" and the "soup months." He said everyone contributed across the city. From September 2015, large numbers of refugees had arrived at the *Bahnhof*. There were not enough places for them, so they were taken to mosques and churches, and even private homes where they slept on floors. "We had to get new rug cleaners to clean every day so they could sleep again. This was all over the city."

The pastor gestured up to the balcony of the church. "They slept there too for a week." Then he took me to the side door and showed me a small enclosure. "We made soup there, huge pots of it, all autumn. We cut up so many vegetables, I cannot tell you, to provide food for the refugees." *All the work was done by Ehrenamtliche.* It was an amazing effort by the people of Hamburg. It lasted from September 2015 to January 2016.

Then the pastor mentioned a man who comes every Friday to the soup kitchen to help them at St Georg's and make sure there are no problems. He knows many languages – Bulgarian, Rumanian, Russian, Turkish, and German. He is Mehmet. I was surprised, that is a Turkish name.

The pastor said that he stands by the side door to keep things under control. The people who came to the soup kitchen used to get into arguments until Mehmet came and was able to mediate. All those who come respect him.

The pastor then went back to the soup area. I hoped to meet Mehmet. Eventually I saw a middle-aged man talking with people by the side door. Could that be Mehmet? He was not tall. I asked someone. I looked toward the pastor who nodded. I went over to him and spoke to him in Turkish. I was right. He was a Turk. He said some friends asked him why he goes to church every Friday. We both smiled. I told him it was *hizmet*, that is Turkish for "service," and favored by God. Clearly he is needed.

He said his own life fell apart ten years ago and slowly he put it back together. He knows what it is to be down and out. Now he owns a cleaning service and a security service. He is respected by those who come for lunch, as well as by the people at church. It is a form of giving back. I watched as he went over to the table, said only a few words, and people quieted down.

I thanked the pastor and Mehmet and went back to the hotel. I had an appointment at two o'clock in the afternoon somewhere in Hamburg.

A Second Visit to the W.I.R. Program

My first attempt to understand the W.I.R. program earlier in the week had taken me across multiple districts and had been only a taste, but it had led to a further appointment. This one was at an even more impressive structure that took up an entire block in yet another section of Hamburg. Where was the appropriate entrance to the enormous building? Once I got in, even access to the elevator required a key. Never let anyone say fieldwork in bureaucracies is easy. But I finally made it to the office on the tenth floor.

To my pleasure there I met Birte Steller, a remarkable municipal leader who knew a great deal about the refugee situation in Hamburg, the labor situation, important cultural differences, and of course the W.I.R. project. She asked why I was in Germany and I explained about my seeking out positive programs for refugees, but that overall my interest was in host reception of refugees.

When I said the phrase "host reception," she almost gasped. She had just come back from Rabat, Morocco, where the German Marshall Fund had a session with top municipal leaders from three countries – Turkey, Morocco, and Germany – all migrant-receiving nations. The purpose of the session was to improve regional structures to receive migrants and serve as "host societies."

Birte Steller mentioned that she had learned at the conference about the city of Gaziantep in Turkey. It has an association run by twenty-six men whose purpose, despite its border location with Syria, was "to protect people," not to enforce borders. Then she contrasted the two cities of Hamburg and Gaziantep. Hamburg has 1.8 million people and 50,000 refugees, whereas Gaziantep has 1.8 million people and 250,000 refugees. And in Germany, 100 per cent of citizens pay taxes. In Morocco 5 per cent pay taxes. She did not know what percentage in Turkey pay taxes.

I said I still thought Germany was doing an amazing job in Europe with refugees. She suggested I check Sweden, too.

I asked about Hamburg. Frau Steller noted that Hamburg is a big city, the second largest in Germany. But it is also a federal state in itself. This made things much easier. The other places like this in Germany are Berlin and Bremen. She noted that in Hamburg, "Every second child has a migrant background. So we are very multi-cultural. People have been coming for fifty years."

She summarized that the Turks had been coming since the 1960s. They had had about 20,000 to 30,000 *Russlanddeutsche* since the 1990s. "We built an area for them in the south of Hamburg. Maybe it was not such a good idea." Those from Yugoslavia came in the 1990s. But they changed the rules then for who was a refugee. "You had to come by the North Sea or by air in order to land first in Germany (for it to be the 'first country of refuge'). So it was impossible to be a 'refugee' for most, only 1 to 2 per cent."

Frau Steller explained that since August, 2016, unless a person came from a safe country, for example from the Balkans, Ghana or Senegal, they had a chance to get refugee status, especially if they came from Syria, Iran, Iraq, Eritrea, or Somalia. However mostly they had people from Afghanistan in Hamburg. I asked why so many from there. She said because so many came from there in the 1980s. So others followed later.

She said the mayor of Hamburg wanted people to integrate as rapidly as possible. This meant schooling for the children, within six weeks. All must go to school until age eighteen no matter the status of the parents, so this is a major means of integration. After that age, from eighteen to twenty-five, there is the *Berufsschule* or trade school that allows one to work three days a week and attend school two days, leading to fulltime work.

"But the real question is how to integrate refugees into the labor market when only 20 per cent have high employment skills. That means 80 per cent do not have formal skills, but some do have work experience." Birte Steller was adamant that earlier measures of competence from Germany were not sufficient. She explained that there was a need to measure both non-formal competencies as well as work experience. "When you add these up, 50 per cent have useful skills for the city of Hamburg. They need extra training for jobs like electrician, nursing, and skilled trades which are in demand. Thus they can be integrated into the labor market."

As for the other 50 per cent, Frau Steller explained that of these 70 per cent have been in school for more than eleven years. They can learn. They are young, eighteen to twenty-five years old, thus they do not have work experience. So they are motivated. Her point was that they will integrate them into practical working companies. "We must do this since only 12 per cent of the jobs in Hamburg are for unskilled workers. We need skilled workers here."

But there was even more to this than I realized. It was not just the new refugees who needed to be trained. As Birte Steller explained, "There are 50,000 refugees in Hamburg, 30,000 are of working age." Of these only 6,000 are in good jobs like the daughter of the Syrian woman I met in the library. "Of these, 15,000 came recently. That means 9,000 came ten years ago. How to manage for those who came a while ago to become skilled workers?" She elaborated that the regular system cannot deal with this. "People come to the job system. But after one visit, they do not return. But there is massive volunteering in Hamburg. The idea is to insert the volunteer, and combine the administrator with volunteers. They will connect a mentor with a refugee to explain how to dress for an interview for a job, how to do a CV. What volunteers can do is be a part of a private network. That is what refugees lack – a private network to help get a job. A company may want to hire a refugee, but is nervous. If they deal with a volunter, it may help bridge the fear."

"With the W.I.R project, the new approach is to advise people when they first come in about labor market integration. This involves a holistic approach in counseling each person. It involves measuring non-formal competences of each person and, with analysis, an attempt to integrate them into higher skilled work."

To do this, the interviews needed to be done in the native language of the refugee. They need good translations too. Then they would evaluate after six months to see how the approach was working.

I asked Birte Steller my usual question, "What do you think is hardest for the refugees here?"

She answered, "Cultural adaptation. They do not feel comfortable with our behavior. They feel we are cold and excluding and too formal. Too rule-based. We are so structured here. A lack of humanity in normal contact." She had lived in the Americas and had even adopted two children from Mexico. She clearly had thought about this at length.

I told her that I talked to people on trains. "And they answer, don't they?" she said. I must have paused. "At least the young people do." "Yes," I said, "but they never initiate conversations." "No," she said, "We are educated not to disturb."

I told her about the Syrian women on the bridge in Bamberg. How I stopped to talk with them for about half an hour. They were so happy to talk. The older woman was so lonely. She said her German neighbors did not even say hello when she greeted them. I said, "You know visiting is the main activity for Syrian women when their work is done. They love to talk."

She said, "It is hard to get contact with us. And they do not just think we are cold. They think we are impolite. We start directly to talk about something instead of asking how they are." I told her how I had to learn Albanian manners in the Albanian community in Detroit. I learned how to always ask about family members at first contact. It was expected. But that was true of Middle Easterners too.

Her boss called her on the phone. She had given me much time. I thanked her for her time and expertise. She is also a lawyer. I wished I could talk with her further. She also has much experience in the welcome center here.

Getting people into work situations sooner is critical to morale and adaptation. It helps with language learning and integration. The learning of non-formal competences and personal counseling is also wise.

The special place of the *Ehrenamtliche* to facilitate possible connections with a possible new work place is also creative. It is a program worth evaluating, refining, and hopefully duplicating.

Church Services

The next day I heard about F.B.I. Director Comey making allegations about Hillary Clinton's emails. I had a terrible sinking feeling about my homeland.

I went to a Catholic service in the morning and in the evening I went to St Georg's Lutheran Church. The pastor had invited me to the monthly evening service for people with AIDS and their friends. It was already dark when the service started. It began with a young tenor at the piano singing a song in English, that I later learned came from "Elegies," about people who had died. It set the tone. Then we all sang a song from the AIDS pastoral care pamphlet. People stood and sang the songs they knew with gusto.

We had two testimonials. The first was from a young German man, only twenty-two years old. He talked about trying to lead an authentic life. The second was by an Arab who had lived in Saudi Arabia, although he was not a Saudi. He read it in German. In Germany he could live with freedom. But he had to struggle with German, and work was hard. His work in Arabia did not count. Yet he had dignity.

We had another song. Then the Arab man came up on the stage again. And two women put a thick rope around him in a dramatic fashion. Then they took the rope off him in the name of God. A priest with a rainbow collar gave a sermon. He spoke about Soren Kierkegaard in Copenhagen and his philosophy concerning what was the right life for him from Jesus. We sang a handsome rendition of the Lord's Prayer from the hymnal.

Then the pastor whom I had met on Friday and who had told me to come to the service at six o'clock in the evening led the Communion. He had all of us come in a circle up front. Then more good songs and organ music and one more song from the man who played the piano and could really sing.

We went out. This was the best and most intimate church service I had been to in all Germany. Bless the gay community and St Georg's Church.

Hamburg's Initial Response to Refugees: **Hamburger Abendblatt**
When I asked local people what would be the best newspaper for
accounts of when the refugees first came to Hamburg, they all
recommended the *Hamburger Abendblatt.* So I spent several hours in the
Hamburg Reading Room of the University Library. There I asked for the
September and October 2015 editions of the *Hamburger Abendblatt.* It is a
large paper and there was so much I only ended up looking carefully at
the first two weeks of September.

There were two interviews with Angela Merkel from that period,
which was impressive for a local newspaper. Recall her family is
originally from Hamburg. These interviews were personal and telling.
In the first one, Merkel encouraged Hamburgers to cope with the refugee
crisis, reminding them that Germany was a "country of hope," and
telling them "Keep distance from those who hate in their hearts."[5] In a
later exclusive interview for the *Hamburger Abendblatt*, she reiterated that
"There should be given zero tolerance for hate and xenophophobia. That
is not Germany ... and not that of the overwhelming majority of its
citizens."[6]

There were accounts of *Ehrenamtliche* and the different sorts of work
people could do to help. By 6 September there was a list of seventeen
help organizations that people could contact to join.

There were short biographies of refugees that made them personal and
real with photographs of each refugee and a map of the city showing
where they currently resided. The short bios of the refugees were very
well done with good questions. They included next to the photograph:

- the refugee's name, their parents' names;
- the refugee's earliest memories of the war;
- the first time they thought of being a refugee;
- how long they have lived in Hamburg, status here;
- why they came to Germany;
- what they miss most;
- in five years what they would like.

All in all the *Hamburger Abendblatt* is an excellent local paper, read across
the city of Hamburg and the surrounding areas but not beyond. There
was even an account of thirty neo-Nazis coming from Bremen to the
Hamburg train station where there were 300 refugees. Bremen had not

allowed them to demonstrate so they had taken the train to Hamburg. The refugees in the Hamburg station had been frightened of them. So 7,000 citizens of Hamburg had gathered in front of the *Rathaus* to say, "*Hamburg bekennt Farbe*," "Hamburg stands by its values."

What I found in early September 2015 were civic demonstrations of thousands of Hamburgers coming out to make the new refugees feel welcome, to offer them food and lodgings, and to impress for their diversity. At the same time, there were questions of where the refugees would live, what work they would do, and so forth.

The refugees were referred to as "coming from Hungary" and Hungary's policy was heavily criticized. Denmark's closing its borders was seen as strange. Some of the refugees who came to Hamburg went on to Sweden, so the context of the north was important.

As I sat in the library reading about the early days of September 2015, I realized I was spending my last days in Germany looking back at the beginning of the refugee influx. Much had gone on since then. Germany had found accommodation for hundreds of thousands of refugees and initiated processing of applications for asylum. Not all would be allowed to remain, but many would. It was a generous act of a country far from the Middle East. I only wish my own country had been so generous.

Beginning of the 500th Anniversary of the Reformation

That night on television I watched Pope Francis in Sweden help celebrate the beginning of the 500th anniversary of the Reformation. I also watched the ceremony in Berlin when 499 years ago to that day Martin Luther had nailed his 95 theses to the door in Wittenberg in 1517.

I watched the entire Berlin ceremony on television from the Konzerthaus with the opening words of Berlin Mayor Müller, followed by a Jewish cantor and a Syrian oud player. The Minister of Culture Monika Grütters spoke briefly, and then President Gauck spoke on Luther's contributions broadly. Gauck will soon be leaving the presidency at the end of his term; he will be missed. It ended with people in the audience who had a birthday choosing from 95 pieces of music.

I packed and called the Syrian woman I had met at the library to wish her and her family well. Hamburg had been as moving as I had expected. The *Weichenstellung* mentoring program was expanding to other German states. The experimental W.I.R. program was tackling the crucial element of getting refugees into work earlier and into the sort of work in which they were more likely to be successful. The dedication and vision of civic leaders in this city that was its own state continued to impress me.

I looked out at the steeple of St Georg's for the last time. Then I headed for the station. I had a six-hour journey from Hamburg to the south. My long research journey had come to an end.

Reflection

I had traveled all over Germany from south to north, from small villages to large cities of over a million inhabitants. Everywhere there were refugees and everywhere there were *Ehrenamtliche*, people volunteering on a regular basis to work with refugees in all manner of ways. The refugees had all been accommodated in hostels with some having moved out into private housing when they received positive notification of asylum. Many were still waiting however because the decision was a three-step process and the numbers of asylum-seekers were so high. The greatest stress for the refugees was in waiting – for language classes, for notification for asylum, for work opportunities – all beyond their control.

The refugee children were all in school. The adults were in German classes or trying to get into the classes. There was a hierarchy in that those most likely to get approved for asylum were given the language classes first. This meant Syrians and northern Iraqis first. Other refugees had to wait unless their communities had programs for everyone which was true of the smaller communities and older camps. Language knowledge in German was seen as a necessary prerequisite to employment in the skilled economy of Germany.

The villages and towns and smaller cities with good leadership were able to reach out and establish effective networks that helped refugees make personal connections. This was essential to moving forward in language and beginning to feel at home in the new cultural setting. Small size was not enough though. Refugees could be isolated in smaller communities as well. In the large cities refugees had the company of more of their countrymen. There were also a greater variety of programs and more work opportunities in the large cities.

It was the second year since the major influx and the policies toward the refugees had tightened up. It was harder to bring family members.

People could not move wherever they wanted to in Germany. Residency was no longer given for three years but for one year. Each year they would have to prove they could not safely return to their home country. At the same time benefits were extended so that if a refugee were in a three-year work program, they could not be deported. The language and integration classes were extended. There were added trial programs, like W.I.R. in Hamburg, to get the refugees into appropriate work and work training situations even before the final notifications had been given.

The political costs of accepting the refugees were felt by Merkel's party in the 2017 election. A cap of 200,000 was put on the numbers of refugees to be accepted in Germany each year. Nevertheless, the refugees from war-torn countries were slowly but largely being absorbed in the long-term process of integration. Could people be patient enough to let this play out, or would politicians and the political winds from the rest of Europe that was more anti-refugee endanger this process?

CHAPTER 7

TOWARD INTEGRATION

Across Germany, there is special concern for integration of the new refugees. This is especially true of those positively inclined to the refugees, including those who are working with them. The difficulty is that integration is a long-term process. Rightist politicians are quick to jump on any incident. This, however, is not new.

Integration of immigrants became increasingly politicized beginning in the 1990s.[1] This was due to concerns for security, national identity, employment, and discrimination. In Germany citizenship had also become a possibility for the first time for migrants at the end of that decade.[2] But what people often forget, as mentioned in the introduction to this book, is that integration in complex liberal democracies is a problem that exists prior to the problem of integration of immigrants.

In addition, liberal democracies have conflicting dynamics that pull in different directions with respect to integration of immigrants. For example, representative and nationalist aspects of liberal democracies pull toward restricting immigration, while constitutional and capitalistic aspects of these same democracies pull toward encouraging immigration.[3] The societies themselves are multidimensional and complex; similarly the migrants and refugees are diverse and integrate at different rates in different ways in economic, social, and cultural realms.

All this is to say that integration, or "becoming a full member of a host society," is a truly complex process. It needs to be a two-way accommodation. The more this is politicized, the more it appears to be a question of identity and belonging. However scholars emphasize that rather than focusing on the rhetoric of identity, focusing instead on improvements in education and employment opportunities would likely do more to improve integration indices.[4]

Much of the recent research of integration of refugees in Germany has resonance for Americans with earlier civil rights and bilingual education from the 1960s and 1970s. The importance of having teachers with *Migrationsintergrund*[5] and having media representatives with *Migrationsintergrund* echoes the importance Americans learned earlier of having minorities represented in teaching and media professions.

Yet here I would remind readers that Germany took in close to one million asylum-seekers in 2015. Germans across the country have worked with their impressive social systems to help integrate those who came from war-torn countries into their schools, their economy, and their society. We have much to learn from them.

Specifics of Integration in Germany

Integration begins immediately for refugees when they come to the new country. The first days matter. Impressions from those days last. Refugees can all tell the exact day they arrived. That is why the work of the *Ehrenamtliche* is so important.

The more there is a personal approach and people are treated as individuals and families, the better the chance there is of people being integrated into the society as contributing members. That is why the approach in smaller, medium sized-towns, and in some large cities where a volunteer welcomes the refugee or refugee family, helps them to register, and accompanies them to where they will be staying, is so wise. A volunteer may then serve, as Daniela Dinser described, like a "godparent," in accompanying the refugee to learn about stores, medical clinics, language classes, or registering children for school. This is someone who cares enough to spend time making sure things work out. Someone who knows more and can show one the ropes, but above all cares. Remember the refugee student in the class near Cologne immediately could tell when the teacher did not care about him.

In contrast, the longer refugees remain in large refugee accommodation, with say 200 or more other refugees, without personal interaction with local people, waiting for their *Bescheid*, forbidden to work legally, or do meaningful activity other than language class that take months to begin, the more they will develop networks only with other refugees. If their immediate families are in Turkey or Syria, their minds will be partially with their families.

Integration is a long-term, participatory two-way process. But to make it culturally two-way, the refugees need interaction with local people. They need to hear German spoken by Germans. They need to see how Germans interact with each other. And they need to feel that they might have a place in this town or city. Again the *Ehrenamtliche* are crucial here. Only individuals can give this. Meanwhile a central problem in facilitating interactions is the delay due to housing and bureaucratic constraints.

In any society, integration involves access to the workplace, education, planning at multiple levels, and social cohesion.[6] I will deal with each of these areas with regard to Germany, as well as Germany's recent policies to promote integration. I will also consider the question of terrorism as a question of security. But first it is important to look at Germany's recent positive experience with integration.

Germany's Most Successful Experience with Integration

One of the important successes of German policy in mid-twentieth century was the integration of 12–14 million expellees from the Sudetenland, East Prussia, north Yugoslavia, Hungary, and Rumania into postwar Germany. The expellees were nominally German, although one-tenth did not speak German. Most were women, children, and old people. But they were not welcomed, nor were they planned for. When they arrived from 1945 to 1947, they were totally destitute. Germany itself was in shambles from the war.

How did Germany accommodate them and how did they fit in? It was truly remarkable. They were seen as refugees, as *Flüchtlinge*. It was ultimately the policies of Adenauer in the early 1950s, with some help from the Marshall Plan allowing the expellees to have special rolling loans for homes. With these homes came the requirement that they also rent to another refugee family. The expellees were accorded social pension benefits as if they had always lived in Germany. Politicians also reportedly listened to their longing for their homelands so that they did not feel so bereft.

What can we learn from this about integration? First, careful policies that respond to basic need and accord people dignity matter. To measure this, there is documentation of steady growth of home ownership through the 1950s of the people who had arrived in Germany between 1945–47. Second, this integration did not happen over night, but took time. Third, refugees are the hardest working people around, for they came to a war-torn Germany, themselves from war-torn regions, with no material possessions and had experienced trauma getting there. Clearly if Germany could integrate people in postwar circumstances, it can do so in these much better ones.

The New Refugee Influx of 2015

Nevertheless, the refugee influx of 2015 has been a special challenge for integration in Germany. In the context of the Syrian civil war almost one million asylum-seekers entered Germany in such a short period of time that they could not initially be screened. This was a bureaucratic nightmare and a humanitarian crisis. The pastor at St Georg's in Hamburg referred to it as the "soup months" when volunteers made soup for refugees from September to January, and they slept in churches, mosques, theaters, homes, industrial buildings, tents, and school athletic arenas.

Between the time of this influx and the earlier successful integration of the expellees, however, there had been less successful experiences in Germany with integration. Here I refer to the experience with both the Turks and the Russian Germans. These experiences left Germans more nervous about integration of new refugees.

Germany did not want to replicate problems with the Turks, who were Muslim like many of the new refugees, although the situation with the Turks evolved from special circumstances. Germany also did not want to replicate the separate colonies and the extent to which "Russian culture" had persisted with the Russian Germans.

2016 Government Policies to Promote Integration[7]

Earlier I made the point that Germany had evolved a more pro-immigrant stance than other European countries in the twenty-first century. However the German government's ability to maintain this consensus, with the growth of anti-immigrant political parties like the AfD, depends on whether it can demonstrate success in controlling immigration and asylum, and effectively managing integration.[8]

In July 2016 Germany instituted major policies to promote integration of the new refugees. These new policies were also meant to reassure public opinion that the government was in control.

The new policies were a combination of "*fördern und fordern*," "support and challenge," emphasizing the two-way responsibility of those seeking asylum. They provide for more integration classes, vocational training, and employment opportunities. They also constrained where refugees could live. The integration classes begin sooner, last longer and, besides the language component, have more emphasis on teaching values of German society. Asylum-seekers who do not attend these integration classes lose access to the government benefits they need to stay in the country legally.

Relating to training and work, during a three-year vocational training grant, a refugee will not be deported. Such a grant can begin after twenty-one years of age. To foster refugees into the labor market, the government provides 100,000 low-level jobs. Priority regulations relating to EU members are relaxed in some states for the first three years.

Authorities also have the power to assign refugees where they will reside. This helps prevent the growth of migrant ghettos in major cities. Refugees can gain permanent residency after five years if they show language proficiency in German and the ability to earn their own living. If they show superior language skills and meet other requirements, they can receive it after three years.

Another form of control to reassure the German public is the cap on numbers of asylum-seekers, limited to 200,000 allowed into Germany each year. Merkel was made to agree to this after the September 2017 election. Although as mentioned, this number can vary somewhat depending on circumstances.

Major Issues in Integration as Seen Through this Study

Let us consider major issues in integration – labor market access, education, urban planning, and social cohesion – as seen through the communities in this study.

Major Issues in Integration: Access to the Labor Market

Germany's predicted severe lack of workers in the coming decades, particularly skilled ones, has been frequently cited in the media and by political and public leaders.[9] Support for labor migration has fueled pro-immigration views. In September 2017 Germany's labor office noted that 773,000 jobs were available.[10] But there are problems of training and matching people with positions. Some may just take time. Let us look at specifics.

Remember the Syrian men above Monika's workshop in Elzach, the Syrian doctor in the third village who had waited so long for language classes, the Iraqis from the *Unterkunft* in Bruchsal whom I later saw at the church International Cafe, the Syrian man in Nürnberg who was waiting for language class and after ten months did not have his asylum decision, and the young Afghan in Hamburg who had been there a year, did not have his permit and was afraid he would be sent back. What all these men had in common was they were in a sort of bureaucratic limbo.

None had their residency permit. None had work. Some did not have language classes, let alone integration classes. Recall it takes three interviews to qualify for the permit, but the decision may not be positive, as happened to the young Syrian man in Munich. Only Assad in Elzach, the Pakistani who had been in Germany for three years, had work in a mattress factory, and came with a knowledge of English and work experience, had his permit. He even speaks the local German dialect now.

In fairness though, Germany needed to screen the asylum-seekers since they had not been screened on entry. Those who did not qualify needed to be sent back to their homelands.

The frustration of waiting for months is telling on the young men. Many, like the tailor in the third village or the silk embroiderer in Macedonia, did not have obviously useful professions for Germany and would need training. Meanwhile they had to wait for language training. But some do have higher skills and professions, like the Syrian pharmacist in Hamburg, her engineer husband, and the Syrian doctor. Yet there is a problem in that foreign credentials do not tend to translate. What does a university degree from Syria mean in Germany? Is an engineer still an engineer? A doctor still a doctor? A law degree is especially difficult. Some refugees in utter frustration have set up websites where they advertise themselves and their backgrounds to future employers. They can explain if they have IT backgrounds. But they must know German. Can they legally work? The men are young and most willing to learn and want to work.

In all my experience in refugee accommodation, I saw much frustration among competent men who felt that the process of waiting for language classes, waiting for integration classes, and waiting for job center interviews was not productive.

The W.I.R. program in Hamburg, "Work for Integration of Refugees" as described, tries to get refugees into work while they are still waiting in the early period of the first year. It is designed to employ careful counseling to learn of non-formal competences, and volunteer mentoring so the refugees end up in work that is better suited for them. It tackles both the new refugees and refugees who have come over the last ten years and were not yet suitably integrated in the work force.

This access to the labor market and training is essential since Germany has a knowledge-based work force. There are a limited number of jobs for unskilled workers and most are filled by EU migrants. The refugees must train to fit in. It will take time.

Major Issues in Integration: Education

Related to employment is education. This was a major lesson of the experience with the Turks. Germany had not seen them as staying in Germany and so had not bothered with education of their children. It will not make this mistake again.

Refugee children enter school within six weeks of arriving in Germany. The first year is seen as an integration year and they are expected to learn German. Sometimes this stretches to two years, especially if students have been out of school due to war or living in camps without schools. The apprentice programs and other vocational training are well organized. They have wisely raised the age limit for these.

In Bruchsal, I met young Syrian students in the *Unterkunft* who had just come back from school and they were already speaking German. The journalist in Cologne described the program in a high school where she was a volunteer for refugee students, with an excellent teacher, sponsored by a chemical company. The AWO, the Workers Welfare Federation, administrator in Cologne told of 600 volunteers in the schools who worked one-on-one with refugee children.

I highly advocate replication of the *Weichenstellung* program, the mentoring program in Hamburg, where university students work with small groups of three to four refugee students, for four hours a week, all through the school year. The mentors serve as academic guides and role models, and are especially effective when they themselves come from migrant backgrounds. This program has now spread to three other states in Germany.

Another question I have concerns how many teachers of Germany's schools have migrant backgrounds. If you want children to succeed, there are studies that show that students do better when the teachers are like them. How many school principals have migrant backgrounds? It is important to consider this in hiring.

Major Issues in Integration: Urban Planning

The fear is that ghettos emerge like those in France outside big cities, or to a lesser extent, of Russian Germans in Germany. But it is natural to have poorer areas in a city where immigrants live for a while, areas where the rents are less in less attractive areas.

Everywhere I went in Germany, people talked about the shortage of rental housing units for refugees when they leave the refugee accommodation. Landlords are reluctant to rent to them, but finding vacant units in the first place is also most difficult. This is true for Germans as well.

Clearly the coordinator in Nürnberg and those in charge in Cologne and Hamburg have worked to make sure that the main refugee accommodation were spread out across the city. These cities all have thousands of refugees. They will assist the refugees in finding apartments.

What Germany wants to avoid is the eventual construction of ethnic ghettos. The longer refugees remain in large *Unterkünfte*, buildings of 200 to 500, or even 800 to 1,000 people, the more the networks of people they create will be with other refugees. People depend on people they know.

Elzach's decision to have refugees in nine different locations helped spread them out. It did not guarantee integration, but it made it more possible over time.

In the middle-sized town of Bruchsal, German volunteers worked with people in the *Unterkunft*. They helped them find housing, and continued contact with them when they left it. This is ideal for integration.

In Schwäbisch-Gmünd, there was less pressure on housing as people could live in the outer villages in smaller groups. The transition to living the way other Gmünders lived was nominal. Again, the main problems are in the large cities where housing is limited. Clearly there needs to be additional housing built, and some sort of rent control if lower income families are not to be pushed out.

Major Issues in Integration: Social Cohesion

Again in social cohesion, it is easier to see where the villages and towns have advantages. It would take more time to research personal interactions in the large cities. Sports clubs or other clubs may become important here. In all places initially it is the actions of the *Ehrenamtliche* that are critical.

The backroom of Rita Andris' Bioladen was a place for gatherings of refugees and local people. It was relaxed and positive. International cafés, where local Germans and refugees could gather on a weekly or biweekly basis, like the Sunday evening one I attended in Bruchsal, or the Friday afternoon one I attended the previous spring in Schwäbisch-Gmünd, were also good places for initiating social contacts. They were good for language practice for the refugees. They always include free cake, tea, and coffee.

German volunteers were leaders in reaching out to refugees to help meet different needs, thereby promoting social cohesion. The more Germans got to see refugees as people, the less the stereotypes hold sway from both sides. But for these contacts to grow into something stronger, people will need to engage in activities together. It will take time. The platforms that Daniela Dinser spoke of, where locals and refugees did things together, were important. Those thirty-two refugees who tried out for the volunteer fire department in Schwäbisch-Gmünd, most of whom did not qualify in the end, were still in regular intense weekend contact with trainers and local men who also wanted to be volunteers over the year, are a good example. That refugees saved a car from the flood in the spring of 2016 is known throughout the region. Again it will take time.

Security: The Questions of Crime, Terrorism, and Attacks on Refugees

In the winter of 2018, a Germany university study noted a 10 per cent increase in crime in southern Germany in 2015 and 2016 when the influx of refugees occurred.[11] A more detailed study by a Swiss university of crime in Lower Saxony at this time noted that those who committed it were significantly more likely to be young male migrants from North Africa, not those from the Syria, Iraq, or Afghanistan.[12] This supports the point I have made several times that the refugees from the war-torn areas of Syria, Iraq, and Afghanistan are less likely to be involved in crime. It also makes clear the need to deport those, like the North Africans, who will not receive asylum. A problem for society is that people do not make the distinction.

With almost a million new refugees, Germany has had relatively few terrorist incidents. The 2016 Berlin Christmas market truck rampage that caused the most deaths was by a Tunisian migrant who had been denied asylum and whom Tunisia had initially refused to take back. The next most deadly terrorist act was in Munich in the summer of 2016 by an Iranian-German youth, born in Germany. He was not a refugee.

There were, however, several deeply violent acts as well as terrorist acts carried out by refugees. Among the violent acts, there was the young Afghan man with the machete on the train near Würtzburg, the young Afghan who raped and killed a German medical student near Freiburg, and the Afghan who killed the young woman in Kandel. These were by unaccompanied minors. While truly violent, they do not appear intended to create fear in the general population. Among the terrorist acts, there was a Syrian who was denied asylum who then tried to bomb the entry to a park area; no one was killed thankfully. There was also the Syrian in Chemnitz in the East who received explosives. He then escaped only to be apprehended by other Syrians who held him and called the police on him. He hanged himself in his jail cell.

The above incidents, although highly regrettable, are very few in number, especially when compared to the numbers of attacks on refugee shelters during the same time period. In 2015 there were 1,029 attacks on asylum shelters. The total number of attacks on refugee shelters in 2016 was 988, a slight drop. However if the number includes as well the attacks on individual refugees for 2016, it is 3,533, or about ten attacks every day.[13] Recognize that most refugees will not report attacks in the first place, so the situation is worse than reported.

Overall

How to integrate newcomers effectively in a society so that they become productive members of that society and want to stay? I add the last part because in modern society, when new people come in, depending on how they feel about how they are treated, they may want to leave for work elsewhere. I was told earlier in Berlin about well-educated Turks who felt they were discriminated against and so moved to the Netherlands. It behooves societies to treat newcomers well so they want to stay. It is not just humane. As birth rates go down in the modern developed world, what people call "the migrant dividend" will become more important. The more a people feel welcomed into a society, the more they are likely to want to remain, and to give back to that society. The initial years do matter.

CONCLUSION

The refugee crisis of 2015 in Europe was unprecedented and unexpected. Refugees streamed through to Greece and up through Eastern European countries toward Western Europe. Germany's response to take in almost one million asylum-seekers was worthy of both respect and study. I went from working in refugee transit camps along the Balkan Migrant Trail in Macedonia to studying "host reception" of how Germany was coping in 2016, the second year after the major entry of refugees. Since Chancellor Merkel had insisted that all communities in Germany take at least 1.5 per cent of their populations in refugees, there was an amazing variety of programs across the land. I sought out positive programs with the understanding that we learn best from such programs. I studied the communities in three groups according to size: villages under 10,000 people; towns and smaller cities of 40,000 to 70,000 to half a million people; and cities over a million people. I talked with people who were working with refugees including volunteers, heads of programs, teachers, civil servants, mayors, priests, imams, and with taxi drivers, and others who had perspectives on the situation. I sat with refugees, drank coffee with them, and listened to their experiences. I came away with much respect for people from war-torn lands and with the people who were working with them in different ways in their own land.

I would add that while some people still think that refugees belong in camps in isolated places, like the Zaatari camp for 83,000 Syrian refugees in Jordan, or the Dadaab refugee camp for over 300,000 Sudanese refugees in Kenya, refugees themselves vote with their feet. In almost every instance when they have a choice they choose to live in urban areas, not in isolated camps. Most seek the best place for education for their children as voiced by many families who made the sacrifices to reach Germany.

What then are the most important positive initiatives and ways of operating that we should take away from this study of transit responses of Macedonians and then local host responses of Germans to the refugee crisis from the 2015 influx?

Positive Initiatives and Strategies for Success

Initiatives for Helping Refugees Transit in Macedonia
Looking first at Macedonia, initiatives of individual people mattered. Here it took special courage to aid the refugees since the government was explicitly against this.

Lence Zdravkin, a middle-aged mother and grandmother, fed and cared for refugees who passed by her home in central Macedonia for several years. This was vital to the refugees who especially needed food and water at that point in their journey. Unfortunately her generosity did not spread in her region and remained largely an individual initiative.

A more extensive and long-lasting initiative has been that of Jasmin Redjepi and his friends who founded Legis.mk, an NGO that aided the refugees on their long walk across Macedonia, testified against the inhumane Gazi Baba detention center, and lobbied the Macedonian Parliament to change the law so that the refugees were finally allowed to use the train to cross Macedonia. After Parliament changed the law in June 2016, Legis.mk regularly brought necessary supplies to the refugees at the two refugee transit camps on the southern and northern borders. Their volunteers are made up of local people of different ethnic groups in Macedonia as well as several internationals. They have continued to be an effective voice in Macedonia for refugees.

Volunteers as Essential Personnel for Integration of Refugees in Germany
In Germany, Merkel's initial opening of the trains in early September 2015 to allow in refugees who were languishing in Budapest was well received by thousands of Germans in Munich and other German cities. "Helpers" met the refugees at train stations all over Germany. Thousands

of these helpers brought food, blankets for sleeping, welcome signs, and directed people to where they could stay temporarily.

As I found in the *Hamburger Abendblatt*, in the first days there were at least seventeen listed groups in one large city that people could join to assist the refugees in a more organized fashion. These were the *Ehrenamtliche*, volunteers with specific ongoing duties. No doubt there were more groups that were not even listed, like those at St Georg's who cut up vegetables and made soup in large cauldrons for the refugees for the next four months.

In Angela Merkel's speech in December 2015, she thanked the volunteers directly. I want to note that in every village, town, and city in Germany that I visited there were volunteers working in all manner of ways to assist the refugees – teaching German classes on a regular basis, tutoring refugees in German, helping refugee children in schools, taking them to doctors, doing work counseling, taking care of children when the parent went for trauma counseling, helping their children with homework after school, giving music lessons. The list is endless. One of my favorites was the retired man in Schwäbisch-Gmünd who had set up his small factory to train refugees in the use of German tools and small machinery. The Bertelsmann Foundation estimates the number of volunteers to be any where from half a million to a million people.[1]

There should be a new quotient, GDK, "gross domestic kindness". But it is more than that. The extent to which the new refugees are integrated will be largely thanks to the individual actions of *Ehrenamtliche* across Germany.

As the priest in Bruchsal noted, people volunteered for all manner of reasons. Some were religious, some not. There were different classes of people, although the coordinator in Nürnberg thought they included the more educated. In general there were more women, although I met many men as well. Many were children of people who themselves had been refugees, that is, German expellees.

In the W.I.R. (Work for Integration for Refugees) program in Hamburg for bringing refugees into the work force sooner and more appropriately, volunteers are vital. They serve as personal mentors and translators. They help refugees construct CVs and apply for jobs. They potentially serve as bridge people for a particular refugee with a company. They lessen the fear people may have in dealing with refugees.

Volunteers give a human face to the community and interact with the newcomers in ways they understand. They see what the newcomers need and also what newcomers can offer, and pass that on to the local group working with them. For example much earlier in Michigan, I worked with a Kosovar refugee family. The father of the family was an artist who painted a special painting for the church that had sponsored his family. We organized an event for presenting it. This builds social cohesion and makes people feel competent and valued. People want to give back but it often takes volunteers to make this possible and memorable.

Matching volunteers with appropriate tasks however is a special skill as was made clear by Angelika Blickhäuser, the AWO manager, who had worked in this for eighteen years. Further, volunteers sometimes need training and should not try to do too much. As with other personnel, they need to be appreciated and should meet regularly to share their experiences.

A Classic Mentoring Program for Young Refugees: Weichenstellung *in Hamburg*

Helping young refugees succeed in the local school system is crucially important. Besides involving volunteers throughout the system, the second positive initiative I advocate is the excellent mentoring program known as *Weichenstellung* from the Zeit Foundation in Hamburg. It involves matching small groups of three to four refugee students with the same university student for four hours a week across the academic year. There is also a cultural activity on a monthly basis in the city to acquaint the students more broadly and to foster solidarity. This is a small group-learning situation organized around a personal tutor, a role model, and a counselor to whom the students can relate. It is especially beneficial if the university student plans on becoming a public school teacher and if the university student has similar refugee or migrant background. The mentors should also be supervised and have monthly meetings to share what they learn. There should be input from the classroom teachers.

After meeting two of the mentors in the Hamburg program, and seeing a video of the interaction of mentor with mentees in the school, I am not surprised that it has expanded into other German states. This mentoring program should be duplicated wherever there are refugees in schools.

Three Strategies for Success in Integrating Newcomers in Germany

In addition to involving volunteers across the board, and implementing the mentoring program as described above, I also advocate the following three strategies for integrating newcomers based on my experience in different communities across Germany.

The communities that were the most successful in integrating newcomers built on work with earlier refugees and migrants where possible, and they refused to be over-bureaucratized despite the large number of new refugees arriving in the short period of time. They listened to local voices and initiatives. What do I mean by this?

Elzach is a good example. It had taken in Bosnian and Iraqi refugees in the early 1990s. People remembered this and there was a fairly positive sense that this should be done. Recall this is a small village at the end of a valley with its own dialect. The mayor's first idea was to put all the refugees in the poor house outside the village and expand the building. This is a bureaucratic response. But voices in the village convinced him that it would be wiser not to do this. He was advised instead to spread out the refugees so more people would be involved in their care. They would learn German better this way. Now they reside in nine different dwellings.

Schwäbisch Gmünd had worked with both *Russlanddeutsche* and earlier Turkish migrants on integration issues in the 1990s. They had called in help from the Schader Stiftung to evaluate their procedures and recommend how they could improve. Herr Gaugele, the head of integration, reported that eventually this led the community to develop what they now call the *"Gmünder Weg,"* the five-step process for integrating newcomers. They were able to test it under fire with the refugees from Gambia, Nigeria, and Afghanistan who came in 2010. So there were three groupings of peoples that Schwäbisch-Gmünd had actively worked on integrating before the new refugees came in 2015.

And as for bureaucratic response, the Oberbürgermeister, who had lodged two refugees with his parents at one time, favored placing three to four refugees in outlying villages with the owner of the house so they could interact and learn German faster. At one time 40 per cent of the refugees in Schwäbisch-Gmünd were living in private homes. This is a testament to leadership.

This is the opposite of bureaucratic responses, which would have dictated putting all the refugees in one building and following dictates from the state or federal government in rigid order. In contrast the most successful programs honed their practices with each experience with refugees and refused to wait to give language classes until refugees received official notification. They provided what they saw was needed as soon as possible.

A second strategy for success in integration was participation of both hosts and newcomers together in community events where people could temporarily forget boundaries. Again Schwäbisch-Gmünd was stellar in this aspect. The head of integration spoke not of walking around fairs, but having refugees participate in them. The refugee officer spoke of shared platforms with refugees where she invited her three children, like the planting of tulip bulbs all around the town. There was the preparation for the town flower show where volunteers, including refugees, who gave fifty hours or more, were given jackets and hats and bags all alike. The Staufer Festival that takes place every four years in July is another event wherein townspeople, including refugees and migrants, participate, to the tune of 1,300 people. They need not all perform. There is staging and publicity and other work to be done together. Art is a natural breaker of boundaries.

Ritual, an age-old art form, breaks down boundaries as well. It opens people's hearts in ways that logic and reason do not. Schwäbisch Gmünd held an *iftar* dinner, a meal signifying the breaking of the fast of Ramadan, on the square behind the main Catholic church, with food and tables and a stage for the imam and the mayor. One thousand people from the town attended and shared this Muslim feast together. The Muslim townspeople, especially the Turks I talked to, felt a part of the town more than ever before. Then on 1 October there was a Christian feast of the Breaking of the Bread, in the same area with a priest and a sharing of the bread.

In America we have memorable ceremonies in the courthouse or on the town square when people become American citizens. I love to go and listen to the judge talk about what it means to become American. The new citizens are always from many countries. They always stand, one by one, and we all clap for each one. They are given their papers and an American flag. It is special for the families and everyone in the room or gathered around the square.

Germany does not have ceremonies like this. What migrants in Germany have told me however is that they are proud to be Berliners, or Hamburgers, Kölners or Stuttgarters. There is much city pride. Perhaps this is a better way for the world to go. We should lessen nationalism, and move to civic and municipal pride. But we do need ceremonies and rituals. They help us come together despite our differences. Often allegiance to sports clubs involves civic pride.

Finally, a third strategy for success in integration is communication across affected parties and honest evaluation. Elzach had its Asylum Circle that met regularly. The Bruchsal volunteers met every two months for pizza dinners. Dr Uli Glaser in Nürnberg has regular meetings and sends out weekly newsletters. Schwäbisch Gmünd has the Integration Roundtable of seventy community leaders that meets four times a year. Hamburg has the welcome center. With these communication settings, evaluations should be shared.

Evaluation of how refugees are doing in the programs matters. Schwäbisch Gmünd publishes yearly reports of all its programs. Evaluation of experimental programs is also important. This includes the *Weichenstellung* project and the new W.I.R. program. The ideas behind them are excellent, but especially with the W.I.R. program, how it is carried out is crucial and only evaluation of the three steps can guide people to make sure it actually leads to refugees finding stable employment.

Emphasis on Leadership at the Local Level

This book began with reflection on what affects people's attitudes toward refugees in Europe. Leadership by national leaders certainly does and here I brought out the contrasting leadership and actions of German Chancellor Angela Merkel and Hungarian Prime Minister Viktor Orbán. It was Merkel's decision, along with the prime minister of Austria, to let in refugees stuck in Budapest in late summer of 2015 that opened Germany up to the refugees. Earlier historical knowledge of refugees, and experience with refugees from the world wars can also affect people's attitudes to refugees in Europe. In Macedonia and in Germany there have been refugees postwar as well. But more important in Germany has been the experience with Turkish migrants. I made the point that many people confuse migrants and refugees.

Yet when people have actual personal experiences with refugees, earlier attitudes, which have often led to stereotypes, can fall by the wayside. That is why I always encouraged people to volunteer and meet refugees as people. That is the best way to challenge one's views of refugees and ethnic groups, and to broaden one's horizons.

Those in Macedonia and Germany who had done this most effectively are among the following *local leaders* I met in my work and long study journey. They are dedicated to helping refugees, helping them become part of their society, or are themselves part of this process. I include them here to remind readers of their remarkable qualities. With many I include their responses to my question, what they saw as most difficult for the refugees.

In Macedonia *Jasmin Redjepi* stands out. He not only founded the NGO Legis.mk with friends in Skopje that aided refugees both before and after they were allowed to use public transportation in Macedonia. He also became an affective spokesperson for refugees in Macedonian media. His NGO was inclusive with Muslim and Slavic Christian volunteers in a country deeply divided. Legis.mk continues to support refugees and marginalized people in Macedonia.

Also in Macedonia, *Lence Zdravkin* took food to the refugees as they passed by her home along the railroad tracks by Veles, a city in the center of the country, as soon as they began to pass by in 2013 and 2014. Word grew and she found herself taking out greater quantities of food and water on a regular basis. The NGO Legis.mk brought her added supplies. She continued to help refugees at the transit camps even after they were allowed to use public transport.

In Germany there is *Rita Andris* from Elzach, a person of faith who lives her faith. I first learned of her through her action of regularly buying four monthly train passes for the refugees to share so they had mobility from Elzach, the small village at the far end of the valley, to Freiburg and back. Her actions inspired others in the village. She had been the one to tell the mayor to spread out the housing of the refugees, and he listened. When I met her, the first thing that she said to me was that the refugees had lived through hard times. What they needed was eye contact and interaction, not someone to help them. What was most difficult for the refugees, according to Rita, was contact with German people.

Pastor Dr Jörg Sieger is a middle-aged Roman Catholic theologian who had been head of Caritas, the Catholic charity, in Heidelberg. He helped me understand changes in recent German social history, and how people of all sorts and conditions in Heidelberg had responded to helping the new refugees. When I asked him what was most difficult for the refugees, he said, "Waiting. Most have their family in Syria. It diminishes their strength. Their flight is not ended since their family is not here."

Rolf-Dieter Gerken, formerly an IT specialist, is the coordinator for volunteers in Bruchsal in Baden-Württemberg. There were 100–120 volunteers who work regularly with refugees in adult teaching, helping with children, and other areas. He has them meet in groups every two months in restaurants for pizza dinners to talk with other volunteers who do similar work. He is especially interested in integration.

Dr Ulrich Glaser, the professional coordinator in Nürnberg, worked in what I consider a most challenging environment of high refugee numbers and restrictive Bavarian laws. Only someone with his energy level, organizational skills, and fortitude could survive and thrive. He had established 172 refugee dwellings across the city of half a million. He would go into residential areas, before refugees would be settled there, and work with local residents to assure them their property values would not decrease. He publishes weekly newsletters to keep people informed.

Hajji Imam Alhout of the oldest mosque in Nürnberg, a tall young Syrian imam, had been in Germany for four years and was doing a degree in theology at a local university. He passed on his respect for Germans and called Germany, "the country of work." He counseled his people that the way to show gratitude to Germany was to give back in work.

Daniela Dinser, officer of refugees in Schwäbisch Gmünd, saw her work as taking care of any need the refugees had as it arose. She herself was a mother of three who was trained in family law. She reflected on people's fear of foreigners – something I had had trouble understanding in Europe – as from not coming to terms with one's own roots. She mentioned that for Germans until recently this had not been easy. Now, however, she can say that she is proud to be German and happy to live there.

Oberbürgermeister Arnold of Schwäbisch Gmünd, a man of vision who never stops, is passionate about community building. He referred to the ritual events of "the Breaking of the Bread" and the *Iftar* dinner as celebrating *Gemeinschaft*, community. The *Gmünder Weg* for integrating refugees is a contribution he helped build. He cautioned, "We Germans like to argue and reason. But it is not through reasoning that this comes. It is a feeling." I asked him of what he was most proud. He answered immediately, "That we have over 1,000 refugees living in town and that we still feel responsible for each other. We still have strong social cohesion in town."

The AWO manager, *Angelika Blickhäuser*, who has worked eighteen years in matching volunteers across Cologne, told me spontaneously that the greatest difficulty for refugees was their false hopes of what life would be like, impossible dreams that they bring with them. She added, "We also have unemployment. And we have no work for men without education or training." As far as integration is concerned, Frau Blickhäuser insisted that patriarchy is the problem for all. That is why women have to struggle, and foreign men too.

Finally, *Birte Steller*, a remarkable municipal leader of the W.I.R. (Work for Integration of Refugees) program in Hamburg, insisted on new ways of assessing refugees' work potential. They should also include non-formal competencies and number of years of work experience. The W.I.R. program itself treated refugees as individuals. It also began before the asylum decision had been made which was the earlier stumbling block. Her response to my question on what she thought was hardest for the refugees reflected much experience with people of other cultures. She answered, "Cultural adaptation. They do not feel comfortable with our behavior. They feel we are cold and excluding and too formal. We are so structured. A lack of humanity in normal contact." She added, "It is hard to get contact with us."

I thought back to Rita Andris who had said that what the refugees needed was to interact with Germans. That is what I had been doing for the past months. But I had been initiating it all the time. And yet Birte Steller was someone I would have enjoyed talking to at much greater length, and I think working with as well.

Some cultural differences will remain. But perhaps this is an area where the refugees can contribute. They are masters of social interaction. The art of conversation is truly an art in the Middle East. But it will take time and both sides being open. I am sure good food will help, like the wonderful Syrian dinner Maria Frank-Seiferling and I had in Bruchsal, or the delicious Turkish meal with the family in Schwäbisch Gmünd.

In particular, I hope that the refugees I met in Germany will develop friendships with Germans, and that Germans will get to know them. Both peoples have deep abilities for lasting friendship and loyalty. They only need time and trust.

Purpose Rexamined

The purpose of this book was to present a human perspective on host and refugee interaction. The ethnographic approach of this book foregrounds the humanity of both the people working with refugees, and the refugees themselves. That is why I described directly how I met them and learned about their work and their experiences. They are memorable and worthy of our respect. The purpose of this book was also to help dispel fear. The refugees from the war-torn countries of Syria, northern Iraq, and Afghanistan did not bring problems as they traveled through Macedonia, nor, apart from a few incidents, have they brought harm to the communities in Germany where they have begun to settle. Their needs are human needs, made temporarily more pressing by the hardships they have suffered and complicated somewhat by cultural differences. At the same time they bring energy and hope for a new and congenial future.

The other main purpose of the book was to inspire people to work with refugees in new ways. Communities of different sizes in Germany have risen to the challenge. Why should not communities in other parts of the world do the same? All communities have their own constraints and strengths. I have given specific examples of how individuals operated and of different programs in communities in Germany, like the skilled tools program in Schwäbisch Gmünd or the mentoring program in Hamburg, which could be adapted to other places in the world. In all places volunteers are crucial, as are regular evaluations of how programs are working. I emphasized the importance for communities not to be taken in by simplistic bureaucratic solutions, like putting refugees all into one building. I also emphasized the importance of having refugees and local people participate together in activities where boundaries are forgotten, like ritual, artistic, and community events, all of which promote social cohesion.

I also hope researchers will learn from this book. I chose to study the situation of host reception of almost one million refugees in Germany a year after the influx at a time when the policy was being established. This was a crucial time and so I was able to make clear how the policy tightened and became more restrictive even after people had received a positive notification. At the same time the language and integration classes were extended, and people would not be deported if they were already in apprentice programs. The *Ehrenamtliche* continue to be essential to ongoing integration. I encourage other researchers to work in host response in developed countries to reception of refugees.

In particular there needs to be a similar study done in Sweden, a country of 9.5 million people, that eventually took in 160,000 asylum-seekers.[2] Also Canada has taken in a substantial number of refugees. Again I recommend looking for positive programs so we can all learn from their experiences. In the United States, ACCESS (Arab Community Center for Economic and Social Services) in Dearborn, Michigan, has been working with Syrian refugees and in six months in 2017 was able to bring twenty-four out of twenty-five to basic subsistence.[3] A crucial element was having one person totally dedicated to each family.

As always, it is the personal contact that is essential. We need to build networks of refugee assistance so that people learn from each other, just as refugees themselves build such networks. Again, it is my hope that the recommendations of this book inspire others working with refugees to try new ideas in their own contexts.

NOTES

Prologue

1. Stephanie Wang, "Pence stops Syrian refugee resettlement in Indiana," *Indianapolis Star*, 16 Nov. 2015. With the election of Trump, Pence was also elected vice-president.
2. See Frances Trix, *Urban Muslim Migrants in Istanbul: Identity and Trauma of Balkan Immigrants* (London: I.B.Tauris, 2017).
3. There are very fine books on refugees coming to Europe including: Wolfgang Bauer and Stanislav Krupar, *Crossing the Sea: With Syrians on the Exodus to Europe* (London: Tetragon, 2016); Hugh Eakin, et al., *Flight from Syria: Refugee Stories* (electronic, 2012–15); and Patrick Kingsley, *The New Odyssey: Europe's New Refugee Crisis* (London: Guardian Books, 2016).
4. The legal expert Benjamin Wittes described the infamous executive order as "malevolence tempered by incompetence," and noted that the order reads "as if it was not reviewed by competent counsel at all" – which is a good way to lose in court.

Introduction

1. The killing in the town of Kandel near Karlsruhe of a fifteen-year-old German girl by an Afghan refugee is such an incident. See "Opinion: Murder of German girl will have political consequences," *Deutsche Welle*, 29 Dec. 2017 at http://www.dw.com/en/opinion-murder-of-german-girl-will-have-political-cons equences/a-41975314.
2. It is not the refugees from war-torn countries that contributed to the earlier rise in crime reported in the German press in the winter of 2018. Rather, these have been attributed to North African asylum-seekers, a small percentage of the refugees who have almost no chance of receiving asylum. See Morris Mac Matzen, "Violent crime rise in Germany attributed to refugees," *Reuters*, 3 Jan. 2018,

https://www.reuters.com/article/us-europe-migrants-germany-crime/violent-crime-rises-in-germany-and-is-attributed-to-refugees-idUSKBN1ES16J.

3. Sweden, a much smaller country, actually took in more refugees in proportion to its population.

4. Pegida is a far-right political movement, founded in Dresden in former East Germany in 2014. It is against immigration and is anti-Islamic. The name comes from the German for "Patriotic Europeans against the Islamisation of the West." I discuss this more thoroughly in chapter one of this book.

5. When the Balkan Migrant Trail was effectively closed by actions of countries along in it in the spring of 2016, refugees continued to try to enter Europe through other ways – through Italy or still through Greece where they have ended up stuck in camps.

6. See Robert G. Rabil, *The Syrian Refugee Crisis in Lebanon: The Double Tragedy of Refugees and Impacted Host Communities* (Lexington Books, Lanham, Maryland: 2016).

Chapter 1 What Affects Attitudes toward Refugees

1. David Francis, "'Mama' Merkel May Win Germany, But Not the Eurozone," *Newsmax*, 22 Sept. 2013.

2. Ibid.

3. I listened to YouTube videos of sections of the speech and include them below. As for commentary, the German and Anglo commentary on the speech were quite different. I cite what I consider the most interesting commentary. I note where applause came.

4. The German Wings crash occurred when the German co-pilot, Andreas Lubitz, locked the pilot out of the cockpit and then purposely crashed the airplane with 144 passengers aboard into a mountain in a suicide event.

5. These were a series of terrorist attacks in which 130 people were killed, 368 wounded. They were the deadliest attacks in France since World War II.

6. A useful summary of this speech is by Joanna Schuster-Craig, "Merkel's Speech at the CDU Party Meeting," *Spartan Ideas: New Europe – Europe and Migration* (17 December 2015).

7. Thomas Vitzhum, "CDU feiert Merkel für grenzenlose Flüchtlingspolitik: Adenaeur, Erhard, Kohl, Gott und Ich," *Die Welt*, 24, 14 December 2015 (GmbH 2016).

8. Tony Patterson, "Angela Merkel vows to 'tangibly reduce' refugee numbers – gets seven-minute standing ovation from party," *The Independent Online*, 14 Dec. 2015.

9. Der Spiegel Staff, "Merkel's refugee policy divides Europe," *Der Spiegel*, 21 Sept. 2015.

10. Philip Faigle, Karsten Polke-Majewski und Sascha Venohr, "Refugees: It really wasn't Merkel," *Die Zeit*, 11 Oct. 2016.

11. "Hungary PM Viktor Orbán: Antagonising Europe since 2010," BBC News, 5 Sept. 2015, http://www.bbc.com/news/world-europe-16390574.

12. Full text of Viktor Orbán's speech at Băile Tușnad (Tusnádfürdő) of 26 July 2014 at https://budapestbeacon.com/full-text-of-viktor-orbans-speech-at-baile-tusnad-tusnadfurdo-of-26-july-2014/.

13. "Hungary's PM Orban calls EU refugee quota plan 'mad,'" 8 May 2015, EURACTIV.com with AFP at https://www.euractiv.com/section/migrations/news/hungary-s-pm-orban-calls-eu-refugee-quota-plan-mad/.

14. "Europe Set for bruising battle over sharing refugee burden," *The Guardian*, 4 Sept., 2015 at https://www.theguardian.com/world/2015/sep/04/eastern-european-leaders-reject-concerted-policy-on-sharing-refugee-burden.

15. Michael R. Marrus, *The Unwanted: European Refugees in the Twentieth Century* (New York: Oxford University Press, 1985), p. 6.

16. Ibid., p. 8.

17. Matthew Carr, *Fortress Europe: Dispatches from a Gated Continent* (New York: The New Press, 2012), p. 20.

18. Marrus, *The Unwanted*, p. 113.

19. Ibid., p. 162.

20. Hannah Arendt, "Walter Benjamin, part I, the Hunchback," *Men in Dark Times* (New York: Harcourt Brace Jovanovich, 1955), "Walter Benjamin, Part I, the Hunchback," pp. 153–71.

21. Albanians' protection of Jews during World War II did not become known until after 1991 when communism fell there because at the end of World War II Albania was in civil war. It then became a Stalinist communist country for forty-seven years, uninterested in relations with Western countries including Israel.

22. Norman Gershman, *Besa: Muslims who Saved Jews in World War II* (Syracuse: Syracuse University Press, 2009).

23. R.M. Douglas, *Orderly and Humane: The Expulsion of the Germans after the Second World War* (New Haven, Connecticut: Yale University Press, 2012), p. 18.

24. Ibid., p. 168.

25. Ibid., p. 1–2.

26. Ibid., p. 193.

27. Ibid., p. 363.

28. John V.A. Fine and Robert Donia, *Bosnia and Hercegovina: A Tradition Betrayed* (New York: Columbia University Press, 1994), p. 247.

29. Vincent Rigby, *Bosnia-Hercegovina: The International Response*, BP-374E.

30. Barbara Crossette, "U.N. details its failure to stop '95 Bosnia massacre," *The New York Times*, 16 Nov. 1999.

31. Douglas, *Orderly and Humane*, p. 315.

32. To understand this much better, see Erika's own account in Erika C. Stevenson, *Fighting for Road Apples* (Bloomington, Indiana: iUniverse, Inc., 2012), p. 70.

33. Douglas, *Orderly and Humane*, p. 321.

34. Ibid., 321–5.

35. Matthias Bartsch, Andrea Brandt and Daniel Steinvorth, "Turkish immigration to Germany: A sorry history of self-deception and wasted opportunities," *Spiegel Online*, 7 Sept., 2010.

36. "Arson attack in Mölln," *One Germany in Europe*, 28 Nov. 1992.
37. Wolfgang Bosswick, "Asylum policy in Germany," Philip Muus (ed.), *Exclusion and Inclusion of Refugees in Contemporary Europe* (Utrecht, Research Centre on Migration and Ethnic Relations, 1997).
38. Veysel Özcan, "Germany: immigration in transition," *Migration Policy Institute*, 4 (June 2004).
39. Ibid.
40. Irina Liebenstein, *Integrationsprobleme von Russlanddeutschen* (Hamburg: Diploma Verlag, 2010), p. 19.
41. Ruth Mandel, *Cosmopolitan Anxieties: Turkish Challenges to Citizenship and Belonging in Germany* (Durham, North Carolina: Duke University Press, 2008), p. 217.
42. Ibid., p. 28.
43. Ibid., p. 38.
44. Maryellen Fullerton, *"Germany For Germans," Xenophobia And Racist Violence In Germany* (New York: Human Rights Watch, April 1995).
45. Simon Green, *The Politics of Exclusion: Institutions and Immigration Policy in Contemporary Germany* (Manchester: Manchester University Press, 2004), p. 84.
46. Fullerton, *Human Rights Watch Report*, 1995.
47. Irwin Suall (ed.), "Germany," *The Skinhead International: A Worldwide Survey of Neo-Nazi Skinheads* (New York: Anti-Defamation League, 1995).
48. Fullerton, *Human Rights Watch Report*, 1995, p. 223.
49. Ibid.
50. Ibid.
51. Ibid.
52. Ibid.
53. Friedrich Heckmann, *Understanding the Creation of Public Consensus: Migration and Integration in Germany, 2005 to 2015*, Report of the Migration Policy Institute, Washington, DC, June 2016.
54. Green, *The Politics of Exclusion*, p. 103.
55. Ibid., 104.
56. James Hampshire, *The Politics of Immigration: Contradictions of the Liberal State.* (Cambridge: Polity, 2013), p. 122.
57. Jessica Bither and Astrid Ziebarth, "In it for the long run: Integration lessons from a changing Germany," Integration Strategy Group (Washington DC: German Marshall Fund, Oct. 2016), p. 19.
58. Report from German Chamber of Industry and Trade, cited in Heckmann, p. 9.
59. Heckmann, "The creation of consensus," p. 10.
60. Thilo Sarrazin, *Deutschland Schafft Sich Ab ("Germany Does Itself In")* (Munich, 2010).
61. Translatlantic Trends, 2011 (Washington DC: German Marshall Fund of the United States, 2011. www.gmfus.org/publications/translatlantic-trends-2011.
62. Heckmann, "The creation of consensus," 2016, p. 6.
63. *"Protest-Märsche: De Maizière zeigt verständnis für Pegida-demonstranten".* Der Spiegel Online, 12 Dec. 2014.

64. Thomas Meaney, "The new star of Germany's far right," *The New Yorker*, 2 October 2016.
65. Ibid.
66. Kate Connolly, "AfD co-leader quits after party election's breakthrough," *Guardian*, 25 September 2017.
67. Cas Mudde, "What the stunning success of AfD means for Germany and Europe," *Guardian*, 24 Sept. 2017.
68. Ibid.
69. Melissa Eddy, "Germany's Angela Merkel agrees to limits on accepting refugees," *The New York Times*, 9 Oct. 2017.

Chapter 2   NGOs and Local Responses

1. Frances Trix, "Ethnic Minorities of Macedonia: Turks, Roma, and Serbs," in Sabrina Ramet (ed.), *Civic and Uncivic Values in Macedonia: Value Transformation, Education, Media* (New York: Palgrave, 2013), pp. 194–213.
2. Doneo Donev, Silvana Oneeva, and Ilija Gligorov, "Refugee Crisis in Macedonia during Kosovo Conflict in 1999," *Croatian Medical Journal*, vol. 43, no. 2 (2001), pp. 184–9.
3. See Leon Trotsky, *The War Correspondence of Leon Trotsky: The Balkan Wars 1912–1913* (New York: Pathfinder, 1980), pp. 328–34, for descriptions of the killing of Muslims.
4. "International commission to inquire into the causes and conduct of the Balkan Wars," *Report of the International Commission to Inquire into the Causes and Conduct of the Balkan Wars*, Carnegie Endowment for International Peace, no. 4 (Washington DC, 1914), p. 72.
5. Amnesty International, *Europe's Borderlands: Violations against Refugees and Migrants in Macedonia, Serbia, and Hungary* (London: Amnesty International, 2015), pp. 14–15.
6. I found this out in my work with refugee assistance in the 1990s. The most generous people were often retirees on fixed incomes, not younger people with larger salaries.
7. Amnesty International, *Europe's Borderlands* (2015), p. 5.
8. Ibid., pp. 14–15.
9. Ibid., pp. 6, 20.
10. Ibid., p. 30.
11. Francesca Rolandi, "Macedonia, the refugee emergency, *International Federation of Red Cross*, 23 Sept. 2015, p. 3.
12. The *Mavi Marmara* was a Turkish ship that the Turkish NGO IHH, a humanitarian charity, purchased, and with peace activists from thirty-seven countries and six other smaller ships, proceeded to sail to Gaza with ten tons of humanitarian aid supplies. Several days out from Cyprus, in the middle of the night of 31 May 2010, masked Israeli commandos landed on the convoy in international waters to stop its progress toward Gaza. There was violence, nine

of the Turkish peace activists were killed, and the convoy was forced to sail into an Israeli harbor.

13. Edward Said, *Orientalism* (New York: Pantheon Books, 1978).
14. Karen Armstrong is a former Catholic nun who writes exceedingly clearly on religion. For students who know nothing about Islam, her book on the Prophet Muhammad (1993) is an excellent introduction.
15. Islam spread to the Balkans later than across the Middle East. There are very fine Ottoman archival documents showing the gradual growth of Islam in the Balkans.
16. We did not however talk about the theological problems of translating the Qur'an from Arabic.
17. www.Legis.mk, *Who We Are.*
18. The most famous account of the Dabaab Camp is Ben Rawlence's *City of Thorns: Nine Lives in the World's Largest Refugee Camp* (New York: Picador, 2015).
19. Rolandi, "Macedonia, the Refugee Emergency."
20. Ibid., p. 3.
21. Personal Interviews, "Legis team is a real portrait of multicultural Macedonia," *Portrait*, 1 Mar. 2016.
22. Rolandi, "Macedonia, the Refugee Emergency." p. 7.
23. "Lence Zdravkin," *Al-Jazeera Balkan*, 7 Jul. 2015.
24. Ibid., p. 6.
25. Mother Teresa, a Roman Catholic of Albanian ethnicity, was born in Skopje in Ottoman Macedonia. She is revered by all groups in the region, Christian and Muslim.
26. "From where I stand, Lenche Zdravkin," *UN Women* (15 Sept. 2015). Available at http://www.unwomen.org/en/news/stories/2016/9/from-where-i-stand-lenche-zdravkin#sthash.YEnyB2vK.dpuf.

Chapter 3   Refugee Transit Camps

1. See the Albanian interview by Mensur Krasniqi, "Maqedonsja Mare Bojkovska: unë, krah për krah shqiptarëve në ndihmë të refugjatëve," ('Macedonian Mare Bojkovska: I, shoulder to shoulder with Albanians to help the refugees,') *Te Sheshi Olitec*, Prishtina, Kosova, 20 January 2016.
2. The French were still most negative toward Middle Eastern refugees due to the November 2015 terrorist attacks in Paris. There were refugees from East Africa, sleeping underneath the raised metro tracks of the nineteenth arrondissement of Paris, who the French largely ignored. I met with them during my time in Europe in the fall of 2016.

Chapter 4   Responses of Villages

1. In English see Inge Jens (ed.), *At the Heart of the White Rose: Letters and Diaries of Hans & Sophie Scholl* (New York: Harper & Row, 1987).

2. Alemanic is a group of dialects of the Upper German branch of the German language family and is spoken from eastern France across Switzerland to Austria. In the case of the name of the Bioladen, the Alemanic is a Low Alemanic dialect of the Upper-Rhine of Southwestern Baden and its variant Alsatian. It is also spoken by the Amish in Allen County, Indiana.
3. I have changed his name for privacy.

Chapter 5 Responses of Towns and Smaller Cities

1. "Tonlage verstimmt Bischöfe," *South German News*, 21 Sept. 2016.
2. Stefan Luft, *Die Flüchtlingskrise: Ursachen, Konflikte, Folgen* (München: Verlag C.H. Beck, 2016).
3. Heckmann, "Creation of Public Consensus," 2016.
4. Friedrich Heckmann, *Integration von Migranten: Einwanderung and neue Nationenbildung* (Heidelberg: Springer Verlag, 2015).
5. Early in my career, I had taught English for a summer in Turkey.
6. I am referring here of course to Douglas' book, *Orderly and Humane: The Expulsion of the Germans after the Second World War*, 2012.
7. Lea Hampel, "Ein Leben im Transit," photos Jens Schwartz, locally brought out, Nürnberg, Germany.
8. See the intriguing discussion on *Leitkultur*, protecting the Constitution, and the Muslim man in Katherine Pratt Ewing's *Stolen Honor: Stigmatizing Muslim Men in Berlin* (Stanford, California: Stanford University Press, 2008), pp. 200–21.
9. See the edited volume, Monika Boosen and Joachim Haller (eds), *Emanuel Leutze: Leben und Werk* (Schwäbisch Gmünd: Museum im Prediger, 2016), for information on Leutze's life and works.
10. "Europäisches Forum für Migrationsstudien", *Miteinander in Schwäbisch Gmünd: Integrationskonzept* (Bamberg: University of Bamberg, 2009).
11. See Ruth Mandel's book, *Cosmopolitan Anxieties: Turkish Challenges to Citizenship and Belonging in Germany*. It focuses especially on Berlin that prides itself on being cosmopolitan and yet has not found room for Turks in this tolerance.

Chapter 6 Responses of Large Cities

1. One was the attack in July 2016 on the train near Würzburg where an Afghan unaccompanied minor had brandished a machete and wounded a German passenger before he was killed by security. The other was worse. In October 2016 a nineteen-year-old German medical student was riding her bicycle home after a party in the early hours outside Freiburg. The Afghan unaccompanied minor refugee raped and killed her, and then threw her body in the river. He was eventually identified by DNA.
2. There were eventually over 700 complaints by women filed with police in Cologne for treatment by men on New Years by the cathedral. See Victor

Brechenmacher, "Lessons from Cologne: Reckoning with refugees in Germany," *Brown Political Report*, 31 Jan. 2016.

3. Angelike Blickhäuser, "Engagement in Zeiten der Flücht: Ein Blick aus der Praxis" in Wolfgang Stadler (ed.), *Theorie und Praxis der Socialen Arbeit: Mehr vom Miteinander. Wie Bürgerschaftliches Engagement sozialen Zusammenhalt stärken kann* (Munich: Sonderband, 2016), 140–4.

4. Angelika Blickhäuser und Bete Ahrends *Ehrenamtlich Eengagiert – Wwie kann es ggehen? Ein Handbuch von* (Köln: AWO, 2014).

5. "Merkel interview," *Hamburger Abendblatt*, 1 Sept. 2016, p. 1.

6. "Exclusive interview with Merkel," *Hamburger Abendblatt*, 5–6 Sept. 2016, p. 6.

Chapter 7   Toward Integration

1. James Hampshire, *The Politics of Immigration* (Malden, Massachusettss: Polity Press, 2013, 2016), p. 131.

2. Mandel, Cosmo*politan Anxieties*, p. 316. She also describes the complexity of this decade.

3. Hampshire, *Politics of Immigration*, p. 12.

4. Ibid., p. 153.

5. Reiner Lehberger, Reiner and Tatiana Matthiesen, "Der Schülercampus 'Mehr Migranten werden Lehrer' orientiert den pädagogischen Machwuchs," special edition on migration in *Journal für Lehrer Innenbildung*, 3 (3/2013, 2013), pp. 41–5.

6. Jessica Bither and Astrid Ziebarth, "In it for the long run: Integration lessons from a changing Germany," *Integration Strategy Group* (Washington DC: German Marshall Fund, October 2016).

7. Jenny Gesler, "Germany: Act to integrate refugees enters into force," *Global Legal Monitor*, Library of Congress, 15 Aug. 2016.

8. Heckmann, "Creation of Public Consensus," p. 16.

9. Ibid., p. 9.

10. Eddy, 9 Oct. 2017.

11. Grace Guarnieri, "Migrants in Europe linked to soaring violence and crime in Germany, study finds," *Newsweek*, 3 Jan. 2018. Available at http://www.news week.com/migrants-europe-violence-crime-germany-study-770105.

12. Ibid.

13. *Deutsche Welle*, "More than 3,500 attacks on refugees in Germany in 2016: report," *Deutsche Welle*, 26 Feb. 2016.

Conclusion

1. Manasi Gopalakrishnan, "German volunteer finds his calling helping refugees," *Deutsche Welle*, 22 Aug. 2016 http://dw.com/p/1JdQg.

2. Of these 165,000, 32,000 have been offered asylum. A main problem in Sweden is unaccompanied minors. When they do not qualify for asylum and are scheduled for deportation, they often "disappear." Tove Lifendahll, "How Sweden became an example of how not to handle immigration," *The Spectator*, 3 Sept. 2016.

3. I heard a panel on this project in the fall of 2017 at the Arab-American Museum Annex in Dearborn, Michigan, where they reported the importance of having one person dedicated to each family. Contact Meredith Steih at ACCESS for information. There is also an article on the program from its early stage. See Andrea Blum, "Syrian refugee families in Michigan get aid through newly launched fund," *Press & Guide*, 11 Jan. 2017. Available at: http://www. pressandguide.com/news/syrian-refugee-families-in-michigan-get-support-through-newly-launched/article_1295ec93-8cda-5c41-be0f-b9a41d04ae74. html.

BIBLIOGRAPHY

(with some Background and Contrastive Sources in English, German, and French)

Amnesty International, *Europe's Borderlands: Violations against Refugees and Migrants in Macedonia, Serbia, and Hungary.* (London: Amnesty International, 2015).
———, *Living in Insecurity: How Germany is Failing Victims of Racist Violence* (London: Amnesty International, 2016).
Anonymous, *A Woman in Berlin: Diary 20 April 1945 to 22 June 1945* (originally published New York: Harcourt, Brace Jovanovich, 1954); (published in German as *Eine Frau in Berlin* in 1960); (again in 2002, after the death of the anonymous author, multiple times in English and German).
Aoun, Elena, "The EU and the Management of the Refugee Crisis in Lebanon: Small Stitches on Huge Wounds," *Studia Diplomatica*, LXVIII-1 (2015), pp. 49–62.
Appadurai, Arjun, *Fear of Small Numbers: An Essay on the Geography of Anger* (Durham, North Carolina: Duke University Press, 2006).
Arendt, Hannah, *Origins of Totalitarianism* (New York: Harcourt, Brace, Jovanovich, 1948).
———, *Men in Dark Times* (New York: Harcourt, Brace, Jovanovich, 1955).
———, *On Violence* (New York: Harcourt, Brace, Jovanovich, 1969).
Armstrong, Karen, *Muhammad: A Biography of the Prophet* (San Francisco: HarperCollins, 1993).
Asylum Quarterly Report, Eurostat statistics explained, "Decisions on Asylum Applicants," Data from 15 June 2017.
Barber, Benjamin R., *If Mayors Rule the World: Dysfunctional Nations, Rising Cities* (New Haven, Connecticut: Yale University Press, 2013).
Barber, Martin, *Blinded by Humanity: Inside the UN's Humanitarian Operations* (London: I.B.Tauris, 2015).
Basso, Keith, *Wisdom Sits in Places: Landscape and Language Among the Western Apache* (Albuquerque, New Mexico: University of New Mexico Press, 1996).
Bauer, Wolfgang and Stanislav Krupar, *Crossing the Sea: With Syrians on the Exodus to Europe* (London: Tetragon, 2016).

Beise, Marc, *Wir Brauchen Die Flüchtlinge! Zuwanderung als Herausforderung und Chance: Der Weg zu einem neuen Deutschland* (München: Süddeutsche Zeitung Edition Streitschrift, 2015).

Bell, Gertrude, *Syria: The Desert and the Sown* (London: I.B.Tauris, 2016 (original date, 1907)).

Bither, Jessica and Astrid Ziebarth, "In it for the long run: Integration lessons from a changing Germany," *Integration Strategy Group*, Washington, DC: German Marshall Fund, Oct. 2016.

Blickhäuser, Angelike, "Engagement in Zeiten der Flücht: Ein Blick aus der Praxis", Wolfgang Stadler (ed.), *Theorie und Praxis der Sozialen Arbeit: Mehr vom Miteinander. Wie Bürgerschafliches Engagement sozialen Zusammenhalt stärken kann* (Sonderband, 2016), pp. 140–4.

Bode, Sabine, *Kriegsspuren: Die deutsche Krankheit German Angst* (Stuttgart: Klett-Cotta, 2016).

Boosen, Monika and Joachim Haller (eds), *Emanuel Leutze: Leben und Werk* (Schwäbisch Gmünd: Museum im Prediger, 2016).

Bosswick, Wolfgang, "Asylum policy in Germany" in Philip Muus (ed.), *Exclusion and Inclusion of Refugees in Contemporary Europe* (Utrecht: European Center on Migration and Ethnic Relations, 1997).

Brechenmacher, Victor, "Lessons from Cologne: Reckoning with refugees in Germany", *Brown Political Report* (31 Jan. 2016).

Brochmann, Grete and Elena Jurado (eds), *Europe's Immigration Challenge: Reconciling Work, Welfare and Mobility* (London: I.B.Tauris, 2013).

Carr, Matthew, *Fortress Europe* (London: Hurst, 2012, 2016).

Celiker, Anna Grabolle, *Kurdish Life in Contemporary Turkey: Migration, Gender and Ethnic Identity* (London: I.B.Tauris, 2013).

Connolly, Kate, "AfD co-leader quits after party election's breakthrough," *Guardian* (25 September, 2017).

Dhume-Sonzogni, Fabrice, *Liberté, Égalité, Communauté? L'état français contre le communauté* (Paris: Éditions Homnisphères, 2007).

Douglas, R.M., *Orderly and Humane: The Expulsion of the Germans after the Second World War* (New Haven, Connecticut: Yale University Press, 2012).

Eakin, Hugh, et al. *Flight from Syria: Refugee Stories* (Pulitzer Kindle Book: 2012–2015) (published separately in al-Jazeera, BBC News, NPR, etc.).

Eddy, Melissa, "Germany's Angela Merkel Agrees to Limits on Accepting Refugees," *The New York Times* (9 October 2017).

Emcke, Carolin, *Gegen den Hass* (Frankfurt am Main: S. Fischer, 2016).

Erden, Özlen, "Building bridges for refugee empowerment," *International Migration & Integration* (2016), pp. 1–19. DOI 10.1007/s12134–016–0476-y.

Europäisches Forum für Migrationsstudien, *Miteinander in Schwäbisch Gmünd: Integrationskonzept* (Bamberg: University of Bamberg, 2009).

Ewing, Katherine Pratt, *Stolen Honor: Stigmatizing Muslim Men in Berlin* (Stanford, California: Stanford University Press, 2008).

Faigle, Philip, Karsten Polke-Majewski und Sascha Venohr, "Refugees: It really wasn't Merkel," *Die Zeit*, 11 October 2016.

Feffer, John, "Not all the migration after the fall of the Berlin Wall was from East to West," *Guardian* (11 October 2013).

Ferris, Elizabeth, and Kemal Kirişci, *Consequences of Chaos: Syria's Humanitarian Crisis and the Failure to Protect* (Washington, DC: Brookings Institute, 2016).

Fine, John V.A. and Robert Donia, *Bosnia and Hercegovina: A Tradition Betrayed* (New York: Columbia University Press, 1994).

Fischer, Nicolas and Camille Hamidi, *Les Politiques Migratoires* (Paris: La Découverte, 2016).

Fottorino, Eric (ed.), *Pourquoi les Migrants? Comprendre les Flux de Population* (Paris: Philippe Rey, 2016).

Friedrich, Sebastian, *Der Aufstieg der AfD (Alternative für Deutschland): Neokonservative Mobilmachung in Deutschland* (Berlin: Bertz & Fischer, 2015).

Fuccaro, Nelida, *The Other Kurds: Yazidis in Colonial Iraq* (London: I.B.Tauris, 1999).

Fullerton, Maryellen, *"Germany For Germans" Xenophobia And Racist Violence In Germany* (New York: Human Rights Watch, April 1995).

Funder, Anna, *Stasiland: Stories from Behind the Berlin Wall* (London: Granta Publications, 2003).

German Marshall Fund of the United States, *Translatlantic Trends* (Washington, DC: German Marshall Fund of the United States, 2011) www.gmfus.org/publications/translatlantic-trends-2011.

Gershman, Norman, *Besa: Muslims Who Saved Jews in World War II* (Syracuse: Syracuse University Press, 2009).

Gesler, Jenny, "Germany: Act to integrate refugees enters into force," *Global Legal Monitor*, Library of Congress (15 August 2016).

di Giovanni, Janine, *The Morning They Came for Us* (New York: Liveright Publishing Corporation, 2016).

Gmelch, Michael, *Refugees Welcome: Eine Herausforderung für Christen* (Würzburg: Echter, 2016).

Goffman, Erving, *Forms of Talk* (Philadelphia: University of Pennsylvania Press, 1981).

Gopalakrishnan, Manasi, "German volunteer finds his calling helping refugees," *Deutsche Welle* (22 August 2016) http://dw.com/p/1JdQg.

Grandahl, Mia, *In Hope and Despair: Life in the Palestinian Refugee Camps* (London: I.B.Tauris, 2003).

Green, Simon, *The Politics of Exclusion: Institutions and Immigration Policy in Contemporary Germany* (Manchester: Manchester University Press, 2004).

Guarnieri, Grace, "Migrants in Europe linked to soaring violence and crime in Germany, study finds," *Newsweek* (3 January 2018), http://www.newsweek.com/migrants-europe-violence-crime-germany-study-770105.

Hampshire, James, *The Politics of Immigration: Contradictions of the Liberal State* (Cambridge, UK: Polity Press, 2013, 2016).

Heckmann, Friedrich, *Integration von Migranten: Einwanderung and Neue Nationenbildung* (Heidelberg: Springer Verlag, 2015).

————, *Understanding the Creation of Public Consensus: Migration and Integration in Germany 2005–2015*, Report of the Migration Policy Institute, Washington, DC (2016).

Heimbach-Steins, Marianne (ed.), *Begrenzt Verantwortlich? Sozialethische Positionen in der Flüchtlingskrise* (Freiburg: Herder, 2016).

Holmes, Seth M. and Heide Castenada, "Representing the 'European refugee crisis' in Germany and beyond: Deservingness and difference, life and death", *American Ethnologist*, vol. 23, no. 1 (2016), pp. 12–24.

Holtkamp, Jürgen, *Flüchtlinge und Asyl: Herausforderung – Chance – Zerreissprobe* (Kevelaer, Germany: Lahn Verlags, Topos Group, 2016).

Jens, Inge (ed.), *At the Heart of the White Rose: Letters and Diaries of Hans & Sophie Scholl* (New York: Harper & Row, 1987).

Kaddor, Lamya, *Die Zerreissprobe: Wie die Angst vor dem Fremden Unsere Demokratie bedroht* (Berlin: Rowohlt, 2016).

Kastrinou, Maria, *Power, Sect, and State in Syria: The Politics of Marriage and Identity among the Druze* (London: I.B.Tauris, 2016).

Kermani, Navid, *Vergesst Deutschland: Eine Patriotische Rede* (Berlin: Ullstein, 2012).

Kingsley, Patrick, *The New Odyssey: Europe's New Refugee Crisis* (London: Guardian Books, 2016).

Krasniqi, Mensur, "Maqedonsja Mare Bojkovska: unë, krah për krah shqiptarëve në ndihmë të refugjatëve" ("Macedonian Mare Bojkovska: I, shoulder to shoulder with Albanians to help the refugees") *Te Sheshi Olitec*, Prishtina, Kosova (20 January 2016).

Kroet, Cynthia, "Violence against refugees rising in Germany: Minister," *Politico* (30 May 2016).

Langer, Freddy, "Das One-Hit-Wonder in der Malerei," *Frankfurter Allgemeine Zeitung*, 119 (24 May 2016), p. 9.

di Lauri, Antonio, *Politics of Humanitarianism: Power, Ideology and Aid* (London: I.B.Tauris, 2015).

Lehberger, Reiner and Tatiana Matthiesen,"Neue Lehrer braucht das Land: Der Schülercampus 'Mehr Migranten werden Lehrer' als Modell zur Rekrutierung von Lehrkräften mit Migrationshintergrund," in Bräu, Karin, Viola B. Georgi, Yasemin Karakaşoğlu, and Carolin Rottin (eds), *Lehrerinnen und Lehrer mit Migrationshintergrund: Zur Relevanz eines Merkmals in Theorie, Empirie und Praxis* (Tübingen: Waxman, 2013), pp. 246–58.

———, Lehberger, Reiner and Tatiana Matthiesen,"Der Schülercampus 'Mehr Migranten werden Lehrer' orientiert den pädagogischen Machwuchs," special edition on migration in *Journal für Lehrer Innenbildung*, 3 (2013), pp. 41–5.

Liebenstein, Irina, *Integrationsprobleme von Russlanddeutschen* (Hamburg: Diploma Verlag, 2010).

Lifendahl, Tove, "How Sweden became an example of how not to handle immigration," *The Spectator* (3 September 2016).

Luft, Stefan, *Die Flüchtlingeskrise: Ursachen, Konflikte, Folgen* (Munich: Diploma Verlag C.H. Beck (2016).

Mac Matzen, Morris, "Violent crime rise in Germany attributed to refugees," *Reuters* (3 January 2018), https://www.reuters.com/article/us-europe-migrants-germany-crime/violent-crime-rises-in-germany-and-is-attributed-to-refugees-idUSKBN1ES16J.

Malkki, Liisa H., *Purity and Exile: Violence, Memory, and National Cosmology among Hutu Refuees in Tanzania* (Chicago: University of Chicago Press, 1995).

———, "Refugees and exile: From 'refugee studies' to the national order of things," Annual Review of Anthropology 24 (1995).

Mandel, Ruth, *Cosmopolitan Anxieties: Turkish Challenges to Citizenship and Belonging in Germany* (Durham, North Carolina: Duke University Press, 2008).

Mansel, Philip, *Aleppo, Rise and Fall of Syria's Great Merchant City* (London: I.B.Tauris, 2016).

Marconi, Giovanna and Elena Ostanel (eds), *The Intercultural City: Migration, Minorities and the Management of Diversity* (London: I.B.Tauris, 2016).

Marrus, Michael R., *The Unwanted: European Refugees in the Twentieth Century* (New York: Oxford University Press, 1985).

Meany, Thomas, "The new star of Germany's far right," *The New Yorker* (2 October 2016).

Meinhold, Corinne und Anja Lerz (eds), *Warum Wir das Schaffen Müssen: Flüchtlinge – und was Wir als Christen Damit zu Tun Haben* (Moers, Germany: Brendow & Sohn Verlag, 2016).

Meininghaus, Esther, *Creating Consent in Ba'thist Syria: Women and Welfare in a Totalitarian State* (London: I.B.Tauris, 2016).

Mudde, Cas, "What the stunning success of AfD means for Germany and Europe," *Guardian* (24 September 2017).

Münkler, Herfried and Marina Münkler, *Die Neuen Deutschen: Ein Land for Seiner Zukunft* (Berlin: Rowohlt, 2016).

ORSAM (Ortadoği Stategiik Araştırmalar Merkezi/Center for Middle East Strategic Studies), *Effects of the Syrian Refugees on Turkey*, ORSAM Report No 195 (Ankara: ORSAM, and TESEV, January 2015).

Ortega, Veronika, *Mehr als Wörter: Leitfaden für Sprachvermittler in der Flüchtlingshilfe* (Weissenburg: Flüchtlingshilfe Wald E.V., Hetzner Online, 2016).

Otto, Konrad, *Zuwanderung und Moral: Was Bedeutet das Alles?* (Stuttgart: Philipp Reclam, 2004).

Özcan, Veysel, Germany: "Immigration in transition," *Migration Policy Institute*, 4 (June 2004).

Podier, Claire, *Migrants & Réfugiés: Réponse aux Indécis aux Inquiets et aux Réticents* (Paris: La Découverte, 2016).

Prantl, Heribert, *Im Namen der Menschlichkeit Rettet die Flüchtlichtlinge!* (Berlin: Ullstein, 2015).

Primo Levi, "Persécutés au pays, déboutés en France: Rapport sur les failles de notre procédure d'asile" (Paris: Centre Primo Levi, 2016).

Rabil, Robert G., *The Syrian Refugee Crisis in Lebanon: The Double Tragedy of Refugees and Impacted Host Communities* (Lexington Books, Lanham, Maryland, 2016).

Rawlence, Ben, *City of Thorns: Nine Lives in the World's Largest Refugee Camp* (New York: Picador, 2015).

Reker, Henriette, *Mein Beruf ist Köln* (Köln: Kiepenheuer & Witsch, 2016).

Rennefanz, Sabine, "East Germans are still different," *Guardian* (30 September 2010).

Rescke, Anja (ed.), *Und das ist erst der Anfang: Deutschland und die Flüchtlinge* (Hamburg: Rowohlt, 2015).

Rohe, Mathias, and Mahmoud Jaraba, "Paralleljustiz: Eine Studie im Aftrag des Landes Berlin, vertreten durch die Senatsverwaltung für Justiz and Verbracherschutz," *Erlangen Zentrum für Islam und Recht in Europa* (November 2015).

Rolandi, Francesca, "Macedonia, the refugee emergency", *International Federation of Red Cross* (23 September 2015), p. 3.

Rowe, Timothy, *The Experience of Protest: Masculinity and Agency among Sudanese Refugees in Cairo* (London: I.B.Tauris, 2016).

Sarrazin, Thilo, *Deutschland Schafft Sich Ab* (Munich: DVA, 2010).

Sassoon, Joseph, *The Iraqi Refugees: The New Crisis in the Middle-East* (London: I.B.Tauris, 2008).

Schley, Fridolin (ed.), *Fremd* (München: P. Kirchheim Verlag, 2015).

Severin, Thorsten, "Germany records 300 attacks on asylum shelters so far this year," *World News* (Reuters, 5 April 2016).

Stevenson, Erika C., *Fighting for Road Apples* (Bloomington, Indiana: iUniverse, Inc., 2012).

Suall, Irwin (ed.), "Germany," in *The Skinhead International: A Worldwide Survey of Neo-Nazi Skinheads* (New York: Anti-Defamation League, 1995).

Süssmuth, Rita, *The Future of Migration and Integration Policy in Germany, Migration Policy Institute, May, 2009*. www.migrationpolicy.org/transatlantic.

Tekkal, Düzen, *Deutschland ist Bedroht: Warum Wir Unsere Werte Jetzt Verteidigen Müssen* (Munich: Berlin Verlag, 2016).

Thiede, Rocco und Susanne van Volxem, *Deutschland: Erste Informationen für Flüchtlinge* (übersetzun ins Arabishche von Ali Hamdan unde Munzir Mohamed) (Freiburg: Herder, 2015).

Trix, Frances, *Spiritual Discourse: Learning with an Islamic Master* (Philadelphia: University of Pennsylvania Press, 1993).

—— *The Sufi Journey of Baba Rexheb* (Philadelphia: University of Pennsylvania Museum of Archaeology and Anthropology with University of Pennsylvania Press, 2009).

——"Ethnic Minorities of Macedonia: Turks, Roma, and Serbs," in Sabrina Ramet (ed.), *Civic and Uncivic Values in Macedonia: Value Transformation, Education, Media* (New York: Palgrave, 2013), pp. 194–213.

—— *Urban Muslim Migrants in Istanbul: Identity and Trauma among Balkan Immigrants* (London: I.B.Tauris, 2017).

Trotsky, Leon, *The War Correspondence of Leon Trotsky: The Balkan Wars 1912–1913* (New York: Pathfinder, 1980).

Wang, Stephanie, "Pence stops Syrian refugee resettlement in Indiana," *Indianapolis Star*, 16 November 2015.

Watson, Peter, *The German Genius: Europe's Third Renaissance, The Second Scientific Revolution, and the Twentieth Century* (New York: Harper, 2010).Wecker, Konstantin, *Dann Denkt meit dem Herzen: Auf Aufschrei in der Derbatte um Flüchtlinge* (München: Güterloher Verlagshaus, 2016).

Wecker, Konstantin, Dann Denkt meit dem Herzen: Auf Aufschrei in der Derbatte umFlüchtlinge (Mü nchen: Gü terloher Verlagshaus, 2016).

Weil, Patrick, *Liberté, Égalité, Discriminations: L' "Identité National" au Regard de L'histoire* (Paris: Gallimard, 2008).

Yazbek, Samar (translated by Nashwa Gowanlock and Ruth Amedzai Kemp), *The Crossing: My Journey to the Shattered Heart of Syria* (London: Rider Books, 2015).

INDEX

Lightning Source UK Ltd.
Milton Keynes UK
UKHW021910280520
363987UK00010B/628

9 780755 617753